Identity in the Shadow of Slavery

THE BLACK ATLANTIC

General Editor: Polly Rewt, The Open University and University of Stirling

Series Advisers: Caryl Phillips, novelist; David Dabydeen, Centre for Caribbean Studies, University of Warwick; Vincent Carretta, Professor of English, University of Maryland; Angus Calder, writer.

The cultural and theoretical parameters of the Black Atlantic world are explored and treated critically in this timely series. It offers students, scholars and general readers essential texts which focus on the international black experience. The broad scope of the series is innovative and ambitious, treating literary, historical, biographical, musical and visual arts subjects from an interdisciplinary and cross-cultural perspective.

The books address current debates on what constitutes the Black Atlantic, both geographically and theoretically. They include anthologized primary material and collections of seminal critical value to courses on the African diaspora and related subjects. They will also appeal more widely to a readership interested in biographical and other material that presents scholarship accessibly.

IDENTITY IN THE SHADOW OF SLAVERY

edited by Paul E. Lovejoy

Continuum
London and New York

Continuum

Wellington House, 125 Strand, London WC2R 0BB

370 Lexington Avenue, New York, NY 10017–6503

First published 2000

British Library Cataloguing-in-Publication Data

A catalogue record for this book is available from the British Library.

ISBN 0–8264–4724–4 (hardback)
 0–8264–4725–2 (paperback)

Library of Congress Cataloging-in-Publication Data
Identity in the shadow of slavery / edited by Paul E. Lovejoy.
    p. cm.   (The Black Atlantic)
    Papers originally presented at the UNESCO/SSHRCC Summer Institute, "Identifying Enslaved Africans: the 'Nigerian' Hinterland and the African Diaspora," held at York University in Toronto, July 14–Aug 1, 1997.
    Includes bibliographical references and index.
    ISBN 0-8264-4724-4 (HB)   ISBN 0-8264-4725-2 (PB)
    1. Africans—America—Ethnic identity—Congresses. 2. Afro-Americans—Ethnic identity—Congresses. 3. Slavery—Social aspects—America—History—Congresses. 4. Slavery—America—Psychological aspects—History—Congresses. 5. Group identity—America—History—Congresses. 6. Slaves—America—Social conditions—Congresses. 7. African diaspora—Congresses. I. Lovejoy, Paul E. II. Series.
E29.N3 I34 2000
306.3'62'08996—dc21

                                                                99-086059

Designed and typeset by Ben Cracknell Studios
Printed and bound in Great Britain by Biddles Ltd, Guildford and King's Lynn

Contents

List of Illustrations

List of Contributors

Lillian Ashcraft-Eason is Associate Professor of History and Director of African Studies at Bowling Green University, Ohio, USA.

Christine Ayorinde completed her PhD in history at the University of Birmingham in 1999 and is currently a post-doctoral fellow associated with the UNESCO Nigerian Hinterland Project at York University.

Hilary McD. Beckles is Professor of History and Pro Vice-Chancellor of the University of the West Indies in Jamaica.

Douglas B. Chambers is Assistant Professor of History at Southern Mississippi University.

Alberto da Costa e Silva, former Ambassador to several countries, is an associate of the Ministério das Relações Exteriores, Brazil.

Manolo Garcia Florentino is Professor of History at the Universidade Federal do Rio de Janeiro, Brazil.

Sandra E. Greene is Associate Professor of History at Cornell University and former President of the African Studies Association (USA).

José Roberto Góes teaches at the Universidade Federal do Rio de Janeiro, Brazil.

Jane Landers is Associate Professor of History at Vanderbilt University, USA.

Paul E. Lovejoy is Distinguished Research Professor of History, York University, Toronto, Canada, and a Fellow of the Royal Society of Canada.

Francine Shields completed her PhD thesis at the University of Stirling in 1998 and is now at the University of Edinburgh.

Maureen Warner-Lewis is Professor of Literatures in English at the University of the West Indies, Jamaica.

Olabiyi Yai is Professor of African Languages and Literatures and Chair of the Department of African Languages and Literatures at the University of Florida and is currently the representative of the République du Bénin to UNESCO.

Acknowledgements

This volume represents a sample of the papers presented at the UNESCO/SSHRCC Summer Institute, 'Identifying Enslaved Africans: The "Nigerian" Hinterland and the African Diaspora', held at York University in Toronto, July 14–August 1, 1997. The Summer Institute was funded by the Social Sciences and Humanities Research Council of Canada and also received the support of York University. This support is here gratefully recognized. The Summer Institute was affiliated with the UNESCO Slave Route Project of the Division of Intercultural Projects, Doudou Diene, Director.

Brenda McComb, J. J. Shafer and Paul E. Lovejoy collaborated in copy-editing the volume. In addition, Ann O'Hear compiled the bibliography and in the course of doing so caught various mistakes. Maureen Warner-Lewis read the completed manuscript, and her suggestions have been largely incorporated. The Summer Institute, from which this volume is derived, could not have taken place without the intellectual and personal commitment of Robin Law, to whom this volume is dedicated.

To Robin Law, for his inspiration and friendship

1

Identifying Enslaved Africans in the African Diaspora

Paul E. Lovejoy

Following individuals along the slave routes traces western African history across the Atlantic. That such routes begin in Africa suggests that the study of the African diaspora look outwards across the Atlantic.[1] This approach, which might be called 'Africancentric' or even 'Afrocentric', introduces a perspective that is *not* centred in the history of Europe or colonial America but instead in trans-Atlantic origins.[2] The essays in this volume tentatively explore this perspective and indeed issues of perspective in examining trans-Atlantic slavery, and hence contribute to an understanding of the roles, functions and influences of Africans in relation to what we recognize as the modern world.

By including 'Africa' in the discourse, the essays in this volume to some degree redefine 'western' and 'Atlantic', placing western Europe and western Africa into an Atlantic context that incorporates both north and south Atlantic, white and black. They focus on culture, language, class, gender, family and ethnic plurality, specifically relating the African background of the enslaved and their descendants to their sense of identity in the diaspora. They reveal that the ways in which enslaved Africans adjusted to the conditions of racialized servility in the Americas involved continuities and discontinuities, invention and re-invention.

An 'African-centred' focus, in contrast to one centred in Europe or the Americas, reveals the often neglected and misunderstood impact of the

African background upon the societies of the Americas and hence the relationship of slavery to modernity itself. It challenges the assumption that not much African history is relevant to the study of the Atlantic because the enslaved population was too diverse in its origins to sustain the continuities of history; or the corollary that the enslaved population, newly arrived from Africa, was comprised of autonomous individuals with such mixed experiences that they rapidly assimilated into the 'new' societies of the New World, whether characterized as 'American' or 'creole'.[3] The shift in focus renders evidence confirming complex links across and around the Atlantic that are surprising, mostly because of the degree to which they have been ignored or denied. It becomes clear that western Africa was not isolated from the Atlantic world.

The essays in this volume demonstrate that the processes of cultural change under slavery, and the importance of human agency in those processes, can be traced to every part of the slave route and have their beginning in Africa. Those enslaved found creative if also often desperate ways of adjusting to their bondage, of course relying heavily on familiar ideas and practices but adopting innovation out of necessity. The struggle for survival began in Africa, which certainly helped to shape the struggle that continued in the Americas. The emphasis on Africa is important because it places the 'middle passage' in the middle. What happened before the shipboard trauma had ramifications affecting the historical development of the African diaspora, the other side of the 'middle' for the enslaved. Those born in Africa had considerable adjustments to make all along the slave route; like all immigrants, whether moving voluntarily or in response to force, the journey itself was new, and the geographical setting of the final destination was unfamiliar. The Africanist approach compares the processes of history that affected enslaved Africans in the Americas with the experiences of those who remained in Africa.

In following the slave route, it is important to consider those among the enslaved who never left western Africa. As Francine Shields demonstrates in her study of enslaved Yoruba women in this volume, the southward push of the Sokoto *jihad* and the Yoruba wars generated a substantial population of slaves, many of whom experienced their captivity in Yorubaland, not in the Americas. Shields shows the particular outcomes of the slave experience to have been a matter of fate; whether those recently enslaved were kept relatively near their original homes or whether they reached Cuba or Brazil seemed to be the result primarily of chance. Indeed, the enslaved could find themselves on board ships that were intercepted by British anti-slave-trade patrols, which resulted in their liberation in Sierra Leone, Trinidad or elsewhere. Thus slaves faced a range of possible experiences that shaped the ways people thought about themselves and others in Africa and in the Americas. As Shields demonstrates, those slaves who remained in Yorubaland and were not deported themselves, none the less found they too had to adjust to their predicament.

By concentrating on the African, I am suggesting that we need to know how people were enslaved and the circumstances of their enslavement. Clearly, individuals resisted slavery at the point of enslavement, and often before, not only when they found themselves enslaved on board ship bound for the Americas or when they disembarked in the Americas and first came into contact with those who had already 'adjusted' to racialized slavery.[4] The individual accounts of the enslaved can be used to broaden our understanding of African history and the history of Africans in diaspora so that the timing and degree of the deracination process are placed in context. The view from Africa shows that this process was often complex.[5]

African backgrounds were diverse; there was no single cultural heritage in Africa that could provide a collective baseline when trying to survive in the Americas.[6] Still there were broad cultural and historical influences, as examined in this volume by Christine Ayorinde's treatment of the origins of Santería or in other studies that follow Muslims or Yoruba, Igbo and Kongo. Specific historical events and conditions in Africa sometimes influenced the adjustments and strategies of the enslaved in the Americas, especially when the patterns of trade concentrated people of similar background. The development of the new societies of the Americas depended to a great extent on cultural creativity in the New World, but historical events and developments in Africa would still have been significant in the consolidation of African heritage.

In focusing on the African, biographical materials can be invaluable. They can link shipping records to cultural changes corresponding to demographic patterns.[7] The approach is empirical in locating and studying texts, following people along the slave route and then crossing the Atlantic. It individualizes the slave trade and connects the enslaved to actual historical settings and events. It questions the assumptions of rapid assimilation of enslaved Africans into the slave systems of the Americas and of the 'newness' of the cultures of the Americas. Enslaved Africans may have found themselves in a 'melting pot', but they did not melt at the same rate or uniformly. A methodology that attempts to follow individual enslaved Africans to the Americas asks this melting-pot-of-slavery theory to explain when and how the melting occurred.

The method of identifying individual enslaved Africans and following their routes into slavery reveals that individuals were enslaved most often for political purposes and occasionally for more narrowly defined judicial or religious reasons. Individuals are rooted in specific places at exact times. From an Africanist perspective how and when each person reached the Americas has to be analysed in historical context, using rigorous historical methodology. Individuals, it can be assumed, reflect their communities of origin, providing details of events in particular places during the experience of enslavement and sometimes revealing other historical information as well. During different stages of forced reaction and adjustment, individuals were exposed to the vagaries of slave status, which were complex in Africa as they were across the Atlantic but in different ways. The recognition of stages of adjustment in the struggle for survival is a forward step in understanding the long route that individuals followed in slavery.

Western Africa in the Atlantic world

The place of the Atlantic is central in the debate over the Africanization of the Americas. The study of European merchant firms and commercial institutions requires a broad Atlantic perspective because their networks crossed national, ethnic and geographical boundaries and thereby shrank the Atlantic. The Atlantic dimension is clear. As goods of trade, enslaved Africans were channelled within these networks. But Africans were not only commodities of trade and units of labour power for the development of the Atlantic world; they were also people, and people unlike goods have memories, habits and expectations. An approach that regards the crossing as a link as well as a gap is now called for. Hence studies of the Atlantic world that focus solely on the northern Atlantic risk Eurocentric distortion.[8] The study of the slave trade as a demographic phenomenon largely overlooks the active and direct involvement of Africa in the development of the Atlantic in any way other than passively allowing its population to be stripped away. 'The Atlantic' usually denotes the European Atlantic, not Paul Gilroy's 'Black Atlantic'.[9]

The interface with Africa is a problem for Atlantic history, both conceptually and methodologically. If there was indeed an 'increasingly integrated and cohesive Atlantic world', which despite its 'diverse and heterogeneous' background 'became one – a unitary whole, a single system', as Philip Morgan has argued, then more attention has to be given to Africa's role in its development. Morgan recognizes that 'slavery was a central feature of this emergent Atlantic system', which suggests that the influence of Africa on this Atlantic world was profound. The increasing integration and cohesion that Morgan highlights depended upon the transformation of western Africa into a labour reservoir.[10] The stuff of 'Atlantic history' did not stop at the African coast but penetrated inland.[11] Specific historical events in western Africa were linked to and helped shape the trans-Atlantic slave trade. Western Africa was not a frontier analogous to the Northern Atlantic fisheries, open to all comers who wanted to plunder the stocks, with minimal resistance.[12] There was a sizeable population of people that had to be forcibly integrated into the Atlantic world.

The story of Fenda Lawrence, as told by Lillian Ashcraft-Eason in this volume, demonstrates that parts of western Africa were much more integrated into the Atlantic world than is often thought to have been the case. Fenda Lawrence, a free black woman from the Gambia river, travelled to Charleston, South Carolina, in 1772, a move unusual for a free black woman and even more so since she was a slave trader. Similarly, Alberto da Costa e Silva, in his essay on African royalty in Brazil, provides examples of both free and enslaved aristocrats from the Bight of Benin who were in Brazil in the late eighteenth and nineteenth centuries. Some were students and perhaps political/commercial 'hostages', while others were political prisoners sent into exile. Whether slave or free, these cases demonstrate a greater degree of familiarity with news across and around the Atlantic than is often assumed in attempts to comprehend what people knew about the trans-Atlantic world. There was a pool of common knowledge that was remarkable. The life stories of the élite, from Fenda Lawrence to the notables from the Bight of Benin, indicate that knowledge of trans-Atlantic slavery had to have been more widespread than is generally recognized.

The states and societies of western Africa participating in the trans-Atlantic trade in slaves were not isolated from the Atlantic rim (or, in many areas, from the Islamic world). Indeed, the merchants, seamen and others, both slave and free, who travelled the Atlantic interacted with a broad range of Africans. They filtered and spread cultural influences.[13] From an Africanist perspective, the essays in this volume are informative in examining the extent to which western Africa fitted into a single, trans-Atlantic system and in what ways such integration came about. Western Africa came into contact with the diverse and heterogeneous world around the Atlantic in the sixteenth century through the institution of racialized slavery. In its complexity, the Atlantic world was truly 'modern'. Yet despite the trend towards a unitary whole after the sixteenth century, the transition was not smooth, as the reliance on slavery demonstrates.[14]

The competing autonomy of the Islamic world (*Dar es-Islam*), including large parts of western Africa, was a factor that inhibited the integration of the Atlantic world into a single region, or at least makes it necessary for us to qualify claims regarding the extent to which some uniformity emerged.[15] *Dar es-Islam* experienced a protracted and painful interaction with Christian Europe, even before the exploitation of the Americas began, and this friction continued after the consolidation of an Atlantic world dominated by western Europe. The political and intellectual development of Islamic West Africa was orientated towards the central lands of Islam through heritage, pilgrimage, diplomacy, trade and education, while many of the coastal African ports were linked economically and culturally to the trans-Atlantic world. Indeed the ways in which the ports of coastal Africa were integrated into trans-Atlantic slavery reveal complex patterns that make it imperative to understand the African dimension.[16]

As a dynamic force in western Africa, Islam helped to shape slavery as an institution, including the provision of slaves for the trans-Atlantic market. The interaction between Muslims and Europeans highlights the need to study the history of slavery from a perspective other than one that locates all the forces of change in Europe and the Americas. Rather, the recognition of different worldviews suggests a series of perspectives that can be described as Eurocentric, Afrocentric and Islamic. Such perspectives can distort history through exclusivity and hence fail to 'situate' knowledge.[17]

Africans in diaspora

Who became assimilated and to what partly depended upon the relative numbers of people who crossed the Atlantic and the extent to which there were concentrations of people of similar origins in reasonably close settlement and within overlapping periods of arrival. The demography of trans-Atlantic migration is sufficiently well understood for it to be possible to establish the existence and location of such concentrations. The trade in enslaved Africans exceeded 11.5 million people, not all of whom arrived, but of those who did, most crossed the Atlantic in the 150 years after 1680.[18] Given the scale of this movement, it would be surprising if there were not concentrations of people of similar background. Many ethnic, geographical, linguistic and other designations can be identified. Several ethnic groups, representing different cultural backgrounds, stand out. Those studied in this volume include Yoruba (Warner-Lewis, da Costa e Silva and Yai), Gbe (Ewe/Fon) (Greene on the Anlo, da Costa e Silva and Yai), Igbo (Chambers), and the closely related 'Bantu'-speaking groups from West–Central Africa (e.g. Kongo, Mbundu) (Florentino and Góes).

By the 1780s, the slave trade brought five and a half million Africans to the Americas, while only one million people born in Europe (British, French, Dutch, Spanish or Portuguese) emigrated to the Americas.[19] The relative scale of these migrations should be noted. As with enslaved Africans, the migration from western Europe also resulted in a high degree of concentration, although Europeans tended to settle in their own colonies, while enslaved Africans found themselves in many different colonies. None the less, the absolute numbers of Africans and the timing of migrations in relation to economic developments meant that in most colonies in the Americas, there was usually one dominant European cultural tradition, and a few dominant African traditions, albeit interacting in ways that were unique and hence 'creole'.

The ratio of males to females also affected the demography of migration and the subsequent growth of population in the Americas. Trans-Atlantic migration in general, whether voluntary or forced, was heavily male. In the case of the slave trade, there were almost two males for every female, although with considerable regional and temporal variation. Despite the relative scarcity of females, enslaved women often constituted the majority, sometimes the overwhelming majority, of available women for procreation. Whether European women were available or not, African women were subjected to sexual exploitation and abuse that influenced both cultural and demographic development, represented most tellingly in the creation of a mulatto population and the institutionalization of racism. As Hilary Beckles discusses in this volume, white attitudes towards gender and race changed; whether the slave population had largely come from Africa or been born in the Americas had a significant impact. Hence from an Africanist perspective, the demography of the enslaved population matters because culture and the dignity of people who have historical roots had to be transferred to the next generation, to those born into slavery in the Americas, and such transfer first and foremost involved child rearing.

The diaspora was clearly not a simple extension of African history, despite such obvious examples of African influences on the Americas as the *jihad* of the central Sudan in Bahia and the transfer of the secret society, *ekpe/abakuá*, from Old Calabar to Cuba.[20] The diaspora reflects layers of influences, and it is not always easy to determine in which directions ideas, or indeed even people, flowed. Fenda Lawrence and the Dahomean aristocracy are not the only examples of the interconnections across the Atlantic. Their personal histories demonstrate that African history did extend into the diaspora, just as the tentacles of Atlantic commerce reached into Africa.[21] There is every reason to postulate the flow of reciprocal influences across the Atlantic, Yoruba influencing Yoruba, whether in Sierra Leone, Cuba, Bahia or the Bight of Benin, and Muslims attempting to adhere to Islamic orthodoxy. Influences were complicated and multilayered, which is why an anthropological approach that telescopes history, establishing a static ethnographic past, has its own methodological weaknesses. The general movement of people was indeed from Africa to the Americas, but ideas moved in many directions around the Atlantic, as did some people.

The interactions between Europe and the larger world, via each individual colony, and the multicultural setting of each slave society take on new meaning from this revised view of the Atlantic world. The task of the historian is to demonstrate how these complex interactions occurred and with what impact, considering the peculiar way in which western Africa, western Europe and the Americas were incorporated through trans-Atlantic slavery. To miss these ongoing, if often intermittent, interactions during and after the era of slavery is to ignore or misjudge the facts and distort the analysis of the processes whereby both African–American and western African societies developed.

Ethnicity

The concept of 'diaspora' has been used to describe the dispersal of enslaved Africans to the Americas.[22] Joseph Harris provides a typology of dispersion in his definition:

> The African diaspora concept subsumes the following: the global dispersion (voluntary and involuntary) of Africans throughout history; the emergence of a cultural identity abroad based on origin and social condition; and the psychological or physical return to the homeland, Africa.[23]

For Harris, the African diaspora is 'the historical relationship between Africans and their descendants abroad' and 'an extension of the African heritage'.[24]

To outsiders, the distinguishing features of diasporas are often hard to see, and hence it is essential to 'deconstruct' the African diaspora in order to 'reconstruct' its history as history situated in Africa.[25] The people who ended up in the Americas left areas that were frequently the scenes of disaster – the stuff of history. When John Thornton reveals the influence of the Kongo civil wars on the revolution in St Domingue, he is not only addressing issues of agency in the Americas but also uncovering new material on the Kongo civil wars themselves.[26] How was it that these traditions of Kongo ideological and political struggle could survive in the diaspora? What does this legacy tell us about the nature of the civil wars? These African influences in the Americas are empirical evidence of historical change in Africa. To ignore these 'survivals' is to deprive African historiography of valuable source material, as well as to overlook the individual histories of enslaved Africans and the full extent of their struggle in the Americas.

Ethnic identification implies a mechanism for preserving and highlighting culture and hence is a key concept in examining the construction of diasporas. Applying the concept of ethnicity to slave societies, one would expect to find a series of autonomous or semi-autonomous groups that traced their roots to Africa, often with continuing linkages or later connections that were intended to recreate associations that had been 'lost'. These connections have sometimes been recognized as 'shipboard' bonding, but in most of these cases, bonds were consolidated along spontaneously generated ethnic lines and communicated through a common language, whatever the dialectal differences that had to be overcome. Were these bonds more common on the ships of some nations than on others, in some periods, on particular stretches of the coast? While these kinds of questions may be answerable through an analysis of the extensive source materials that are now known to exist, caution against generalizations is advised. Undoubtedly, assimilation occurred and creole societies were formed that went on to mix populations of diverse backgrounds; when, how quickly, and under whose direction are surely subjects of research and reflection.

Ethnic identifications come into being in specific historical circumstances and require recognition of categories by the participants, both members and outsiders. A historical model of ethnicity looks for interaction and change, not isolation and stasis. A dynamic view of ethnicity emerges where the movements of individuals are traced along the slave routes from Africa to their destinations for as many people as possible.[27] Such an approach, at the very least, allows for the possibility that an African-centred (and Islamic) perspective can correct distorted views of the relationship of the African ethnicity to the lived experiences of slaves in the Americas and Europe. The black diaspora was in fact a series of diasporas of different ethnicities, involving the amalgamation of many sub-ethnicities, which were occasionally revealed, as for example through the use of patronymics and the adoption of other naming practices that were the 'survivals' of kinship networks.

As an examination of caste, class and ethnicity in the interior of western Africa demonstrates, the ways in which people identified themselves and were identified by others were related to complex economic, social and political forces. For example, salt workers and merchants in the central Sudan during the era of the trans-Atlantic and trans-Saharan slave trades had diverse backgrounds, from slave to free, that were sometimes regarded as ethnic.[28] Ethnicity, social identity and even class and occupation intersected in a series of overlapping 'diasporas' within the central Sudan which suggest that the changes under slavery affected people in many different and individual ways.

The Africanist approach recognizes the existence of what Melville Herskovits called 'culture areas', but allows for more than one cultural tradition and does not impose later ethnography on the historical record. As Sandra Greene cautions in her discussion of cultural areas along the West African coast, the relationships among people have to be examined with respect to specific institutions and practices, in historical context. In the case of the relationship between Anlo and Yoruba, the context of the slave trade mattered but does not explain when and how particular cultural, religious and ideological features spread along the lagoons behind the Bight of Benin.

In looking at the specific histories and cultural struggles that were peculiar to slave America, it must be kept in mind that ethnicity is not a *thing* to be discovered by a test conducted either by historians today or by people in the past who applied ethnic categories to themselves or to others. Ethnic identification involved and involves reinterpretation and re-invention of the present and the past. All ethnic categories change, and often they contain contradictions that in themselves have varying degrees of significance. Uncovering the multiple layers of change that are often disguised, but sometimes readily apparent, in ethnic identifications is a useful methodological technique in reconstructing history. The task is to figure out when and how ethnic categories developed and for what purposes, with the ultimate aim of explaining how people established communities in the Americas.

Ethnic designations that were used in the past to identify categories of captives by place of origin, religion and language indirectly provide keys to unlock the ways in which western Africa became integrated into the Atlantic world and the ways in which there was resistance to that integration. These categories were used for purposes of social control and identification, but reveal deep historical roots. The 'ethnolinguistic continuity' along the Atlantic seaboard of Africa has long been recognized, although interpretation of this 'continuity' is subject to debate.[29] As Greene demonstrates, issues of gender and ethnicity were intertwined. Many people in western Africa were preoccupied with issues of status, which related to who their mothers were and whether they had been slave, pawn or 'free'. Ethnic background was closely associated with the status of different wives and sexual partners. Hence the ability of women to form liaisons with important men, including Europeans, was a factor in ethnic identity, as Ashcraft-Eason demonstrates in this volume. Broadened conceptions of ethnicity developed in the diaspora, particularly among Igbo and Yoruba. However, the impact of such developments in the diaspora on the cultural and social history of the homeland is not resolved. Sometimes it is assumed that ethnic identifications became more inclusive as a result of the forced migration of slavery and that ethnic solidarity emerged where none had previously existed, as Chambers argues in his discussion of Igbo in diaspora in this volume. As used by specialists, ethnic terms reveal historical processes that were far from static.[30]

The attempt to identify people with ethnic categories within West Africa dates back well before the opening of the Atlantic trade. In the early seventeenth century, Ahmad Baba of Timbuktu wrote a treatise on ethnicity and slavery in West Africa that is clearly based on widespread usage of certain ethnic terms that did not just suddenly come into existence. As the indigenous Arabic texts of West Africa establish, the use of ethnic concepts was widespread in West Africa during the era of the trans-Atlantic slave trade, as it had been earlier. The etymologies of terms like 'Hausa', 'Bambara' and 'Yoruba' have been traced to questions of the legitimacy of enslavement and efforts to classify people for purposes of protection as well as oppression.[31] Muslims conversant with the debate over ethnicity and slavery were none the less enslaved and deported to the Americas, as well as to North Africa, which helps explain how the use of certain ethnic terms spread to European languages. Changes in the uses of these terms are themselves subjects of historical research, but the terms also have legitimacy for certain purposes of historical analysis in the same way that 'French', 'German', 'Portuguese' and other European ethnic/national terms are used, even while requiring deciphering. The 'national' histories of Europe tend to use broad cultural designations derived from names of languages or geographical areas, but who exactly were 'Portuguese' in the sixteenth- or seventeenth-century Atlantic world? 'Portuguese' in fact could include mulattos, converted Jews, and in south-eastern Africa those with mixed ancestry from India. Complexities like these reveal some of the conceptual problems raised by attempting to explain the meaning of ethnicity among African populations. How the exact mixes came about in each area is subject to standard and rigorous historical research and reconstruction to the degree that it is ever possible or desirable.

Ethnic and linguistic patterns in the Americas were the result of processes of adjustment, sometimes called 'creolization'. However, neither ethnicity nor language was static in western Africa – the processes of historical change did not begin in the Americas. Too often, however, ethnicity and language are treated as static, to the exclusion of the complex ways in which ethnic designations actually came about and were used in the past. Whether or not the Bambara were a 'true ethnic group', for example, misses the dynamic, contradictory and constantly changing conceptions of ethnicity.[32] Yet historical research on western Africa shows that ethnicity has been a key factor in the ways in which people have been identified and identified themselves in the context of historical change. Any static understanding of ethnicity that acknowledges no process, no change, whether in Africa or the Americas, is therefore suspect.[33] As Morgan warns, there is 'a distinct danger . . . in applying terms such as ethnic group and nation indiscriminately in African and African–American studies'.[34] For this reason, the meaning of ethnic and national identity in the early modern era is a central problem in African history, even more so than in any other case.

While scholars who study slavery in the Americas sometimes recognize the African background as 'important', they usually do not examine the specific historical contexts from which the enslaved came. They nod in the direction of Africa, but they do not adopt a perspective from Africa.[35] It is as if individuals stopped being 'Africans' once they were on board

'European' ships. While ethnic communities such as Yoruba and Fon took on new meaning in the Americas, these groupings were more than manifestations of the creative adaptation of people to conditions of slavery through acts of cultural resistance. In Africa, people with diverse origins still recognized cultural and linguistic cohesion when it occurred, and they invented common historical traditions when necessary, as in the case of Asante, Dahomey or the revolutionary Muslim movement of the eighteenth and nineteenth centuries.

The creole generation

The term 'creole' has various meanings in the study of slavery and its aftermath. In some contexts, 'creole' means 'born in the Americas', sometimes applied only to the enslaved population but by extension to the mulatto population and other people of mixed descent, and ultimately to the descendants of European settlers as well. The linguistic term takes on cultural meaning, suggesting a 'new' society arising from the peculiar interaction between people from western Europe and western Africa under conditions of slavery and colonialism. The term is also used in linguistics to refer to the offspring of speakers of dialects, common or trade languages by people working together without a common first language. By extension, the concept of 'creolization' has been used to describe the process of creating and maintaining distinct cultures and societies in the Americas.

There are other meanings of the term, which suggest that an Atlantic-wide perspective must be adopted in considering processes of change and adaptation, and how birth in the 'new' environment of bondage, i.e. the 'creole' setting, affected the lives of people and the nature of their culture. 'Creole' (or 'Krio') was used in West Africa to describe the population of mixed ancestry in Sierra Leone and subsequently along other parts of the West African coast, and hence the term has also assumed ethnic connotations.[36] The origins of this usage can be traced to Portuguese-dominated trade along the western African coast, where a pidgin version of Portuguese was widespread from the sixteenth century onward and was identified with people of mixed European and African origins, including former slaves from the Americas. As in the Americas, the term suggests that people of diverse origins were amalgamated into a new identity, only in this case 'Krio' emerged as an ethnic designation.

The term is often thought to be Portuguese in origin (*crioulo*), deriving from *criar*, 'to nurse or breed'. Maureen Warner-Lewis provides an alternative etymology, arguing persuasively that the term is actually derived from Kikongo, and not Portuguese, specifically from *nkuulolo*, 'a person excluded, an outsider', *kuulolo*, 'excluded', *kuula*, 'to be outside, exiled, excluded'. According to Warner-Lewis, the word was 'co-opted by subsequent generations from the vocabulary of the first generation of Africans but its semantic range broadened to include Europeans as well as Africans' who were 'exiled' from the Old World, and by extension 'born in the Americas' and hence 'culturally of the Americas'.[37]

The various uses of the term 'creole' present a problem in its effectiveness as a concept in analysing the cultural and social adjustments experienced by enslaved Africans in the Americas. While initially referring to those born in the Americas of African descent, whether or not racially mixed, by extension the term became associated with culture and was applied to mixed populations, whether or not of African descent, as long as they were born in the Americas.[38] In some constructions, moreover, birth in the Americas is not an essential feature. Ira Berlin uses the term 'Atlantic creoles' to designate 'those who by experience or choice, as well as by birth, became part of a new culture that emerged along the Atlantic littoral – in Africa, Europe, or the Americas – beginning in the 16th century'.[39] And as we have seen, Krio emerged as a name for a language and a people born in Africa.

The difference between first and second (and subsequent) generations is fundamental to the concept of 'creole', as applied in the Americas. The term implicitly distinguishes those born in the Americas under slavery from those born in Africa, whatever their status had been there. Where one was born, and most especially on which side of the Atlantic, was a crucial feature of slavery. Whether an individual slave had been born into slavery or had been retained in a society and culture as a slave had an influence on status, identity and cultural autonomy. Those who had gained some familiarity with the culture and society of their masters acquired a recognizable status distinct from a newly bought slave, whether in western Africa or the Americas. In the sense that 'creole' is often used in the Americas, those born into slavery in western Africa were usually called 'slaves of the house', sometimes referred to as 'domestic' slaves, but it is significant that the distinction between generations was also important. However, in the Americas even those slaves born in Africa found it extremely difficult if not impossible to re-establish African cultural and societal systems as they had known them in Africa within the institution of racialized slavery and the political environment of colonized America, whereas slaves in the non-racialized environment of western Africa might find themselves familiar with local society and culture.

According to Kamau Braithwaite, 'creolization' is a cultural process that identified those of slave status and African origin with a distinctive and separate culture in opposition to the dominant culture and society of European origin. This opposition between dominant culture and subordinate status was specific to slavery in tropical plantation colonies:

> Within the dehumanizing institution of slavery . . . were two cultures of people, having to adapt themselves to a new environment and to each other. The friction created by this confrontation was cruel, but it was also creative. The white plantations and social institutions . . . reflect one aspect of this. The slaves' adaptation of their African culture to a new world reflects another.[40]

Specifically Braithwaite envisioned creolization in Jamaica as the emergence of 'authentically local institutions' and a 'little tradition' among slaves that reflected a division between two *separate* traditions. Cultural polarity was the basis of the 'creole' society, which was defined more by its divisions than by its shared elements and hence was not a 'plural' society that came to share increasingly common values. Braithwaite placed 'creole' society along a 'historically affected social-cultural continuum . . . [of] interrelated and sometimes overlapping orientations'.[41] For Braithwaite, the 'submerged mother of the creole system' was Africa.[42]

Sidney Mintz and Richard Price have used 'creolization' to emphasize the cultural creativity of the enslaved in the Americas. Despite the oppressive conditions in the Americas, enslaved Africans demonstrated a degree of resourcefulness that produced Afro-Caribbean and more generally Afro-American cultures which were 'creole' because these hybrid cultures were 'born' in the Americas. They argue that creolization involved a period of adjustment that was remarkably fast. Given that slaves faced the seemingly insurmountable problem of establishing any relationships based on African experiences, Mintz and Price postulate a situation in which social relationships had to face the problem of a virtual vacuum, and that under such oppressive conditions inventiveness was rewarded, not tradition. Hence, they conclude, that 'distinctive, "mature" African–American [i.e. creole] cultures and societies probably developed more rapidly than has often been assumed', indeed occurring 'within the earliest years of slavery'.[43] Their assumption is that not much of African culture could have been conveyed to the Americas because of the heterogeneity of the enslaved population and the absence of appropriate institutions.[44]

Certainly the disruption that characterized the forced movement to the Americas was crucial in the lives of the enslaved, but the 'resistant response' to the oppression of slavery did not just happen in the Americas when enslaved Africans were incorporated into 'new', hybrid cultures.[45] It does appear that there was rapid change in language, as suggested in Olabiyi Yai's discussion of early Fon and Yoruba texts from Brazil, and Maureen Warner-Lewis's discussion of Yoruba songs in Trinidad, both in this volume. Moreover, Jane Landers (also in this volume) demonstrates that the *cimarrón* communities around the Caribbean often incorporated fugitive slaves from many different backgrounds and therefore were perhaps more 'creolized' than in the plantation areas where slaves of similar origins sometimes were concentrated. However, the extent to which the African background played itself out in the course of adaptation is not a closed question. Certainly, Igbo identity in the diaspora, as examined in Douglas Chambers' contribution to this volume, raises questions about ongoing processes of ethnic definition and redefinition, in which the 'creole' setting of the Americas was important but was only one more setting to which people had to adapt.

None the less, the backgrounds of slaves cannot be depersonalized, reduced only to 'deep-level cultural principles' that miraculously survived the Atlantic crossing. As Mintz and Price note, friendships of oppression (e.g. shipboard bonding) that usually had no institutionalized basis in Africa, provided a basis for social relationships under slavery.[46] According to Mintz and Price,

> the beginnings of what would later develop into 'African–American cultures' must date from the very earliest interactions of the enslaved men and women on the African continent itself. They were shackled together in coffles, packed into dank 'factory' dungeons, squeezed together between the decks of stinking ships, separated often from their kinsmen, tribesmen, or even speakers of the same language, left bewildered about their present and their future, stripped of all prerogatives of status or rank, ... and homogenized by a dehumanizing system that viewed them as faceless and largely interchangeable.[47]

While this context fostered the creation of creole cultures, the historical lens telescopes the 'creolization' process, unless it is recognized that there were significant variations in the common heritage that Africans are sometimes thought to have shared.[48] Claims that 'all African slaves' shared a 'common heritage . . . despite their origins in different parts of Africa' have no more analytical value than the statement that all slaves experienced oppression.[49]

Mintz and Price emphasize the 'rapid' creolization of newly arrived slaves from Africa, but this emphasis faces problems raised by the various studies in this volume, which show that the African people crossing the Atlantic included both slaves and free men and women. Trans-Atlantic patterns of interaction continued much longer and in greater strength than Mintz and Price have allowed, which raises new questions about which aspects of African history are relevant for the study of slavery in the Americas. As Stephan Palmié has observed,

> despite its theoretical sophistication and methodological soundness, the 'rapid early synthesis' model suggested by Mintz and Price fell short of stimulating a thorough historicization of African–American anthropology. Instead, and quite contrary to these authors' intentions, it sometimes seems to have encouraged hypostatizing the concept of creolization to a degree where it allows glossing over history in a manner reminiscent of an earlier inflationary use of the concept of 'acculturation'. This tendency . . . not only trivializes the question of how exactly 'creole' syntheses were achieved, but also obscures the formidable problems presented by cases where covariational 'adhesions' might plausibly be attributed to Atlantic transfer – not necessarily of concrete forms, but of organizational models.[50]

The most serious oversight due to the 'hypostatization' of the concept of creolization is the significance of the difference between first- and second-generation immigrants. Douglas Chambers has attempted to describe the different, but continuous, processes of adaptation in terms of primary and secondary creolization – an initial stage, with a high proportion of African-born slaves, and a later stage, with a predominance of American-born slaves in the population.[51] More than one 'charter generation' was possible, given the uneven development of the larger plantation areas.

As early as 1916, Fernando Ortiz described the adjustments under slavery as a gradual process of incorporation or 'transculturation':

> *Transculturation* . . . expresses the different phases of the process of transition from one culture to another . . . [which] does not consist merely

in acquiring another culture [i.e. *acculturation*] . . ., but the process also necessarily involves the loss or uprooting of a previous culture, which could be defined as deculturation.[52]

Braithwaite describes the phenomenon in similar terms as 'interculturation'. Both terms suggest phases of 'creolization', in contrast to an initial, sudden creation of 'creole' culture for the mass of newly imported, deracinated African slaves who serve as the model for the study of cultural impact in the depiction of slavery conveyed by Mintz and Price.

The reformulation of African norms can be established in different contexts, such as Cuba, where there are signs of ongoing interaction across the Atlantic, even during the days of slavery.[53] As Christine Ayorinde discusses in her essay on the Santería movement in Cuba, the interaction between Ifá divination traditions and the worship of *orisha* has been continuous and has involved ongoing interaction across the Atlantic. Hence, her findings, when placed alongside Sandra Greene's examination of Yoruba influences among the Anlo (Gbe) along the lagoons behind the Bight of Benin, demonstrate that cultural interaction and transformation were not isolated, but affected areas on both sides of the Atlantic. The flow of culture was not one way only, from Africa to the Americas.

For some, the most appropriate model for explaining the evolution of slave culture in the Americas is the image of the 'melting pot', first used to explain the mixing of white people from different parts of Europe in the United States.[54] According to Eltis and Richardson, the melting-pot imagery of European migration also applies to enforced African immigration because

> heterogeneous groups of African peoples [were] thrown together in the Americas . . . drawing on and modifying often very diverse individual and collective experiences and skills in order to build new identities and communities . . . In the final analysis, . . . the cultures of slave-based communities were essentially new and owed more to the conditions that Africans encountered in America than to their upbringing in Africa.[55]

The metaphor of the melting pot overlooks the fact that many did not melt, however. It ignores the persistence of a great range of differences in the Americas, whether in eighteenth-century New York or nineteenth-century Bahia. Sometimes the enslaved melted; sometimes they did not. Rates and degrees of amalgamation varied over time and space. The African background was more than malleable wax, even if perhaps too 'heterogeneous' to be easily traceable in all situations.

On first consideration, the concept of creolization as a gradual or protracted process of cultural invention, subject to the adjustments forced by the 'resistant responses' of slaves, seems to explain the evolution of a common 'American' culture and society (or cultures and societies), and hence the 'miracle' of which Michel-Rolph Trouillot speaks.[56] This 'creolization' model still skips over African history, however. As Palmié has explained, it is not always clear 'how exactly historical human agency makes the respective (formal and functional) variables "stick" in specific instances'. Any explanation of slave behaviour and cultural expression that relies solely on the adaptive responses of slaves to the environment of the Americas 'evades the issue of systemic articulations that may . . . reveal single observational units to be part and parcel of larger, encompassing historical processes operating on a transatlantic scale'.[57]

In discussing the creolization of the enslaved population, it is essential that history not be telescoped, compressing the African past into some generalized shape. Whereas Herskovits romanticized the African context, thinking that the American derivative of the African was self-destructive in the hegemonic structure of imperial European culture and society, the creolization model often mistakes the end result of migration as the beginning. But how and why specific cultural and historical connections were destroyed, when and where contact was maintained or re-established with the African past, and how the past was subsequently re-invented are still subjects of study. In fact there were many links across the Atlantic, including Muslim, Yoruba, Igbo/Efik, Kongo, Akan and others, besides those emanating from Europe.

Conclusion

The fragmented lives of the enslaved Africans who crossed the Atlantic can be reconstructed to reveal an Africa that shaped the creolization of the Americas and does not entirely divorce slaves from their origins. Such an approach opens the door to the findings of a whole generation of African historiography.[58] Anthropological models of slavery and servility in Africa have little to say about the historical processes that influenced trans-Atlantic slavery, unless firmly rooted in specifics of history.[59] Transformations occurred in western Africa that suggest that slavery was not a mere variation of a range of relationships that marginalized people. Rather, enslavement and slave use in Africa increased in response to the trans-Atlantic demand for slaves and continued to do so after the termination of that traffic, particularly in the areas under Muslim control. Because of these transformations, abolition of the trans-Atlantic slave trade did not end slavery in western Africa. The incidence of enslavement remained high, and the numbers of slaves increased in the course of the nineteenth century. Slavery came to a slow and intermittent end under European colonialism in the twentieth century. The former slaves and descendants of slaves who returned to Africa continued to be involved in issues of enslavement and emancipation well into the twentieth century. The reverse migration of 'African–Americans' to Africa is also part of the history of slavery and its termination.

A perspective that focuses on 'creolization' as a process that arises only in the Americas, as Mintz and Price postulate, risks misrepresenting the African dimension and indeed is frequently ahistorical. There is too much reading backwards from a present in which African culture has indeed melted into the larger cultural history of the Americas. From the perspective of Africa, the study of slavery has to be centred in the period in which the slaves who had been born in Africa actually lived. The continuities and disjunctures in their personal and collective lives have to be considered as factors that shaped slave society and ultimately affected the formation of 'creole' culture (or cultures) in the Americas.

The purpose of understanding the African part of slavery is not just to add a chronological or geographical dimension in order to complete the American, particularly North American, and European narratives. The purpose of identifying the individuals and collectives among the oppressed in the trans-Atlantic slavery nexus is to work out a new 'partial perspective' in the study of slavery. The focus on creolization draws attention to the agency of slaves themselves in fashioning an identity within the oppressive conditions of slavery. This America-centric perspective is not wrong; it is only partial. As Haraway has suggested,[60] the task of 'situating knowledge' is an attempt to overcome claims to objectivity by a vision from a largely imaginary 'totalized', universal (unlocated) point of view which in fact is itself far from objective. To reflect and define the partiality of perspective, to 'incorporate' more views means to move in the direction of increased objectivity. Adding the Afrocentric perspective on slavery not only adds another view, but also helps to mark the European/American as partial (and self-interested because Americanist history uses the history of Africans in the Americas to construct 'American' identity). Letting the source materials, particularly the voices of the people from the past, speak for themselves spotlights the crucial issues of who is investigating the past and where the investigation is being conducted. As the interests (race, class, ethnicity, gender, age, religion, etc.) of interpreters become more visible, it becomes increasingly difficult for their interpretations to make claims as 'truth'.

There is every reason to repudiate the all-encompassing domination of the European in analysing the non-European subaltern, but there is no reason to adopt a wholly new paradigm and an alternate language to analyse relationships of oppression that are divorced from history. It is inappropriate, since the relationships between Europeans and Africans, Christians and Muslims, and indeed males and females changed over time. As Haraway advocates, 'the privilege of partial perspectives' allows for the possibility of 'partial, locatable, critical knowledges sustaining the possibility of webs of connections called solidarity in politics and shared conversations in epistemology'.[61] The chapters in this volume constitute such a web of connections. Indeed a search of the African diaspora reveals that enslaved Africans spun their own webs in the course of their forced relocation and deportation to the Americas, which were subsequently reinforced by the movements of people and ideas across and indeed all around the Atlantic. Enslaved Africans were not passive materials moulded by the wills of their masters or by the imaginations of historical interpreters. In recognizing what Haraway calls the 'agency of the objects of research', the aim is to see the enslaved as individuals who had their own existence independent of the interests of the researchers.

The essays in this volume examine the issue of identity in the shadow of slavery. One theme is ethnic separateness as against ethnic mingling and indeterminacy; viz Landers on *cimarrón* ethnicity, Chambers on Igbo, Ayorinde and Warner-Lewis on Yoruba, Greene on Gbe and specifically Anlo-Ewe, Yai and da Costa on Fon and Yoruba, and Florentino/Góes on a population largely from West–Central Africa. Da Costa continues the theme of overseas African personalities treated in Warner-Lewis's contribution, while the final four essays deal with gender issues (Florentino/Góes on family patterns in rural Rio de Janeiro, Beckles on gender ideology, Shields on women slaves in Yorubaland, and Ashcraft-Eason on the unusual career of Fenda Lawrence, originally from the Gambia). The contrast between the wretchedness of the women in Shield's study and Fenda Lawrence's relative independence is worthy of note, while the characters in da Costa's chapter on aristocrats in exile or captivity serve as wonderful counterpoint to Ashcraft-Eason's depiction of Fenda Lawrence.

Jane Landers explores ethnicity and cultural adaptation among fugitive slaves in the Hispanic domains bordering the Caribbean between 1503 and 1763. She demonstrates that fugitive slaves had to adjust rapidly to survive, and in doing so, they often merged cultural features in ways that reflect the adaptive responses of slaves in the Americas, even revealing a willingness to reach an accommodation with the Spanish authorities. 'Creolization' seems to have been particularly intense among those achieving their autonomy from the slave regime. Yet in his chapter, Douglas Chambers follows Igbo into diaspora, demonstrating how a sense of community evolved in the process of dispersion. Chambers shows that dispersed Igbo developed concepts of group identity in the eighteenth century because enslaved Igbo were concentrated in particular parts of the Caribbean and North America.

Christine Ayorinde examines *orisha* worship and Ifá divination, both of Yoruba origin, in Cuba, where these phenomena are commonly referred to as Santería. She shows how religious practice has reflected the ongoing reinterpretation of the sense of Cuban identity. Intermittent links across the Atlantic have been central to the historical development of Regla de Ocha/Ifá, but these institutions, while distinctly Yoruba in origin, have none the less come to represent a much broader community than simply one of the people who can trace their Yoruba ancestry.

In examining the western portion of the Bight of Benin, Sandra Greene demonstrates that cultural zones are elusive constructs that have to be examined historically. Ethnic and cultural constructs are not simply replicated, either within West Africa or in the diaspora. How and when Ifá divination and *orisha* worship spread in West Africa and was then reinterpreted locally are as significant as the spread of these institutions to the Americas under slavery. Hence the process of cultural amalgamation and adaptation examined by Landers was under way in West Africa, also under the shadow of slavery.

As Olabiyi Yai observes, linguistic adjustments in both Fon and Yoruba can be traced through surviving vocabularies and word lists, which he examines for Brazil in the eighteenth and early nineteenth centuries. However, caution is advised; languages may change more rapidly than other aspects of culture as people work out a common dialect or pidgin to ease problems of communication. Maureen Warner-Lewis demonstrates in her chapter that Yoruba recaptives, liberated from slave ships in the nineteenth century and taken to Trinidad, evolved common traditions that were reinterpretations of institutions and symbols that reflected important political differences in West Africa but in diaspora came to help shape a new sense of 'Yorubaness'.

The chapters by Lillian Ashcraft-Eason and Alberto da Costa e Silva demonstrate that there was a limited degree of ongoing contact across the Atlantic during the slave-trade era. As the career of Fenda Lawrence reveals, at least one women slave trader from West Africa travelled to the Americas. Moreover, the travels of West African royalty, both as slaves and as free people, also established some degree of continuity across the Atlantic, so that cultural and linguistic memories were occasionally reinforced by personal contact. An examination of identity under slavery has to allow for these continuing linkages.

Manolo Garcia Florentino and José Roberto Góes show in their study of rural family life and kinship among slaves in the boom economy of Rio de Janeiro between 1790 and 1830 that enslaved Africans, most of whom came from West–Central Africa, tended to (re-)establish familial and kin networks when they could, but that rapid expansion in the economy and the arrival of large numbers of newly enslaved people threatened the creole-born population and reduced the relative proportion of cross-ethnic unions. Their study raises questions about the relative pace of cultural adaptation depending upon the state of the economy and the scale of forced immigration.

Hilary Beckles emphasizes the significant change in gender relation-ships between first and subsequent generations of enslavement in the Americas, a pattern that is particularly relevant in studying Igbo migrants, because relatively more Igbo women were enslaved in the Americas than women from other ethnic backgrounds. Attitudes towards gender and work changed as the demographic profile of the slave population changed. The emphasis on birth in the Americas, the creation of a 'creole' generation, inevitably resulted in new factors shaping people's identities. Finally, Francine Shields examines the lives of Yoruba women slaves who remained in the homeland in the nineteenth century. Her study reveals the complex backgrounds of the enslaved; issues of identity involving the emergence of Yoruba as a distinct ethnic category played themselves out in West Africa as well as across the Atlantic.

As these essays demonstrate, identity is in any case a shadowy concept, one that is open to interpretation, reinterpretation and even misinterpreta-tion. In the context of racialized slavery in the Americas, identity is even more elusive – due to factors of security, social control and resistance. Who people were, how they were seen and how they saw themselves changed depending upon the situation and the perspective of the viewer. The coercion implicit in the slave regime inhibited and thereby shaped to a large degree which cultural features survived and which could not, however embattled.

Notes

1 An earlier version of this essay was presented at the UNESCO/SSHRCC Summer Institute, 'Identifying Enslaved Africans: The "Nigerian" Hinterland and the African Diaspora' (York University, Toronto, 1997). In developing the ideas in this essay, I owe a great debt to many people, but most especially to Robin Law; see our 'Deconstructing the African Diaspora: The Slave Trade of the "Nigerian" Hinterland' (paper presented at the conference 'The African Diaspora and the "Nigerian" Hinterland: Towards a Research Agenda', York University, Toronto, 1996); and (with Elisée Soumonni) 'The Development of an African Diaspora: The Slave Trade of the "Nigerian" Hinterland, 1650–1900' (working paper, UNESCO Slave Route Project, Cabinda, Angola, 1996). Douglas Chambers, David Richardson, Viktoria Schmidt-Linsenhoff, Maureen Warner-Lewis, David Trotman and Jane Landers shared with me important insights, provided references and issued critiques. I owe a special debt to Brenda McComb, whose persistence and skill in editing made me think more clearly. The research for this paper was supported by the Social Sciences and Humanities Research Council of Canada and was undertaken while I was a Killam Senior Research Fellow (Canada Council).
2 The concept of 'Afrocentrism' as developed by Molefi Kete Asante in *The Afrocentric Idea* (Philadelphia, 1987) has been criticized for overrepresenting the diaspora of the North Atlantic. Since the United States was the most 'melted' region of slavery in the Americas, a concentration on North America risks an 'American' bias. For a discussion of 'Afrocentricity' see Asante, 'Afrocentricity', in William Andres, Frances Smith Foster and Trudier Harris (eds), *The Oxford Companion to American Literature* (Oxford, 1997), pp. 8–10.
3 Sidney Mintz and Richard Price, *The Birth of African-American Culture: An Anthropological Perspective* (Boston, 1992 [1976]).
4 Karen Fog Olwig, 'African Cultural Principles in Caribbean Slave Societies', in Stephan Palmié (ed.), *Slave Cultures and the Cultures of Slavery* (Knoxville, TN, 1995), p. 24.
5 According to Mintz and Price (*African-American Culture*, 18):
> The Africans who reached the New World did not compose, at the outset, *groups*. In fact, in most cases, it might even be more accurate to view them as *crowds*, and very heterogeneous crowds at that. Without diminishing the probable importance of some core of common values, and the occurrence of situations where a number of slaves of common origin might indeed have been aggregated, the fact is that these were not *communities* of people at first, and they could only become communities by processes of cultural change. What the slaves undeniably shared at the outset was their enslavement; all – or nearly all – else had to be *created by them*.

It is suggested here that this analysis has too many exceptions to carry much weight.
6 Melville Herskovits, *The Myth of the Negro Past* (New York, 1941).

7 Paul E. Lovejoy, 'Biography as Source Material: Towards a Biographical Archive of Enslaved Africans', in Robin Law (ed.), *Source Material for Studying the Slave Trade and the African Diaspora* (Stirling, Scotland, 1997), pp. 119–40.
8 For studies which reveal this problem of focusing on the north Atlantic to the virtual exclusion of the 'black' Atlantic, see Bernard Bailyn, 'The Idea of Atlantic History', *Itinerario* 20, no. 1 (1996), pp. 19–44; Ira Berlin, 'From Creole to African: Atlantic Creoles and the Origins of African-American Society in Mainland North America', *William and Mary Quarterly* 53, no. 2 (1996); David Hancock, *Citizens of the World: London Merchants and the Integration of the British Atlantic Community, 1735–1785* (Cambridge, 1995); and Marc Egnal, *New World Economies: The Growth of the Thirteen Colonies and Early Canada* (Oxford, 1998).
9 Paul Gilroy, *The Black Atlantic: Modernity and Double Consciousness* (Cambridge, 1993).
10 Philip D. Morgan, 'The Cultural Implications of the Atlantic Slave Trade: African Regional Origins, American Destinations and New World Developments', *Slavery and Abolition* 18, no. 1 (1997), p. 122.
11 Ira Berlin incorporates the African littoral in his conception of the Atlantic but does not explain how far the process of creolization developed in such important enclaves as Bonny and Old Calabar in the Bight of Biafra, nor does he address the differences between Portuguese, English and French influences in that process; see Ira Berlin, 'From Creole to African'. Similarly, Joseph Miller trans-navigates the Atlantic, but presents the history of West–Central Africa, where slaves actually came from, in a cyclical fashion that is difficult to place in chronological sequence and hence cannot be tied easily to specific historical events. Africa is once again treated as marginal; see Joseph C. Miller, *Way of Death: Merchant Capital and the Angolan Slave Trade, 1730–1830* (Madison, WI, 1988). Miller describes his contribution to the study of the Portuguese Southern Atlantic slave trade as an examination of 'a marginal institution on the margin of the Atlantic system'; see Miller, 'A Marginal Institution on the Margin of the Atlantic System: The Portuguese Southern Atlantic Slave Trade in the Eighteenth Century', in Barbara L. Solow (ed.), *Slavery and the Rise of the Atlantic System* (Cambridge, 1991), pp. 120–50. It was marginal only from the perspective of Europe. The same criticism also applies to David Eltis, 'Precolonial Western Africa and the Atlantic Economy', in Solow, *Slavery and Atlantic System*, pp. 97–119.
12 Richard Thomas and Richard Bean, 'The Fishers of Men: The Profits of the Slave Trade', *Journal of Economic History* 34, no. 4 (1974).
13 Morgan, 'Cultural Implications', p. 122. Also see Bailyn, 'Idea of Atlantic History'. Despite the nod to Africanist research, Bailyn has not really come to terms with the extensive material on trans-Atlantic connections, which to some extent verify the approach of Gilroy in *Black Atlantic*, but expanding the analysis beyond the anglophone world of the northern Atlantic.
14 See Philip Morgan, 'Cultural Implications of the Atlantic Slave Trade', p. 122.
15 Ira Berlin and Earl Lewis both look in the direction of Atlantic history, but neither has included African history in his picture; see Berlin, 'Atlantic Creoles'; and Earl Lewis, 'To Turn as on a Pivot: Writing African Americans into a History of Over-lapping Diasporas', *American Historical Review* 100, no. 3 (1995).
16 Robin Law and Kristin Mann, 'West Africa in the Atlantic Community: The Case of the Slave Coast', *William and Mary Quarterly* 56, no. 1 (1999), pp. 307–34; and David Richardson, Paul E. Lovejoy and David Eltis, 'Slave Trading Ports: Towards an Atlantic-Wide Perspective, 1676–1832', in Robin Law (ed.), *The Ports of the Slave Trade (Bights of Benin and Biafra)* (Stirling, UK, 1999).
17 Donna Haraway, 'Situated Knowledges: The Science Question in Feminism and the Privilege of Partial Perspective', *Feminist Studies* 14, no. 3 (1988), pp. 575–99.

18 This estimate is based on the database of over 27,000 slaving voyages compiled by David Eltis, Stephen D. Behrendt, David Richardson, and Herbert S. Klein (eds), *The Transatlantic Slave Trade, 1527–1867: A Database* (Cambridge, 1999).

19 The source for the population estimate of Europeans in the Americas in c. 1780 is Philip D. Curtin, *The Atlantic Slave Trade: A Census* (Madison, 1969).

20 Paul E. Lovejoy, 'Background to Rebellion'; Stephan Palmié, 'Ekpe/Abakuá in Middle Passage', in Ralph Austen (ed.), *Slavery and Memory* (forthcoming).

21 João José Reis, *Slave Rebellion in Brazil: The Muslim Uprising of 1835 in Bahia* (Baltimore, 1993); and Paul E. Lovejoy, 'Background to Rebellion: The Origins of Muslim Slaves in Bahia', in Paul E. Lovejoy and Nicholas Rogers (eds), *Unfree Labour in the Development of the Atlantic World* (London, 1994), pp. 151–80.

22 The term 'diaspora' has also been used to describe the movements of dispersed ethnic minorities that dominated trade in West Africa and elsewhere; see Alusine Jalloh, introduction to Jalloh and Stephen E. Maizlish (eds), *The African Diaspora* (College Station, TX, 1996), pp. 3–5. Curtin has applied the concept in his accounts of commercial networks, but not to explain the African dispersal, and to the best of my knowledge, he nowhere explains his reason for distinguishing between plural societies and diasporas. Curtin has looked at commercial diasporas, but not ethnic diasporas more broadly, and therefore has failed to distinguish his conception of diaspora from ethnic dispersal; see his *Cross Cultural Trade in World History* (New York, 1984). In *The Rise and Fall of the Plantation Complex: Essays in Atlantic History* (New York, 1990), Curtin does not discuss the concept.

23 Joseph Harris, introduction to *Global Dimensions of the African Diaspora*, 2nd edn (Washington, DC, 1993), p. 3.

24 *Ibid.*, pp. 3–4.

25 Robin Law and Paul E. Lovejoy, 'The Changing Dimensions of the African History: Reappropriating the African Diaspora', in Kenneth King *et al.* (eds), *Rethinking African History: Interdisciplinary Perspectives* (Edinburgh, 1997).

26 John K. Thornton, '"I Am the Subject of the King of Congo": African Political Ideology and the Haitian Revolution', *Journal of World History*, 4, no. 2 (1993), pp. 181–214.

27 David Eltis and David Richardson, 'The "Numbers Game" and Routes to Slavery', *Slavery and Abolition* 18, no. 1 (1997), pp. 1–15.

28 Paul E. Lovejoy, *Caravans of Kola: The Hausa Kola Trade, 1700–1900* (Zaria and Ibadan, Nigeria, 1980); and Lovejoy, *Salt of the Desert Sun: Salt Production and Trade in the Central Sudan* (Cambridge, 1986).

29 See P. E. H. Hair, *Africa Encountered: European Contacts and Evidence 1450–1700* (Brookfield, VT, 1997), which reprints various earlier studies on 'ethnolinguistic continuity' along the Guinea coast. More recently John K. Thornton has updated the identification of specific ethnic groups and political units; see *Africa and Africans in the Making of the Atlantic World, 1400–1680* (Cambridge, 1992).

30 Certainly, the use of ethnicity as a substitute for 'tribe' is unacceptable in the view of scholarly literature. For a failure to understand the significance of ethnicity in African history, see, for example, Michael Mullin, *Africa in America: Slave Acculturation and Resistance in the American South and the British Caribbean, 1736–1831* (Urbana, IL, 1992). Moreover, much of the historical research on western African history would not support the conclusions of Olwig that 'clearly defined linguistic and cultural entities corresponding to tribes or ethnic groups' did not characterize western African societies before the colonial period, although she cites only anthropological sources and ignores the vast historical literature that would prove her wrong; see Olwig, 'African Cultural Principles'. Olwig cites Barrie Sharpe, 'Ethnography and a Regional System', *Critique of Anthropology* 6, no. 3 (1986), pp. 33–65, and Elizabeth Tonkin,

'West African Ethnographic Traditions', in R. Fardon (ed.), *Localizing Strategies: Regional Traditions of Ethnographic Writing* (Edinburgh, 1990), pp. 137–51.

31 See Paul E. Lovejoy, 'The Muslim Factor in the Trans-Atlantic Slave Trade' (paper presented at the University of the West Indies, Mona, Jamaica, 1997).

32 Morgan, 'Cultural Implications', p. 139. According to Morgan (*ibid.*, p. 136), 'so-called African ethnic or national identities were often convenient reconstitutions or inventions [in the New World]. Nor could these identities easily remain pristine in the pluralistic Americas.' However, Morgan's argument seems to suggest that ethnicity could be 'pristine', which seems to miss the significance of ethnicity in African history. Eltis and Richardson even argue that 'recent work suggests that in Africa ethnic affiliations may have had only marginal significance – it appears that the concept of "ethnicity" was rather more pliable than has sometimes been assumed'. But what they mean by 'marginal significance' is unclear (see 'Numbers Game', p. 11).

33 See the discussion in Morgan, 'Cultural Implications', p. 123, although Morgan does not seem to distinguish among several different uses of the concept of ethnicity. I would suggest that John K. Thornton (*Africa and Africans in the Making of the Atlantic World*) uses ethnicity as a concept in significantly different ways from how other scholars use the term, including Gwendolyn Hall in her study of Louisiana or Mervyn Alleyne in his analysis of Akan influence in Jamaica, and certainly at variance with Michael Mullin's use of 'tribe' (*Africa in America*) as a substitute for 'ethnicity' in Virginia, all of whom are cited by Morgan.

34 For Morgan ('Cultural Implications', p. 135), ethnicity 'is often a residual term applied when too little is known about some group to be able to label it more precisely'.

35 According to Morgan ('Cultural Implications', p. 135), 'The homogenizing tendency of stressing cultural unity in Africa, of emphasizing the non-random character of the slave trade, and of seeing the dominance of particular African coastal regions or ethnicities in most American settings, is at variance with the central forces shaping the early modern Atlantic world. This tendency should be resisted.'

36 See, for example, George Brooks, *Landlords and Strangers: Ecology, Society, and Trade in Western Africa, 1000–1630* (Boulder, CO, 1993), and Akintola Wyse, *The Krio of Sierra Leone: An Interpretative History* (Washington, DC, 1991).

37 Maureen Warner-Lewis, 'Posited Kikoongo Origins of some Portuguese and Spanish Words from the Slave Era', *America Negra* 13 (1997), pp. 89–91. For an example of the earlier discussion claiming a Portuguese etymology, see Kamau Edward Brathwaite, *Contradictory Omens: Cultural Diversity and Integration in the Caribbean* (Mona, Jamaica, 1974), pp. 5–6.

38 As Berlin observes ('From Creole to African', p. 253 n), 'creole' has been applied to 'native-born free people of many national origins, including both Europeans and Africans, and of diverse social standing. It has also been applied to people of partly European but mixed racial and national origins in various European colonies and to Africans who entered Europe. In the United States, creole has also been specifically applied to people of mixed but usually non-African origins in Louisiana.' See also John A. Holms, *Pidgins and Creoles: Theory and Structure*, 2 vols (Cambridge, 1988–9).

39 Berlin, 'From Creole to African', p. 253.

40 Kamau Edward Braithwaite, *The Development of Creole Society in Jamaica, 1770–1820* (Oxford, 1971), p. 306. Also see Braithwaite, *Contradictory Omens*.

41 Braithwaite, *Creole Society*, pp. 309–11. Braithwaite was responding in particular to M. G. Smith's *The Plural Society in the British West Indies* (Berkeley, 1956), although some of Braithwaite's ideas can be traced back at least as far as Philip D. Curtin's *Two Jamaicas, 1830–1865: The Role of Ideas in a Tropical Colony* (Cambridge, 1955).

42 Braithwaite, *Contradictory Omens*, p. 6.

43 According to Mintz and Price (*ibid.*, p. 48), 'To document our assertions that fully formed African-American cultures developed within the earliest years of settlement in many New World colonies involves genuine difficulties. These stem from the general shortage of descriptive materials on slave life during the initial period, as well as from the lack of research regarding this problem.'

44 See e.g. Karen Fog Olwig, *Cultural Adaptation and Resistance on St. John: Three Centuries of Afro-Caribbean Life* (Gainesville, FL, 1985). The fact that Olwig studied three centuries may have led her to overestimate the adaptation of slaves in her 'ethnographic past' and thereby telescope the ultimate 'creolization' of the population, so that the end result looks like the beginning.

45 Olwig, 'African Cultural Principles', pp. 23–39.

46 Mintz and Price, *African-American Culture*, pp. 2, 8, 14.

47 *Ibid.*, p. 42.

48 *Ibid.*, pp. 42–7.

49 Olwig, 'African Cultural Principles', p. 25.

50 Palmié, 'Ekpe/Abakuá in Middle Passage'. See also Palmié, 'A Taste for Human Commodities: Experiencing the Atlantic System', in Palmié (ed.), *Slave Cultures*, pp. 40–54.

51 Douglas Chambers, 'Eboe, Kongo, Mandingo: African Ethnic Groups and the Development of Regional Slave Societies in Mainland North America' (paper presented at the conference 'The History of the Atlantic World', Harvard University, 3–11 September 1996; Chambers, '"My Own Nation": Igbo Exiles in the Diaspora', *Slavery and Abolition* 18, no. 1 (1997), pp. 72–97.

52 Fernando Ortiz, *Cuban Counterpoint: Tobacco and Sugar* (Durham, NC, 1995), pp. 101–2. But observe Ortiz's general ignorance of African history. According to Ortiz, Africans

> brought with them their diverse cultures, some as primitive as that of the Ciboneys, others in a state of advanced barbarism like that of the Tainos, and others more economically and socially developed, like the Mandingas, Yolofes (Wolofs), Hausas, Dahomeyans, and Yorubas, with agriculture, slaves, money, markets, trade, and centralized governments ruling territories and populations as large as Cuba; intermediate cultures between the Taino and the Aztec, with metals, but as yet without writing. The Negroes brought with their bodies their souls, but not their institutions nor their implements. They were of different regions, races, languages, cultures, classes, ages, sexes, thrown promiscuously into the slave ships, and socially equalized by the same system of slavery. They arrived deracinated, wounded, shattered, like the cane of the fields, and like they were ground and crushed to extract the juice of their labor. No other human element has had to suffer such a profound and repeated change of surroundings, cultures, class, and conscience. They were transferred from their own to another more advanced culture . . .

See also Fernando Ortiz, *Los negros esclavos* (1916; reprint, Havana, 1975), esp. chap. 2. Ortiz drew on an extensive amount of documentation, but his approach was anthropological, not historical. See his listing of ethnic categories in Cuba, pp. 40–66.

53 Palmié, 'Ekpe/Abakuá'.

54 Morgan, 'Cultural Implications', p. 136.

55 Eltis and Richardson ('Numbers Games', pp. 12–13) refer specifically to the analysis of Philip Morgan, 'Cultural Implications'.

56 Michel-Rolph Trouillot, 'Culture on the Edges: Creolization in the Plantation Context', *Plantation Societies in the Americas*, 5 (1998), p. 8. Also see Nigel Bolland, 'Creolisation and Creole Societies', in Alistair Hennessy (ed.), *Intellectuals in the Twentieth-Century Caribbean* (Basingstoke, 1992), pp. 50–79.

57 Palmié, 'Ekpe/Abakuá'.

58 Olwig ('African Cultural Principles') concludes that 'the bulk of the slaves . . . transported to the West Indies between the middle of the seventeenth century and the end of the eighteenth century . . . most likely . . . did not belong to any permanent socioeconomic entities that can be defined as tribes in the later (colonial) sense of the term'. It is not clear what Olwig means by the 'colonial' sense or by the absence of ethnic identities.

59 Igor Kopytoff and Suzanne Miers, 'African "Slavery" as an Institution of Marginality', in Miers and Kopytoff (eds), *Slavery in Africa: Historical and Anthropological Perspectives* (Madison, 1977), pp. 3–81, but see Paul E. Lovejoy, *Transformations in Slavery: A History of Slavery in Africa* (Cambridge, 1983) among other critics. The debate centres on definitions of slavery, especially whether or not slaves were a form of property in various African societies. Also see Toyin Falola and Paul E. Lovejoy (eds), *Pawnship in Africa: Historical Perspectives on Debt Bondage* (Boulder, CO, 1994).

60 Haraway, 'Situated Knowledges', pp. 579–99.

61 *Ibid.*, p. 584.

═ **2** ═
Cimarrón Ethnicity and Cultural Adaptation in the Spanish Domains of the Circum-Caribbean, 1503–1763[1]

Jane Landers

The trans-Atlantic transmission and creolization of African cultural elements such as languages, religious beliefs, worldviews and political and social organizations reflect both cultural persistence and adaptation in the African diaspora.[2] However, by the time enslaved Africans left the African coast, individuals of many distinct ethnic backgrounds had already intermingled, and in the Americas, slaves often moved more than once and thus experienced a variety of settings and slave systems.[3] In some areas, Native Americans, Europeans and Africans had extensive contact for over three centuries. Hence, the study of slave culture must not focus only on the areas in Africa from which people were sent or the areas in the Americas that received them, or even assume that the geographical designations of these areas were uniform.

Europeans often did not record the origins of slaves correctly or use consistent terminology in their classifications. Multiple migrations and interactions with distinct European and Amerindian nations produced complex cultural permutations. For example, Spaniards referred to the people known as the Mossi in Africa as the Gangá in the circum-Caribbean. If Carabalí (Calabarí) joined secret societies in Cuba, Spaniards might refer to them as *ñañigos* or *abakuá*. Sometimes Spaniards also used double designations such as Mandinga Ososo or Carabalí Isuama.[4] Tracing the interactions of these cultures is a Sisyphean task, but it is

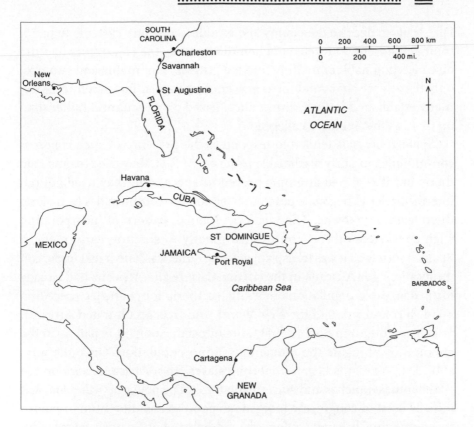

FIGURE 2.1   Map of the circum-Caribbean region, 18th century. *Source: Drawn by the Cartographic Office, Department of Geography, York University, Canada.*

one on which historians and archaeologists of the circum-Caribbean have been collaborating for several decades now.[5]

In the Spanish domains of the circum-Caribbean, including both islands and adjacent mainland territories, enslaved Africans sometimes became free by escaping Spanish dominion and living as *cimarrones*, as fugitive slaves were known. From the early sixteenth century, fugitive communities, variously referred to as *palenques*, *manieles*, *mocambos* or *cumbes*, were common and Spaniards complained that *cimarrones* raided their settlements and enticed away or stole other slaves.

The fugitive communities also challenged Spanish notions of civilized living, as well as the desired racial and social order; however, repeated military efforts to eradicate these *palenques* were, more often than not, unsuccessful. Africans built remote strongholds protected by wooden palisades and camouflaged pits containing sharpened stakes. They laid false trails to deceive the enemy and established sentry systems to patrol their settlements. Moreover, when discovered, the *cimarrones* had the disconcerting habit of melting into the jungles, mountains and swamps, only to coalesce again and form new encampments. But, if left in peace, many established stable communities, based on agriculture, rather than on theft, as the Spaniards alleged.[6]

Spanish officials tended to respond to the presence of such *cimarrón* communities in fairly predictable patterns. At first, they tried to eradicate them, but if repeated attempts proved unsuccessful, they used church intermediaries to negotiate peace and 'reduce' the communities by making them legitimate towns. The medieval Spanish pattern of incorporating such converted 'others' contributed greatly to shaping early modern Spanish society as it was transplanted to the Americas, and it had important implications for Africans in the circum-Caribbean.[7] Africans had already formed sizeable populations in southern Iberia for centuries preceding Spanish colonization of the New World, and free, acculturated Africans, or *ladinos*, fought in Spain's first 'wars of pacification' in Española in the attempt to subjugate the indigenous Taíno population. Once the wars subsided, Spaniards began importing slaves from Africa to work on the island mines, ranches and sugar plantations. The policy of '*reducción*' was initially used to congregate indigenous populations into 'human polity', meaning into Christian settlements modelled after Spanish towns 'with streets and plazas'. These new Christian Indian towns became the model for later free black towns.[8] In this way, *cimarrones* became vassals or allies of Spain, and thereafter many *cimarrones* and their descendants lived freely in their own settlements or among the Spaniards in their towns.

Spanish bureaucrats created a rich documentary record of the Africans living in their empire, capturing moments of their lives in censuses, military rosters, civil and criminal proceedings, land grants and correspondence. And while the Catholic church never attempted a major missionary effort among Africans, as it did among Native Americans, it did try to convert those Africans who lived in Spanish towns and, in the process, it generated some of the oldest extant records on Africans in the Americas – dating from the mid-sixteenth century.[9] Catholic baptismal, marriage and burial registers record not only the names, races and legal statuses of the individuals presenting themselves, but also their African 'nations'. In rare cases they also give birthplaces in Africa. As required by Catholic ritual, African couples chose marriage sponsors, and parents chose godparents for their baptized children. These customs enable

FIGURE 2.2   Handmade St Christopher's medal found at Gracia Real de Santa Teresa de Mose.
St Christopher is the patron saint of travellers and of Havana and is depicted carrying Jesus
over the water, a possible reference to the belief in transmigration to Africa after death.
Source: Courtesy of the Florida Museum of Natural History, Fort Mose Exhibition.

scholars to reconstitute some family and fictive kin networks. Scholars can also use these serial church records to explore a range of other important questions, including mortality and fertility rates, miscegenation and naming patterns, and even rates of manumissions.[10]

In the Caribbean, as elsewhere, the Catholic church was noted for its pragmatic acceptance of religious syncretism, which permitted Africans either to accept or creatively to modify Catholic tenets and the church's pantheon of saints.[11] In Spanish areas, the Day of Kings (Epiphany, January 6) became a day of licence, role-reversal and cultural expression for

Africans. From at least the sixteenth century, African religious brotherhoods (*cabildos* or *cofradías*) organized themselves by nations, elected kings and queens, registered their members, collected dues and bought properties in which to meet, thereby generating additional important documentary sources.[12] In Havana, the Mandinga, Carabalí, Lucumí, Arará, Gangá and Congo paraded through the streets, led by their elected kings and queens, and Spanish witnesses describe participants performing African songs and dances, accompanied by drums, scrapers and hollowed gourd rattles, and wearing elaborate costumes of raffia, feathers, animal skins, dog teeth, horns and beads. Stilt-walkers, masked figures and gymnasts added to the merriment. Art from nineteenth-century Havana depicts many of these elements. How much in these ceremonies had changed since the Atlantic crossing is unknown, but Spanish officials recognized and accepted ethnic, political and social organization. Under the umbrella of Catholicism, Africans expressed distinct cultural forms and retained elements of African languages, music and material culture well into the twentieth century.[13]

Spanish records are somewhat more limited on life in the fugitive slave communities. Contemporary observers did not always appreciate or record what they saw there, but the accounts of priests sent among the *cimarrones*, and even those of military opponents, offer useful clues about the physical layout, demographics and civil, religious and military leadership of the communities, as well as scattered information on subsistence patterns and trade networks with Europeans, Indians and other Africans, free and enslaved. Historical archaeology offers important new insights into the material life of Africans, which is not frequently treated in the documentary record, although little has been done in Hispanic areas of settlement. When unconquerable *palenques* were legitimated, a new level of documentation was generated through town charters, parish registers, militia records, notarial accounts and many of the same materials available in other Spanish towns. In most cases these rich sources have yet to be fully mined.[14]

Most importantly, perhaps, both free and enslaved Africans generated their own historical records in the Spanish colonies. Depending on their individual histories, Africans were sometimes literate in several languages and, just as indigenous groups did, they quickly learned and adapted to the Spanish legal culture. They wrote petitions and corresponded with royal officials and the king, made proclamations of fealty, initiated legal suits and property transactions, and left wills. Their verbatim testimonies also come to us through civil and criminal proceedings, which Spanish notaries recorded and read back to the sworn witnesses for verification, alteration or amendment. Spanish concepts of *buen gobierno* (just government) extended access to groups often excluded by other systems, such as women and slaves.[15]

The earliest *cimarrones* were found in Española. In 1503 Governor Nicolás de Ovando complained to the crown that slave runaways could not be recovered from Taíno hideouts in the mountains and that they were teaching the Indians 'bad customs'. Spain had only recently concluded the war to reconquer Granada and had just expelled Muslims who failed to convert to Catholicism. Ovando feared the potential religious 'contamination' of the Indians, but he also feared that Africans, reputed for their bellicose nature (rather than for their military training), might encourage and assist Indian resistance. Ovando's concern was not unfounded. In 1521 Wolof slaves led the first major slave revolt on Española, leading Spain temporarily to forbid the importation of Africans from areas of Muslim influence.[16] By the mid-sixteenth century, an estimated 7000 *cimarrones* inhabited settlements scattered across Española. At the close of the century the free population on the island, including Europeans, free mestizos and mulattos, numbered only 2000, while the enslaved population stood around 20,000. The same pattern characterized other areas of the circum-Caribbean.

In 1609 the Viceroy of Mexico (New Spain) launched a major expedition against the *palenque* near Vera Cruz, which was led by Yanga, an African of the Bran nation. By then Yanga's town had withstood Spanish assaults for more than thirty years and was already a permanent settlement of seventy houses and a church. Yanga and his Angolan war captain Francisco finally sued for peace. In 1618 Spanish authorities formally recognized the community as the free black town of San Lorenzo de los Negros de Córdova.[17] In Mexico blacks outnumbered whites as early as 1550 and were estimated to number ten times the white population by the early seventeenth century.[18]

Just as repeated campaigns against Yanga's town failed, so did those against *cimarrones* in Española. In 1662 the archbishop attempted to persuade 600 families still gathered into four *palenques* along the mountainous southern coast of Española to make the same transition, but the Bahoruco *cimarrones* had already ignored a previous offer, and they rejected this overture as well, commenting that they did not believe the word of Spaniards. According to the archbishop, the *cimarrones* produced an abundance and variety of crops on their land and were raising livestock. The women panned for gold in the rivers to buy clothing, drink and other items in the capital of Santo Domingo, including iron and steel from which the

FIGURE 2.3   Clay pot crafted by inhabitants of the maroon settlement of José Leta in Española (the Dominican Republic). *Source: Courtesy of Manuel A. García Arévalo. Photo by the author.*

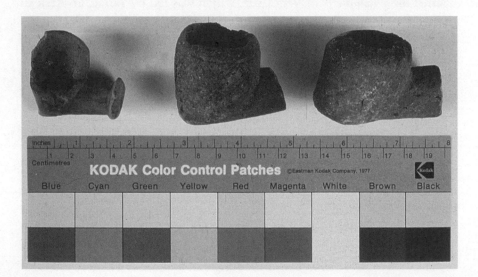

FIGURE 2.4   Clay pipes crafted by the inhabitants of the maroon settlement of José Leta in Española (the Dominican Republic). *Source: Courtesy of the Florida Museum of Natural History, Fort Mose Exhibition.*

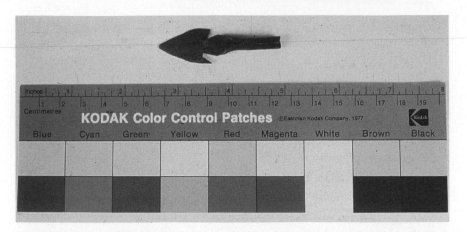

FIGURE 2.5   Copper arrow point crafted by the inhabitants of the maroon settlement of José Leta in Española (the Dominican Republic). *Source: Courtesy of the Florida Museum of Natural History, Fort Mose Exhibition.*

men fabricated arrows and short, broad swords. Four years after the archbishop's visit, the Spaniards launched a series of campaigns against the Bahoruco settlements, almost eliminating them; however, scattered *cimarrón* communities persisted well into the eighteenth century.[19]

Surface collection and shallow excavations at José Leta, an early eighteenth-century *cimarrón* settlement in eastern Española, confirm some of the recorded observations about *cimarrón* life. Researchers found numerous bones indicating that inhabitants subsisted largely on wild pigs, although it is presumed they also grew garden crops and gathered wild honey. The site yielded seventeen copper bracelets, metal arrowheads, incised clay pipes and a variety of iron objects, including tongs and lance points. Iron slag deposits are evidence that the runaways were manufacturing at least some of the objects on this site, as the archbishop observed at Bahoruco. In nearby caves explorers have also found metal daggers, clay water jugs and triton shell trumpets which they identify to be the work of African runaways.[20] Recently, Manuel García Arévalo assembled a collection of pots made by African runaways and retrieved from water-filled caves near Santo Domingo airport. These handmade, low-fired vessels incorporate indigenous elements in decorative patterns and are examples of the type of pottery designated colonoware, spatially defined by being found in areas where blacks and Indians coexisted. The identification of such wares has prompted scholars to re-examine collections once identified as purely Indian for possible African production.[21]

Fugitive communities also challenged Spanish rule on mainland South America. For example, a complex of *palenques* ringed the important slaving port of Cartagena de Indias, despite lengthy Spanish campaigns to destroy them. In 1530, only five years after the first Spanish town, Santa Marta, was founded, slaves burned it down. Thereafter, slaves escaped from gold mines and haciendas with regularity to form *palenques* in the rugged interior provinces. For the next 150 years, Spanish forces tried to eradicate these recalcitrant communities.²² In 1683 they marched against a network of settlements north of the capital of Bogotá and located a strongly fortified settlement from which 'the blacks came out to meet them with much skill and valour', using Spanish arms they had acquired in earlier encounters, as well as lances and bows and arrows. When night fell, the Spanish troops had to suffer in the rain because, before escaping, the *cimarrones* had burned their shelters and destroyed their fields of maize and cassava. The famous *palenque* of San Basilio, outside Cartagena, was 'reduced' to a legitimate and law-abiding town in 1686. It had been in existence for over sixty years and numbered more than 3000 inhabitants. The 'governor' of the settlement commanded six hundred warriors, ruled by four war captains, each of his 'nation'.²³

Other Colombian *palenques* refused *reducción*. In 1691, complaining that runaways had appropriated cattle and 'usurped' 300 gold mines, a sizeable Spanish force attacked the *palenque* of San Miguel, which was defended by 450 men and reinforced by men from the nearby *palenques* of Arenal (sandy ground or quicksand), Coco (coconut), El Limón (lemon), Tabacal (tobacco field), Espino (thorns), La Venta (the wind), and three with African-sounding names, Duanga, Norossi and Masu. After a 48-day siege, the men of San Miguel burned their settlement and dispersed to the settlements of their allies.²⁴

Several years later a Spanish priest, Father Zapata, tried to 'reduce' the *palenque* of Matudere. Although the priest's perceptions may have been culturally skewed, he reported social and ethnic divisions between the Mina and creole inhabitants of Matudere. According to him, they lived in different parts of the camps, pursued different activities and held different attitudes. As Father Zapata approached the settlement, he was met by Matudere's war captain, Pedro Mina, out on patrol with a squad of eight to ten men whose faces were decorated with red and white paint. The priest noted that the Mina controlled the forty-odd guns, while the *criollos* used lances and bows and arrows. He thought the distribution indicated the *criollos'* preference for such weapons, but it may have been that the settlement's most able warriors merited the best weaponry. The priest stressed the exoticism (read 'backwardness') of the Mina when he described them at later festivities as celebrating with their 'customary dances'. In contrast, he referred to the creoles as 'domesticated'. He was impressed that they had built an 'adequate' church, which contained 'paper images' (presumably Christian ones since he stated no objections). His distinctions, and maybe their own, were not based simply on their being African or country-born.

Diego Biafara and Francisco Arará served as 'masters of the church', the leaders of those who 'lived in Christianity, knew the prayers, sustained the church, and prayed the rosary'. The priest observed that the *cimarrones* recited the rosary 'with devotion' during their services and that they knew the proper responses and seemed to understand the liturgy.[25] He urged the assembled *cimarrones* to accept *reducción* and to give up hostilities against the Spaniards. When he proposed to make a census of Matudere's inhabitants, Pedro Mina denounced the peace talks and refused to allow 'his people' to be registered. The priest accused Mina of being a bad Christian and a disobedient vassal. Fortunately for historians, but unfortunately for the *cimarrones*, the *criollos* eventually overruled Pedro Mina, and the census was taken.[26]

Matudere was composed of about 250 members. More than 100 were African-born or had African-born parents. There were twenty-eight Mina, nineteen Arará, ten Congo, nine Luango, five Angola, three Popo, three Yolofe, two Caravalíe, one Bran, one Goyo and at least one Biafara. Those designated as *criollos* were divided into two groups: *criollos de la montaña*, to identify those persons born free in the *palenque*, and *criollos escapados*, to designate creole runaways from Spanish cities (persons who in other contexts are described as *ladinos*, meaning acculturated Spanish-speaking Catholics).

The *criollo escapado* Domingo Padilla, or Domingo Criollo, and his wife, Juana Padilla, became leaders at Matudere in 1681. Domingo called himself Captain, and Juana adopted the Spanish title *Virreina*. This choice of rank may have made a political statement, as only Mexico (New Spain) and Peru then rated viceroys, and the highest Spanish official in Colombia (New Granada) was only a governor. It should be noted that although Spaniards described Domingo as a *criollo* and *ladino*, his father, Domingo, who also lived at the Matudere, was born in Angola.[27]

As was the case at San Basilio and in the Mexican *palenques*, Matudere's war captains were African-born and seem to have commanded squadrons of their own countrymen. Pedro Mina led the most numerous African nation in the settlement, and Francisco Arará led the second largest group. Pacho Congo and Miguel Pantoja (nation unstated) held subordinate military positions such as standard bearer (*alférez*).[28] According to Governor Martín de Cevallos, who eventually destroyed Matudere, African shamans (whom he called *brujos* or witches) used 'diabolic artifacts and inventions' including 'poisoned arrowheads and cords and other demonic ideas' to assure the *cimarrones* they were invincible. Clearly, Catholicism and African religious practices coexisted at Matudere. The inhabitants may have participated in both simultaneously, just as they did in the Spanish cities. Later testimony identified Matudere's shaman as Antonio, the escaped slave of Juan Peña. Residents of Matudere apparently regarded Antonio as a holy man, kissed his hand to show their respect, and obeyed him in everything, including his order to kidnap women from nearby haciendas to be their wives. Antonio reputedly told his followers that they need not fear the Spaniards because he had a cloth full of powder which he would set alight to make the attackers disappear. Emboldened by this supernatural assurance only a month after Father Zapata's visit, warriors from Matudere ambushed and defeated a Spanish force of some sixty men sent against them, appropriated their weapons and returned the commander's testicles, wrapped in a cloth, to the governor in Cartagena.[29]

The citizens of Cartagena were at that moment torturing and interrogating slaves whom they feared were conspiring with the *cimarrones* to launch a major uprising against the capital. The plot was allegedly co-ordinated by Francisco, an Arará slave belonging to the Convent of Santa Clara, and the Arará war captain of Matudere, Francisco Arará. The Spaniards regarded the men as related since they belonged to the same nation, and this may have also reflected an African view. Joseph, another black slave at the convent of Santa Clara, testified that although the Arará of Cartagena had no formal *cabildo*, they had elected as their governor and king one Manuel Arará, a slave belonging to the Jesuits. The Arará gathered at Manuel's house 'to relax' and Joseph collected dues with which to bury their fellow Arará and dispensed alms to the destitute, much as their Catholic counterparts did.[30] The authorities condemned Francisco to death, but before the sentence could be carried out he escaped, and Cartagena's black executioner died of poisoning. A black replacement met the same fate and soon a rumour circulated that the city's meat supply had also been poisoned.[31]

To quell the hysteria, the governor himself led a retaliatory expedition against Matudere. Calling on the patron saint of the Spanish Reconquest, Santiago, or James (known variously as Matamoros, Mataindios or, it would seem, Matanegros, depending on the enemy), the Spaniards launched a spectacular night raid. As if on cue, a lightning bolt hit the house in which the *cimarrones* had stored their arms and munitions and blew it up. Spaniards and Africans alike may have perceived the explosion as a sign of divine intervention. The light of the resulting fires helped the Spaniards to track the scattering *cimarrones*.[32]

Spanish troops caught Domingo Padilla and forty-two others and recovered nineteen Spanish women, who were taken back to Cartagena.[33] There they interrogated the prisoners under oath, beginning with Domingo Padilla, alias Criollo. According to Padilla's testimony, he and his wife and three sons had fled slavery twelve years earlier, in 1681. They spent the first six months living in the jungle in a shelter of branches, then moved to a second spot, where they built two *bohíos* or huts. When they found the land unaccommodating, they moved a third time to the place called Matudere, where some fifty-four men and forty women were already living in huts. Padilla identified the most senior resident as Bentura Paulo. Although they claimed to be Matudere's founders, apparently Padilla and Juana had assumed leadership over a pre-existing settlement. By what means they had done this is unknown. In his testimony, Padilla identified Francisco Arará, rather than Pedro Mina, as the war captain for Matudere and blamed him for specific murders and attacks on the nearby Indian town of Piojón. He confirmed Father Zapata's identification of the creole Miguel as Matudere's standard bearer.

Thirteen of Matudere's defenders, including Domingo Padilla, were hanged and quartered. Their mutilated body parts were posted along the country roadsides 'as an example and terror to others of this class'. The *Virreina*, Juana, who was then approximately sixty years old, received 200 lashes and exile, as did many others, and the sick, very old or very young captives received 100 lashes each before their owners were allowed to post bond and recover them. Before finishing with Juana, Governor Martín de Cevallos brought an artist to the jail to paint her portrait 'for the novelty', but he caustically remarked that the artist favoured her by making her appear more clean and tidy than she really was.[34]

As Miguel Acosta Saignes has documented, Venezuela was yet another part of the circum-Caribbean 'infested' with *cimarrones*. Rich gold deposits near the site of Nirgua led Venezuela's governors repeatedly to attempt its settlement, but the Indians fiercely resisted Spanish encroachment and four towns had to be abandoned. To secure the area in 1601, Governor Arias Vaca designated blacks and *zambos* (persons of mixed African and Indian heritage) as *conquistadors*, with the accompanying perquisites. When whites began to move into Nirgua in the eighteenth century, the black descendants of its founders appealed directly to the king to uphold their privileges, which he did. In 1695 and 1696 the Spaniards legitimated four additional towns, combining Africans and Indians along the Tocuyo river.[35]

Ocoyta, an eighteenth-century Venezuelan *palenque*, was destroyed shortly after it was formed, but its central leadership controlled several sites and had developed an administrative hierarchy. A drawing of Ocoyta locates at the centre of the town the house of the leader of the Mina nation, Guillermo Ribas, his wife and their three sons, one of whom had been born there. Surrounding this house, in a semicircle, were the houses of Guillermo's officials, including his executioner, lieutenant, messenger and aide, and a Mina named Francisco. Only the last-named was married, to María Valentina de Rada, a free *zamba* (a person of African and Indian parentage). The other residents, including two women, one of whom also had three sons, lived in eleven houses forming the outermost semicircle.[36]

Spanish Florida also had a tradition of African resistance, *cimarrón* communities and a free African town dating from the Spanish period – Gracia Real de Santa Teresa de Mose, outside St Augustine.[37] Mose was a product of Anglo-Spanish rivalries. In 1670, the English directly challenged Spain's claim to exclusive sovereignty in the continent by establishing Charles Town in Carolina. Slaves, some of whom were accompanied by Indian wives and guides, began to escape from the English plantations almost immediately and some travelled southwards to Spanish Florida, where they asked for baptism into the 'true faith'. After resolving an ambiguity in their legal status, in 1693 Charles II granted the runaways freedom on the basis of religious conversion: 'The men as well as the women . . . so that by their example and by my liberality others will do the same.'[38] Spain subsequently extended Florida's religious sanctuary policy throughout the Caribbean, encouraging slaves from English, Dutch and even French territories to desert to Spanish territories. It was a cost-effective way for them to undermine competing plantation systems while augmenting their own military and labour forces.

By 1738 a sizeable community of runaways had gathered in St Augustine, and Florida's new governor, Manuel de Montiano, granted them a town about two miles north of St Augustine which was named Gracia Real de Santa Teresa de Mose. In gratitude, the freedmen vowed to shed their 'last drop of blood in defense of the Great Crown of Spain and the Holy Faith, and to be the most cruel enemies of the English'.[39] The Mandinga Francisco Menéndez, who had initiated the group's successful suit for freedom and had led the black militia, oversaw the new settlement. Governor Montiano referred to the inhabitants of Mose as Menéndez's 'subjects', and he probably enjoyed considerable autonomy.[40] Montiano's successor later stated that the villagers of Mose were 'under the dominion of their Captain and Lieutenant', indicating that Antonio Joseph Eligio de la Puente also had an important role in the community, perhaps analogous to that of the war captains found among other maroon groups.[41] Spanish titles and support may have also reinforced these leaders' status. Whatever the nature of their authority, Menéndez commanded the Mose militia for more than forty years, and Eligio de la Puente held his position for at least twenty-six.[42]

As the Spaniards had hoped, Mose became a lure to other slaves of the English. Shortly after the town's foundation, twenty-three men, women and children escaped from Port Royal, Carolina, and made it safely to St Augustine in a stolen launch. Governor Montiano promptly honoured their request for sanctuary, and they joined their fellows at Mose.[43] The following year, on 9 September 1739, a group of 'Angolan' slaves revolted near Stono, South Carolina, where they killed more than twenty whites and sacked and burned homes before heading for St Augustine.[44] South Carolina's governor quickly gathered a retaliatory force, which struck the rebels later that day when they stopped along the road for what the white pursuers viewed as a drunken dance, but which John Thornton identifies as a traditional feature of war in central Africa.[45] Thornton argues that the Stono rebels were probably not from Angola, but from the Kongo (which traders generically referred to as the Angola Coast). Kongo had long been Catholic, with many Portuguese speakers, and Thornton contends, as did contemporary Carolinians, that the rebels could well have understood both the offer of Catholic protection and Spanish, a sister language to Portuguese. He attributes the success with which the rebels fought their way southwards to their training and service as soldiers in Kongo.

Once the initial terror over the Stono Rebellion had subsided, South Carolina planters resumed the importation of African slaves. In 1749

Georgia also legalized the slave trade. Hence many of those who thereafter escaped to Spanish Florida were African-born *bozales*. Because so few men came with wives, they formed new unions with local African and Indian women in Florida.[46]

The parish registers show that there was great ethnic and racial diversity at Mose, which was also true of Spanish Florida in general. Among the African 'nations' specifically identified for the original population at Mose were the Mandinga, Fara and Arará. Later additions further diversified the group, incorporating Congo, Carabalí and Mina in the mix. At St Augustine there were also Gamba, Samba, Gangá, Lara and some persons identified only as Guineans. Florida's governors complained about the 'bad customs' and 'spiritual backwardness' of the *bozales*, and St Augustine's priests did their best to convert them.[47] In 1744 Father Francisco Xavier Arturo baptized Domingo, a Carabalí slave, on his deathbed, with the comment that his 'crudeness' prevented him from understanding Christian doctrine. Two years later, on separate occasions, Father Arturo gave the Congo slaves Miguel and Francisco conditional baptisms because each told the priest he had been baptized by a priest in his homeland and taught to pray in his own language. As Miguel was re-baptized, he blessed himself in that unidentified language. In 1748 Father Arturo gave the same conditional baptism to Miguel Domingo, also a Congo slave who had been baptized in Africa and continued to pray in his native language.[48]

Ethnic identification of Africans in the Spanish records is difficult because of intermarriage. Although children of these mixtures may have known their parents' ethnicities, they probably identified themselves in new ways. Even the first-generation Africans at Mose must have drawn upon several sources when constructing new identities for themselves. Their freedom was dependent upon Catholic conversion and political enmity towards the English; the privilege to live autonomously under their own leaders was tied to Spanish corporatism and concepts of social organization; and the ability to protect both was guaranteed by Spanish legal constructs of community and citizenship, and the expectations of military vassalage. Western and central Africans would have been familiar with similar ideas and systems and could certainly have adapted to them as needed. A few examples should suffice to illustrate.

Tomás Chrisóstomo and his first wife, Ana María Ronquillo, were both Congo. When they married in 1744, Tomás was the slave of Don Francisco Chrisóstomo and Ana María was the slave of Juan Nicolás Ronquillo. Pedro Graxales, a Congo slave, and his legitimate wife, María de la Concepción

Hita, a Carabalí slave, who had married the year before, served as their sponsors. By 1759, Tomás Chrisóstomo was a free widower living at Mose and, the following year, he and the widowed María Francisca were married. By that time Tomás Chrisóstomo's godfather, Pedro Graxales, was free and a sergeant of the Mose militia, but Graxales' wife and at least six children remained enslaved in St Augustine.[49]

Many other examples of ethnically complex families appear in the records. When María Luisa Balthazar, an Indian from the village of Palica, married Juan Chrisóstomo, of the Carabalí nation, he was a slave living in St Augustine. The couple's daughters, María Magdalena and Josepha Candelaria, were born free at their mother's village of Palica. One daughter, María Magdalena, was already the widow of Juan Margarita (who may have been an Indian) when she married Pablo Prezilla, a free mulatto from Cumaná, Venezuela. After Prezilla died, María Magdalena married a third time. Her third husband, Phelipe Gutiérres, was a free man whose race is not given in the record, and thus can be assumed to be white. In 1747, María Luisa and Juan's second daughter, Josepha Candelaria, married an Indian widower in the village of Punta. After María Luisa Balthazar died, the widowed Juan Chrisóstomo married María Antonia, a Carabalí slave. While María Antonia and their children remained enslaved, Juan Chrisóstomo gained his freedom and joined the Mose militia.[50]

The long-term and close contact between Africans and Indians in Spanish Florida led to religious and cultural adaptations of which we have only scattered pieces of documentary evidence. Juan Ygnacio de los Reyes, an Ibaja Indian from the village of Pocotalaca, was among the trusted militia guerrillas on whom Governor Montiano depended during the siege of Florida led by Georgia's General James Oglethorpe in 1740. Once, Montiano ordered Juan Ygnacio to give a reconnaissance report to the captain general in Havana, but '[Juan Ygnacio] having declared to me that he had made a certain promise or vow, in case of happy issue, to our Lady of Cobre, I was unwilling to put him aboard with violence, and I let him go at his own free will to present himself to Your Excellency'.[51] Nuestra Señora de la Caridad del Cobre was, and still is, the black patron saint of Cuba whose miraculous discovery was attributed to two Cuban Indians and an African who were fishing together. La Caridad de Cobre is also the syncretic symbol for Ochun, the Yoruba goddess of pleasure and fertility.[52] Juan Ygnacio clearly understood the saint's function (to ensure happy issue) as well as the Spanish respect for religious vows. It is interesting to speculate how much Juan Ygnacio's contact with Africans in Florida and

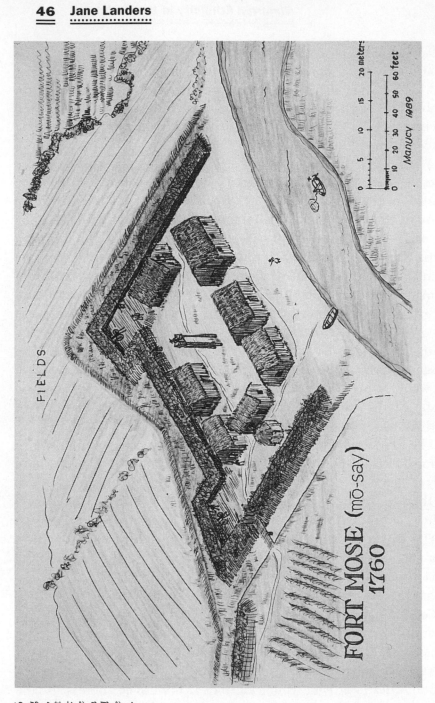

FIGURE 2.6
Artist's rendering
of Fort Mose,
1760, by Albert
Manucy. Source:
Courtesy of the
Florida Museum
of Natural
History, Fort Mose
Exhibition.

Cuba may have influenced his choice of a patron – and how many other Florida Indians may have also been influenced by this and other Cuban traditions.

These examples illustrate the extensive cultural adaptation that went into the formation of the Afro-Indo-Hispanic community of Mose. Many of its members were born in western or central Africa and spent at least some time in a British slave society before risking their lives and escaping. At least some had lived among the Yamasee Indians and fought other Indian nations before reaching Spanish Florida. At least thirty-one became slaves of the Spaniards before litigation brought them freedom. Once free, they associated closely with the remnants of the seven different Indian nations that had been aggregated into two outlying villages, where even some of their children lived. Meanwhile, new infusions of Africans of different nations continued to be incorporated into the original Mose community. After Oglethorpe destroyed their first settlement in 1740, the Mose refugees moved to the ethnically mixed city of St Augustine, and in 1752 they resettled on the frontier at the second Mose.

Mose's second fort had three earthwork walls over two metres high, faced on the outside with marsh clay and planted along the top with prickly pear cactus. The fourth side was open to Mose Creek, which flows to St Augustine. There was an exterior moat about two metres wide and nearly a metre deep, an earthenwork defence line, and large and small interior wooden post structures. One very large structure had posts forty-five centimetres in diameter. A smaller oval structure measured approximately four metres in diameter.[53]

Mose was reoccupied for only eleven years before its inhabitants were forced to evacuate to Cuba with the other Spanish colonists in 1763. Recovered artifacts include military objects such as gunflints, strikers and musket balls, and domestic articles such as metal buckles, metal and bone buttons (including one still in the process of manufacture), thimbles, pins, clay pipe bowls and stems (of both local and European design), nails and a variety of glass bottles and ceramic wares (of English, Spanish and indigenous types). Religious artifacts include amber rosary beads, metal rosary pendants and chains, and a handmade pewter St Christopher's medal. As the Catholic patron of travellers and an appropriate choice for people who were born in western or central Africa and transported to Carolina or Georgia and then relocated to Florida, St Christopher is also the patron saint of Havana, which raises the possibility that the artist may have travelled to Cuba and adopted that devotion. On the reverse side of the medallion is a compass rose – also an appropriate symbol for travellers, and possibly an indication that the maker was a sailor or pilot in the Spanish maritime system.[54]

Mose was located at the head of Mose Creek, and the settlers had access to both fresh- and salt-water resources. The grassy savannahs, pine woods and marshes around Mose were home to buffalo, deer, wild cattle, fowl of all kinds and wild horses, which the men of Mose caught, broke and rode. Around their shelters the freedmen and women broke ground, dug new fields and planted food crops, much as their counterparts in the *palenques* did.[55] According to Elizabeth Reitz, Mose villagers had much the same diet as nearby Indian villagers, relying heavily on estuarine resources and wild foods. In addition to fish (primarily Atlantic croaker, sea catfish and sea trout, drums, silver perch, spots, mullet and sheepsheads, but also sharks and rays) and shellfish, the Mose villagers consumed deer, rabbits, squirrels, raccoons and turtles (pond and chicken turtles, and diamondback terrapin) to supplement the occasional government gifts of beef and corn. These findings suggest a high degree of self-sufficiency at Mose.[56]

Early circum-Caribbean *palenques* seem to have shared certain features, including isolation in remote mountains or jungles, African leadership, semicircular or circular stockades, use of lances, bows and arrows, stakes and pits and heavy rocks, and dependence on locally gathered foods or on goods taken from Spaniards. Once established, the communities sometimes evolved multiple sites based on agriculture and became more self-sufficient, even producing their own metal weapons. Communities also began to reproduce themselves. Civil, military and religious leadership in these communities became more complex over time.[57] The later settlements support Richard Price's theory that maroon leaders of the period were military figures well-versed in European ways and equipped to negotiate their followers' best interests.[58] They established widespread trade and communication networks, profited from contraband trade, read the political winds, participated in local and international wars, and struck deals and made treaties with both Indians and Spaniards. Some of the *cimarrones* had travelled widely around the Caribbean with former masters, in exile or by their own efforts, and it is possible that resistance techniques travelled with them.

As white populations increased, so did military pressure against the *palenques*, and creating free black towns such as San Basilio and Mose was a successful adaptation to these changed conditions. Although coexistence was sometimes made difficult by the resentment of local landowners, metropolitan officials and town leaders saw it as an accommodation worth making. The *cimarrones* gained some autonomy and peace for their families. From the Spanish viewpoint, the towns meant an end to the continuous outlay for military expeditions. They also served Spanish goals of populating contested or inhospitable reaches of the empire with loyal vassals and military reserves. The crown could also claim to have fulfilled its humanitarian and religious duties in converting the *cimarrones* and 'reducing' them to an orderly urban life.

As the preceding case studies suggest, archaeologists working on African sites in the Americas, and historians as well, should reject the fallacy of a common, uniform African culture and pay more attention to the regional and temporal developments on both sides of the Atlantic while searching for ethnic and cultural connections. If, as Merrick Posnansky argues, recycling, functional substitution, innovation and adaptation are constants in West African material production, then searching for exact duplication of African patterns and techniques in the Americas is a fool's game.[59] Further historical and archaeological research on *cimarrón* settlements is needed to discern more accurately the nature and scope of cultural adaptations in the African diaspora.

Notes

1 I would like to thank Paul Lovejoy and the members of the organizing committee of the UNESCO/SSHRCC Summer Institute, 'Identifying Enslaved Africans: The "Nigerian" Hinterland and the Diaspora', for giving me the opportunity to exchange ideas with such a distinguished group of international scholars. Research for this essay was generously supported by the National Endowment for the Humanities, the Vanderbilt University Research Council, and the Program for Cultural Cooperation between the Spanish Ministry of Culture and universities in the United States.
2 Kathleen A. Deagan and Jane Landers, 'Excavating Fort Mose: A Free Black Town in Spanish Florida', in Theresa A. Singleton (ed.), *I, Too, Am America: Archaeological Studies in African American Life* (Charlottesville, VA, 1999) (hereafter cited as *I, Too, Am America*); Jane Landers, 'Gracia Real de Santa Teresa de Mose: A Free Black Town in Spanish Colonial Florida', *American Historical Review* 95 (1990), pp. 9–30.
3 Philip D. Morgan, 'The Cultural Implications of the Atlantic Slave Trade: African Regional Origins, American Destinations and New World Developments', *Slavery and Abolition* 18, no. 1 (1997), pp. 122–45.
4 Pedro Deschamps Chapeaux, *Los cimarrones urbanos* (Havana, 1983), pp. 29, 41, and *El negro en la economía habanera del siglo XIX* (Havana, 1971), pp. 31–46.
5 I am adopting an expanded definition of the circum-Caribbean which includes not only lands touching the Caribbean Sea but also areas which both prehistorically and historically had political and commercial connections to the Caribbean (hence it includes both the Atlantic and Gulf coasts of the United States).
6 See the studies in Richard Price (ed.), *Maroon Societies: Rebel Slave Communities in the Americas* (Baltimore, MD, 1979).

7 William D. Phillips, Jr., *Slavery from Roman Times to the Early Atlantic Trade* (Minneapolis, MN, 1985), pp. 162–3; Ruth Pike, *Aristocrats and Traders: Sevillian Society of the Sixteenth Century* (Ithaca, NY, 1972), pp. 173, 180, 186–9.

8 Declaration of Emperor Charles, 1538, cited in Lyle N. McAlister, *Spain and Portugal in the New World, 1492–1700* (Minneapolis, MN, 1984), p. 172.

9 Because it affected his conversion efforts, the Jesuit Alonso de Sandoval paid particular attention to the bewildering array of ethnicities and languages of the Africans to whom he ministered in seventeenth-century Cartagena, detailing which groups spoke mutually intelligible languages; Alonso de Sandoval, *Un tratado sobre la esclavitud* (Madrid, 1987).

10 For examples of the variety of records and how they can be used see Jane G. Landers, *Black Society in Spanish Florida* (Urbana, IL, 1999). See also Gwendolyn Midlo Hall, *Africans in Colonial Louisiana: The Development of Afro-Creole Culture in the Eighteenth Century* (Baton Rouge, LA, 1992), and Kimberly S. Hanger, *Bounded Lives, Bounded Places: Free Black Society in Colonial New Orleans, 1769–1803* (Durham, NC, 1997).

11 Some of the most significant work on religious syncretism has focused on Cuba and on Brazil. See Fernando Ortiz, *Hampa Afro-Cubana: Los negros brujos* (Madrid, 1906), and Ortiz, *Los negros esclavos* (Havana, 1975); Lydia Cabrera, *El Monte* (Havana, 1954); Cabrera, *Reglas de Congo: Palo Monte y Mayombe* (Miami, 1979); Cabrera, *Yemayá and Ochún* (Madrid, 1974; Miami, 1980); Cabrera, *La sociedad secreta Abakuá* (Havana, 1954); William Bascom, *Sixteen Cowries: Yoruba Divination from Africa to the New World* (Bloomington, IN, 1980). On Brazil see Roger Bastide, *As religiões africanas no Brasil*, 2 vols (São Paulo, 1971).

12 The precedents for these groups were set by Africans living in Spain in the fifteenth century who organized *cofradías* in cities such as Sevilla, Cádiz, Jerez, Valencia and Barcelona; José Luis Córtes López, *Los origines de la esclavitud negra en España* (Madrid, 1986), pp. 151–76; Phillips, *Slavery from Roman Times*, pp. 163, 168.

13 Fernando Ortiz, *Los cabildos y la fiesta Afro-Cubana del Día de Reyes* (Havana, 1992). See also his original article, annotated and translated by Jean Stubbs, 'The Afro-Cuban Festival "Day of Kings"', in Judith Bettelheim (ed.), *Cuban Festivals, An Illustrated Anthology* (New York, 1993), pp. 3–47; and 'Los cabildos Afrocubanos', in Julio Le Riverand (ed.), *Orbita de Fernando Ortiz* (Havana, 1973), pp. 121–34. For artistic evidence from nineteenth-century Havana, see the work of Victor Patricio Landaluze, some of which is reproduced in Ortiz, *Los cabildos*, and in Robert Farris Thompson, *Flash of the Spirit: African and Afro-American Art and Philosophy* (New York, 1984).

14 Records generated by other European powers on 'notorious' African maroons or rebels occasionally add to the historical record of Africans in areas of Spanish settlement. See Landers, 'Gracia Real'.

15 See Charles Cutter, *The Legal Culture of Northern New Spain, 1700–1810* (Albuquerque, NM, 1994). On indigenous use of Spanish law, see Susan Kellogg, *Law and the Transformation of Aztec Culture, 1500–1700* (Norman, OK, 1995). For examples of Africans' use of Spanish law, see Landers, *Black Society*. If Africans could not speak Spanish, court officials used translators, just as they did for non-Spanish-speaking witnesses of other ethnicities. This may have added new layers of linguistic filters, but was, none the less, an effort to understand and record the voice of Africans.

16 Royal Cedula replying to Governor Nicolás de Ovando, 29 March 1503, Indiferente General, Archivo General de Indias, Seville, Spain (hereafter cited as AGI); Slave Codes for Santo Domingo, 6 January 1522, Patronato 295, AGI. For background, see Carlos Larazzábal Blanco, *Los negros y la esclavitud en Santo Domingo* (Santo Domingo, Dominican Republic, 1967), chaps 5 and 6.

17 Colin A. Palmer, *Slaves of the White God: Blacks in Mexico, 1570–1650* (Cambridge, MA, 1976), pp. 125–30; William B. Taylor, 'The Foundation of Nuestra Señora de Guadalupe de los Morenos de Amapa', *The Americas* 26 (1970), pp. 439–46.

18 David M. Davidson, 'Negro Slave Control and Resistance in Colonial Mexico, 1519–1650', *Hispanic American Historical Review* 66 (1966), pp. 235–53.

19 Blanco, *Los negros y la esclavitud*, pp. 151–2; Carlos Esteban Deive, *Los guerrilleros negros: Esclavos fugitivos y cimarrones en Santo Domingo* (Santo Domingo, 1989).

20 José Juan Arrom and Manuel A. García Arévalo, *Cimarrón* (Santo Domingo, 1986), pp. 48–55.

21 Manuel García Arévalo, interview, Santo Domingo, August 1996; Ferguson, *Uncommon Ground: Archaeology and Early African America, 1650–1800* (Washington, DC, 1992), pp. 18–32, 109–16, and Ferguson, 'Looking for the "Afro" in Colono-Indian Pottery', in Robert L. Schuyler (ed.), *Archaeological Perspectives on Ethnicity in America* (New York, 1979), pp. 14–28. See also Ferguson, '"The Cross Is a Magic Sign": Marks on Eighteenth-Century Bowls from South Carolina', and Matthew C. Emerson, 'African Inspiration in a New World Art and Artifact: Decorated Pipes from the Chesapeake', in *I, Too, Am America*.

22 Report of Governor Juan de Pando, 1 May 1683, Santa Fe 213, AGI.

23 Anthony McFarlane, '*Cimarrones* and *Palenques*: Runaways and Resistance in Colonial Colombia', *Slavery and Abolition* 6 (1985), pp. 134–5; Real Cedula, 13 July 1686, Santa Fe 531, libro 11, folio 217, AGI.

24 Autos sobre la reducción y pacificación de los negros fugitivos y fortificados en los palenques de la Sierra de María, 1691–1695, Santa Fe 212, AGI. In Cuba the Archangel Michael is associated with the Yoruba god of iron, Ogun, penetrator of the forests and cultivator of the land as well as a violent warrior who demands justice; Sandra T. Barnes (ed.), *Africa's Ogun; Old World and New* (Bloomington, IN, 1989); Entrada y Derrota del Palenque de Matudere, Santa Fe 213, folios 41–274, AGI. María del Carmen Borrego Pla's study focused on Spanish military and political campaigns against the communities, and she did not explore the ethnographic material in the same documents. Moreover, she also mistakenly refers to Matudere as Matubere; see Pla, *Palenques de negros en Cartagena de Indias a fines del siglo XVII* (Seville, 1973).

25 Father Fernando Zapata to Governor Martín de Cevallos, 21 April 1693, Santa Fe 213, AGI.

26 *Ibid.*

27 *Ibid.* The community was reproducing itself, for there were thirty-four children in the camp, including three orphans whom families had adopted.

28 *Ibid.* Pedro's wife, Teresa, was also a Mina, and the couple had three sons and two daughters living with them.

29 Report of Governor Martín de Cevallos, 29 May 1693, Santa Fe 213, AGI. Robin Law shows that ritual decapitation and castration were important features of warfare in Dahomey until leaders forbade the practices late in the eighteenth century; Law, '"My Head Belongs to the King": On the Political and Ritual Significance of Decapitation in Pre-Colonial Dahomey', *Journal of African History* 30 (1989), pp. 399–415.

30 Testimony of Joseph of Santa Clara, 1 May 1693, Santa Fe 212, AGI. The informal nature of the Arará 'brotherhood' and the social function it performed are reminiscent of those that João José Reis describes for the Malé in Bahia; Reis, *Slave Rebellion in Brazil: The Muslim Uprising of 1835 in Bahia*, trans. Arthur Brakel (Baltimore, MD, 1993).

31 Junta de Guerra, 30 April 1693, Santa Fe 212, AGI; Governor Martín de Cevallos to the king, 2 July 1693, Santa Fe 213, AGI.

32 Report of Martín de Cevallos, 29 May 1693, Santa Fe 213, AGI. The deposed Oyo king Shango allegedly became an *orisha* who used lightning bolts to strike down enemies who angered him; Henry John Drewel, John Pemberton III and Rowland Abiodun, *Yoruba: Nine Centuries of African Art and Thought* (New York, 1989).

33 Pedro Mina escaped capture and ruled the Matudere survivors for two more years, but in 1695 Mina, too, was apprehended at the *palenque* of Norossi; Report of Sancho Ximeno, 22 September 1695, Santa Fe 212, AGI.

34 Cevallos said that he hung the portrait in the governor's mansion; Martín de Cevallos to Antonio Ortíz de Talora, 29 May 1693, Santa Fe 213, AGI.

35 Miguel Acosta Saignes, *Vida de los esclavos en Venezuela* (Caracas, 1961), pp. 260–6; Royal Cedula, 7 March 1704, cited in Richard Konetzke (ed.), *Colección de documentos para la historia de la formación social de Hispanoamérica*, (Madrid, 1953), p. 94.

    The records of Nirgua's town council (*cabildo*) date from 1628 through 1799, and its documentary history also includes correspondence between town leaders and Venezuelan authorities and between Venezuelan authorities and the Crown, Royal Cedulas, a Bishop's pastoral visitation and travellers' accounts. See Irma Marina Mendoza, 'El cabildo de Pardos en Nirgua: Siglos XVII y XVIII', *Anuario de estudios Bolivarianos* 4 (1995), pp. 95–120.

36 Saignes, *Vida de los esclavos*, pp. 297–307.

37 An interdisciplinary team headed by Dr Kathleen Deagan, of the Florida Museum of Natural History, investigated the town in 1987.

38 Landers, 'Gracia Real'; Royal Officials to the King, 3 March 1689, cited in Irene Wright, 'Dispatches of Spanish Officials Bearing on the Free Negro Settlement of Gracia Real de Santa Teresa de Mose', *Journal of Negro History* 9 (1924), pp. 144–93; Royal Cedula, 7 November 1693, SD 58–1–26, in the John B. Stetson Collection, P. K. Yonge Library of Florida History, University of Florida, Gainesville (hereafter cited as PKY).

39 Manuel de Montiano to the King, 3 March 1738, and 16 February 1739, SD 844, on microfilm reel 15, PKY; Fugitive Negroes of the English Plantations to the King, 10 June 1738, SD 844, on microfilm reel 15, PKY.

40 Manuel de Montiano to the King, 16 September 1740, SD 2658, AGI.

41 Colin Palmer describes a similar relationship between Yanga and Francisco Angola, leaders of the maroon community which became San Lorenzo de Los Negros de Córdova, near Vera Cruz, Mexico, in *Slaves of the White God*, pp. 128–30.

42 Menéndez and Antonio Joseph Eligio de la Puente appear first and second on all official Spanish reports on Mose, including those after their evacuation to Cuba in 1763; evacuation report of Juan Joseph Eligio de la Puente, 22 January 1764, SD 2595, AGI.

43 Allan D. Chandler and Lucien L. Knight (eds), *Journal of William Stephens* (Atlanta, GA, 1904–16), p. 358. The runaways arrived in St Augustine on 21 November 1738; Manuel de Montiano to Juan Francisco de Güemes y Horcasitas, 16 February 1739, SD 845, microfilm reel 16, PKY.

44 The most complete analysis of Stono is offered by Peter H. Wood in *Black Majority: Negroes in Colonial South Carolina from 1670 through the Stono Rebellion* (New York, 1974). A more traditional account is found in Eugene Sirman's *Colonial South Carolina: A Political History, 1663–1763* (Chapel Hill, NC, 1966).

45 According to John K. Thornton, the rebels, who stopped along the road and 'set to dancing, Singing and beating the Drums to draw more Negroes to them', were performing dances that were a central element of military training and war preparations in Kongo; Thornton, 'African Dimensions of the Stono Rebellion', *American Historical Review* 96, no. 4, (1991), pp. 1112–13. For more on Kongo war techniques see Thornton, 'African Soldiers in the Haitian Revolution', *Journal of*

Caribbean History 25 (1991), pp. 58–80. See also 'A Ranger's Report of Travels with General Oglethorpe, 1739–1742', in Newton D. Mereness (ed.), *Travels in the American Colonies* (New York, 1916), pp. 222–3; Wood, *Black Majority*, chap. 12; Law, '"My Head Belongs to the King"'.

46 At the time of the census, Francisco Roso, Tomás Chrisóstomo, Francisco Xavier de Torres and his son, Juan de Arranzate, Pedro Graxales, Joseph de Peña, Juan Francisco de Torres, Joseph Fernández and Juan Baptista all had slave wives in St Augustine. The frequency of births is testimony that conjugal rights were honoured by the slave owners, as required by the Church. See Census of Ginés Sánchez, 12 February 1759, SD 2604, AGI.

47 Governor Fulgencio García de Solís condemned not only the original Mose settlers but also 'those who have since fled the English colonies to join them'; Fulgencio García de Solís to the King, 29 November 1752, SD 844, microfilm reel 17, PKY.

48 Baptism of Domingo, 10 December 1744, Catholic Parish Records, Diocese of St Augustine Catholic Center, Jacksonville, FL. (hereafter cited as CPR), on microfilm reel 284 F, PKY; Baptism of Miguel, 29 September 1746, and of Francisco, 14 October 1746; Baptism of Miguel Domingo, 26 January 1748.

49 Marriage of Tomás Chrisóstomo and Ana María Ronquillo, 28 February 1745, CPR, microfilm reel 284 C, PKY. Baptism of Pedro Graxales, 9 December 1738, CPR, microfilm reel 284 F, PKY. Marriage of Pedro Graxales and María de la Concepción Hita, 19 January 1744, CPR microfilm reel 284 C, PKY. Baptisms of their children, María, 4 November 1744; Manuela de los Angeles, 1 January 1747; Ysidora de los Angeles, 22 December 1748; Joseph Ynisario, 4 April 1755; Juana Feliciana, 13 July 1757; Pantaleona, 1 August 1758; and María de los Dolores, 16 August 1761; CPR, microfilm reel 284 F, PKY.

50 Marriage of Manuel (Juan Manuel) Chrisóstomo and Antonia Chrisóstomo, 10 January 1744, CPR, on microfilm reel 284 C, PKY. Marriage of Pablo Prezilla and María Magdalena, 17 June 1743, *ibid.* Marriage of Phelipe Gutiérres and María Magdalena, 25 October 1745, *ibid.* Marriage of Juan Manuel Manressa (of Punta) and Josepha Candelaria, 26 May 1747, CPR, on microfilm reel 284 C, PKY. Baptism of Manuel Rutiner, legitimate son of Juan Chrisóstomo and María Antonia Espinosa, born 30 January 1744 and baptized 4 February 1744, CPR, on microfilm reel 284 F, PKY and Manuel Rutiner's marriage to Felipa Urisa, 19 June 1756, CPR, on microfilm reel 284 C, PKY. Because his mother was still a slave, Manuel was a slave, as was his wife. One of the couple's marriage sponsors was Ygnacio Roso, of Mose.

51 'Letters of Montiano, Siege of St. Augustine', *Collections of the Georgia Historical Society* (Savannah, GA, 1909), pp. 20–43; *An Impartial Account of the Late Expedition against St. Augustine under General Oglethorpe*, facsimile of 1742 edition, intro. and indexes by Aileen Moore Topping (Gainesville, FL, 1978), pp. xv–xvi.

52 Irene Wright, 'Our Lady Of Charity', *Hispanic American Historical Review* 5 (1922), pp. 709–17; Thompson, *Flash of the Spirit*.

53 Deagan and Landers, 'Excavating Fort Mose'; Kathleen Deagan and Darcie MacMahon, *Fort Mose: Colonial America's Black Fortress of Freedom* (Gainesville, FL, 1995). Archaeological investigations at this partially submerged site used remote-sensing, multi-spectral imagery scanning, aerial photography and traditional archaeological survey methods.

54 Another reading may reflect the common western and central African belief that upon death the deceased would be transported again across the waters to their homeland; Georgia Writers' Project, *Drums and Shadows: Survival Studies Among the Georgia Coastal Negroes* (Athens, GA, 1986), pp. 195–6, 220–2.

55 Until the newly planted crops could be harvested, the governor provided the homesteaders with corn, biscuits and beef from the same government stores used to supplement Indian towns; Purchases and Payments for 1739, Cuba 446, AGI.

56 Descriptions of the black and Indian villages can be found in Father Juan de Solana to Don Pedro Agustín Morel de Santa Cruz, 22 April 1759, SD 516, on microfilm reel 28 K, PKY.

Interestingly, many resources available in the Mose estuary (for example, the gopher tortoise) were exploited by neither Indians nor Africans, indicating that the Africans and creoles of Mose may have adapted to Indian traditions of food acquisition. On the basis of cross-cultural analysis of faunal remains from multiple archaeological sites in and around St Augustine, Elizabeth J. Reitz argues that resource use by both Spaniards and Africans reflects 'the local setting rather than previous ethnic traditions'; Reitz, 'Zooarchaeological Analysis of a Free African American Community: Gracia Real de Santa Teresa de Mose', *Historical Archaeology* 28 (1994), pp. 23–40. Reitz compared faunal collections from Mose and from the mission Indian village of Nombre de Dios (the village closest to Mose) and found almost identical use of estuarine resources, especially in the levels of consumption of Atlantic croaker and fingerling mullet. Gopher tortoises appear in all other known faunal collections from St Augustine, with the exception of the Indian and African villages. For comparable work on Spanish, criollo and mestizo household sites see Elizabeth J. Reitz and Stephen L. Cumbaa, 'Diet and Foodways of Eighteenth-Century Spanish St. Augustine', in Kathleen A. Deagan (ed.), *Spanish St. Augustine: The Archaeology of a Colonial Creole Community* (New York, 1983), pp. 151–85.

57 Excavations at Palmares, created in the early seventeenth century by African slave runaways in the colonial state of Pernambuco, Brazil, and finally broken up in 1694, suggest that a mixture of peoples lived there, including Tupinamba Indians, escaped Africans and even some Europeans (primarily Dutch). See Charles E. Orser, Jr., *In Search of Zumbi: Preliminary Archaeological Research at the Serra da Barriga, State of Alagoas, Brazil* (Normal, IL, 1992); Orser, 'Toward a Global Historical Archaeology: An Example from Brazil', *Historical Archaeology* 28 (1994), pp. 5–22; Edison Carneiro, *Os quilombos dos Palmares* (São Paulo, 1988); R. K. Kent, 'Palmares: An African State in Brazil', *Journal of African History* 6 (1965), pp. 161–75.

58 Price (ed.), *Maroon Societies*, pp. 29–30.

59 Merrick Posnansky, 'West African Reflections on African American Archaeology', in *I, Too, Am America*; Christopher DeCorse, 'Culture Contact, Continuity, and Change on the Gold Coast, A.D. 1400–1900', *African Archaeological Review* 10 (1992), pp. 163–96; DeCorse, 'The Danes on the Gold Coast: Culture Change and the European Presence', *African Archaeological Review* 11 (1993), pp. 149–73.

= 3 =

Tracing Igbo into the African Diaspora[1]

Douglas B. Chambers

Everywhere in the Americas, diasporic Africans and their immediate descendants created new worlds. The enslaved were forcibly displaced from their ancestral homes, taken to the coast, and then boarded upon ships bound for far away, although often in the company of others culturally not unlike themselves. After their Atlantic crossing, these peoples drew on familiar ethnic-African ways of being and of doing in order to survive as slaves. Initially, distinct 'nations' of Africans, and perhaps distinctively 'African' notions of nationalism, emerged from the Atlantic crossing and initial confrontation with chattel slavery. The survivors (and their children) also filtered through their shared experiences functional borrowings from other Africans, from their masters and from Amerindians as well, to fashion distinctive local and regional cultures.

The worlds that the slaves made, however, represented at least partial extensions of their various ancestral cultures (and cultural logic) within the constraints of the plantation/slavery regimes in which they commonly found themselves.[2] Diasporic ethnogenesis, or the creation of new African-derived ethnic identities outside the continent, seems to have been the first step in the historical creolization of these forcibly displaced populations. To understand the process, one must connect African histories (local as well as regional) with the subsequent historical experiences of those taken as slaves to the Americas.

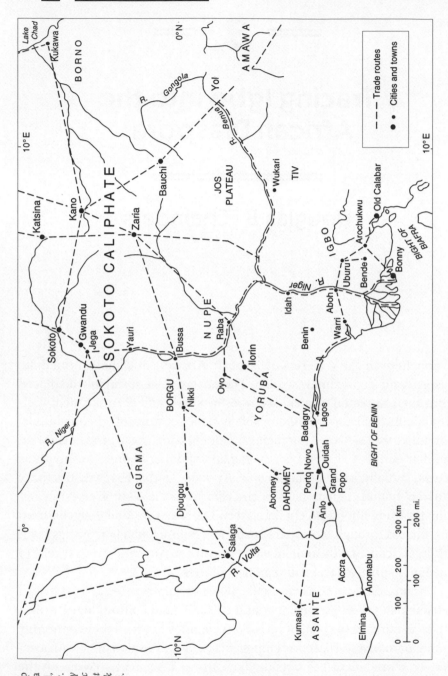

FIGURE 3.1 Map
of Lower Guinea
and hinterland,
early 19th century.
*Source: Drawn by
the Cartographic
Office, Department
of Geography, York
University, Canada.*

Igbo peoples constituted one of the largest 'nations' of the trans-Atlantic slave trade, and thus of the early modern history of the Americas. They were found in sizeable numbers throughout the Caribbean and North America, especially anglophone areas, from the late seventeenth through the mid-nineteenth century. But just as the peoples of the hinterlands of the Bight of Biafra had earlier created a plethora of local societies and yet united in a way that justifies their being characterized as all sharing 'Igboness',³ so their uprooted cousins creatively adapted themselves to their own particular historical circumstances in specific times and places, by mixing the familiar with the functional, and not in simply random ways.

About 1.7 million people were transported from the Bight of Biafra over the course of the trans-Atlantic slave trade, the vast majority (1.5 million) after 1700. Over 90 per cent of these people were taken by British slavers, and were thus bound for the anglophone Americas (but they also wound up in some numbers in places like St Domingue and Cuba). In general, I estimate that eight in ten diasporic Biafrans were Igbo-speaking (and presumably also Igbo-acting), with the rest divided between Ijaw (Kalabari) and Cross River peoples (so-called 'Moko').⁴ But since Igbo were the modal group of 'Calabars' (and probably also of Ibero-American 'Carabalí') this paper will focus on tracing people (and peoples) in and from what I call Eboan Africa, the hinterland of the Bight of Biafra.

Enslaved Igbo often reconstituted themselves as a diasporic 'nation', perhaps based on the Igbo concept of the *ebo* [ehbo] (clan, set of kindreds) or on particular ideas associated with being *igbo* [iboe], and at times reproduced this collective identity in communal performance such as foodways, 'powerways', dances, orature, religious praxis and other aspects of slave-village *habitus*.⁵ As with other diasporic African nations, such as Coramantee (Akan), Nago or Lucumí (Yoruba), Congo or Angola (western Bantu), Arada or Popo ('Gbe') and so forth, these initial African ethnic identities in the New World may have been newly constructed, the result of diasporic ethnogenesis, as a first step in the process of creolization. I am suggesting, therefore, that a historically operational 'Eboe' meta-ethnicity in the diaspora was derived from the cultures of the Biafran interior. An 'Eboan' collective identity developed, as slaves, once thrown into the diaspora, discovered ways of doing and of being which Igbo-speaking and Igbo-acting slaves shared.

Social and cultural artifacts termed 'Ibo' or 'Eboe' in the New World are signs of a historical Igbo presence, varied in different times and places. It may be possible to construct a series of definitions or historical understandings of what it meant to be Eboe in Virginia, in Jamaica or in St Domingue (or Carabalí in Cuba), and so forth, but it would be anachronistic to read these social and cultural assemblages back into African history as core signs of continental Igbo ethnic identity. Instead, the challenge is to follow Eboan African (Igbo) peoples and history *from* the hinterland *into* the diaspora.[6]

Central to the problem of defining 'Eboe' social signs and cultural referents is that, in the process of creolization, diasporic Igbo responded to the often brutal conditions of slavery in ways that require more subtle analyses than searching for New World 'carryovers' or 'retentions' of Eboan African 'traits'. Using a metaphor of formal linguistics to describe the cultural change which the term 'creolization' (also borrowed from linguistic theory) evokes, it seems that Igbo may have tended to 'calque', that is, to copy-translate into another cultural code behaviours (including words and phrases and other social 'things') from the ancestral set. Therefore, even 'basilectal' (root) things such as yam-growing and -eating, especially the reliance on *D. rotundata*, became identified as of 'Guinea' rather than from Igbo specifically (that is, in the anglophone Americas).[7] Other aspects of slave culture may be termed Igboesque creolisms, while still others were clearly Igbo.[8]

If people displaced from certain other ethnic groups tended towards being 'apports', bringing 'words' and 'things', in or nearly in their original form and function, to New World situations, such as Coramantee (Akan/Ga) ancestral dayname systems (or, at the least, the names themselves), or Nago/Lucumí (Yoruba) *shango* worship, Igbo may have tended to copy-translate ancestral cultural forms and functions into creole (or even Euro-American) forms, that is, acted as 'calques'. For example, on Carriacou in the Grenadines, so-called 'Ibo nation-dances' included not just 'Ibo' but also 'Jig-Ibo' and 'Scotch Ibo'.[9] In Haiti, Igbo created independent *nanchons* (*vodun* nations) informed by their own *loa* (gods), and with their own drumbeats and songs and ceremonials, but these took hyphenated names such as Legba-Ibo or Ibo-Lazile, transparent calques like *Un Pied Un Main Un Je* (One Foot, One Hand, One Eye), apparently a translation of a common Igbo name, or other names that may have evoked directly ancestral Igbo deities (perhaps *alosi*) (*Barak, Akoupi, Takwa, Ibo Hequoike*).[10] These socio-religious forms were creolized – that is, most likely created in the diasporic context through an internal process of 'bricolage'. Igbo in Haiti, however, invested their hyphenated *loa* with 'the ancestral principle [which] is the point of cosmic departure' for members of the several Igbo-named *nanchons* there, so that even in the mid-twentieth century these Igbo *loa* were believed to be 'intimately authoritative for Ibo families'.[11] In other areas, identifying Igboisms (as well as Eboe-isms) in slave and African–American folk lifeways, especially where the people did not use 'Ibo' to denote their ancestrally influenced forms, often requires a step or two of interpretation and, therefore, a qualified reliance on inference.

Diasporic Igbo used a variety of ethnonyms to group themselves, or were so grouped by others, in different times and places. In the early seventeenth century, as attested by Sandoval (1647), Igbo were seen as a subset of 'caravalies' (Kalabaris), as they also seemed to the Dutch in the second half of the century.[12] Throughout the eighteenth century, however, British slave traders and planters usually equated Calabar and Eboe. In late-eighteenth-century Jamaica, and in the Lesser Antilles in the nineteenth century, another term for a subset of 'Calabars' was 'Moko', whom European slave traders such as Hugh Crow learned were called 'Kwa' in Bonny and were 'mortal enemies to the Eboes'. Earlier, Sandoval (1647) had included 'moco' in his list of 'caravalies particulares', and Dapper (1668) thought they originated in the vicinity of Bonny to the north; in the late eighteenth century Captain Adams explicitly stated that 'Ibibbys' (Ibibio) were the same as 'Quaws' and were called 'Mocoes' in the West Indies. In the 1840s, however, Koelle learned in Sierra Leone that people called 'Moko' came from east of the Cross River (and perhaps from the grassland areas even further east) and were sold through Old Calabar. In the twentieth century, the Kalabari (New Calabar) word for Ibibio as a group was *Mboko*; likewise, Ngwa-Igbo call Ibibio *Nmogho*. One surmises, therefore, that in the seventeenth and eighteenth centuries most 'Moko' were Ibibio (and perhaps others from the lower Cross River), but that in the nineteenth century the term was extended to others enslaved farther to the north and east.[13]

In nineteenth-century Cuba the term Calabar ('carabalis') reappeared as a general ethnic marker used by slaves, freedmen and masters to gloss various Biafran (including Igbo) connections when naming *cabildos* (mutual aid societies), which led Fernando Ortiz to note that 'many of the *ibos* entered Cuba as carabalis'. For example, in Havana circa 1900 one *cabildo* had the title 'carabali ibo'. Ortiz also noted that in Havana 'there existed a rich cabildo of the carabalis *isuama isieque*'.[14] Curiously, the term 'Moko' was apparently not used in Cuba.

The shift in terms descriptive of 'nations' from the Bight of Biafra may have reflected shifting patterns in the slave trade from the hinterland to the coast. In the seventeenth century, 'Carabalis' referred to a mix of eastern Ijaw, southern Igbo and western Ibibio; in the eighteenth century, Igbo predominated or, as Edwards (1793) put it, 'All the Negroes imported from these vast and unexplored regions [in the Bight of Biafra hinterland], except a tribe which are distinguished by the name of *Mocoes*, are called in the West Indies *Eboes*'.[15] In the nineteenth century the pattern shifted again, with a greater proportion of non-Igbo, sometimes called Moko and sometimes not, and perhaps representing more people taken from groups like the Ekoi and Ejagham in present-day western Cameroon, as well as Efik from Old Calabar itself, bound for places such as Cuba.[16]

Over these centuries, Carabalí (initially Ijaw, later perhaps southern and eastern Igbo), Eboe (Igbo) and Moko (Cross River) peoples influenced in various ways the creolization (Africanization) of various American slave societies. In the case of Igbo, and because of the relatively high proportion of women in displaced Eboan populations, it may be that their influences were felt most directly in domestic spheres of life; that is, they were highly gendered. Or, possibly, the classical Igbo impetus to localism resulted in a constantly changing mosaic of folkways (cultures) as small groups of displaced people struggled to make sense of their new worlds, creating many constantly changing common traditions from loosely shared ancestral ones.[17]

The very multiplicity of terms used by and for 'Calabars' is of interest for clues to the historical, geographical and cultural provenances of people enslaved from the interior. This variability is also important for hints about the process of what I have elsewhere called 'primary creolization' (initial regrouping, or diasporic ethnogenesis) in the early building of communities out of the shared experiences of upbringing, enslavement, displacement and oppression. In the process of creating these communities, diasporic Igbo (in particular) fashioned new, African-derived identities in America (and Sierra Leone). Since the people who identified as 'Eboe' learned this term only after being taken out of Igboland, it may have signified a meta-ethnicity that seems fluid and essentially new and yet rooted in shared historical experiences.[18] Thus, for enslaved Eboan Africans (Igbo), the term 'Eboe' was a diasporic sign (word), but one with important African meanings.

In the various dialects and subcultural areas of present-day southeastern Nigeria, the term *igbo* contained a variety of meanings. There seem to be at least three categories of meanings associated with *igbo* and close cognates; classificatory, geographical and mythic. The first set of meanings are the best-known historiographically; that is, *igbo* used as a pejorative signifier for linguistically similar 'others' or 'slaves' or 'strangers', especially those associated with upland (forested) areas by riverine or lowland dwellers (*olu*).[19] Other 'types' of people covered by *igbo* included 'yam-eaters' and, generically, the 'community of people', as well as 'group of old ones' (*ndigbo*).[20] 'Thus,' wrote Oriji, 'whenever an Igbo man's life was threatened outside his cultural environment, he simply shouted *Igbo neri ji na ede unu nokwa ebea?* (Igbo who eat yams and cocoyams), meaning "Who domesticated these crops, are you around?"'[21]

Other words, phonetically closer to 'ebo' (e.g. *ibo, oyibo*), also had classificatory meanings. In 1832, R. A. K. Oldfield recorded that on the middle reaches of the Niger near 'Eboe' (Aboh), locals hid in the bushes and called out to them what he heard as 'Oh, Eboe! Oh, Eboe!' (meaning 'White man, white man!'); in the 1850s at Onitsha another such 'stranger', Revd J.C. Taylor, was called by the people *oibo*, to mean 'whiteman'.[22] Isichei has noted that in southern Nigeria *oyibo* was a term used to denote 'Europeans'.[23] In the early twentieth century, *ebo* (without the labial-implosive *gb* phoneme) could also mean various things, including 'the man to whom a slave runs' (Asaba area), 'man who finds a thief', 'breaking down of wall by rain' (an interesting metaphor that would be for 'slaves'!) and, in the case of *igbwo*, a long or English type of bead (obviously, a trade bead).[24]

'Igbo' was also used as a geographical term, both by outsiders as well as by people in Eboan Africa, though not particularly frequently, given the meanings suggested above. By the mid-nineteenth century, Europeans had learned to call the general country inhabited by various Igbo-speaking peoples 'Igbo' (Eboe).[25] Some Eboan Africans also used the term, though more specifically. For example, in Isuama and Orlu (and indeed further south, in Owerri, Ikwerre and Ngwa) some people claim that their ancestors migrated from a place called 'Amigbo' (Igbo Homeland), perhaps mythic, perhaps real, but in any case founded by a man named 'Igbo' (whose family was associated with the domestication of yams and cocoyams) and whose putative descendants were considered to be living in 'the homeland, cultural centre' of southern Igbo.[26] In fact, Ja Ja of Opobo, an Nkwerre-Igbo, was born in Orlu division about 1821, in a village that was also called Amigbo.[27]

In the nineteenth century there existed a town called 'Azigbo' in the Nri-Awka area (north–central), where the 'Igbos' owned a market called *Nkwo Igbo* (that is, the 'Igbo' market on *nkwo*, one of the four days of the Igbo week).[28] Farther to the north, near Nsukka, people called a main road running south *uzigbo* ('road [of the] Igbo').[29]

As might be expected, individuals (usually men) named 'Igbo' (or variations thereon) show up in the charter myths of a number of the more important village-groups (*obodo*), as well as of quarters and villages (*ogbe*) that were part of them. The original inhabitants are often described as having been expelled from earlier settlements for some violation or conflict and then migrating to their current places (where, ideally at least, the direct patrilineal descendants retained the original staff of authority *ofo*). For example, in the Nnewi district, the founder is remembered as *Digbo* (*di*: husband; husband of Igbo); in 'Anioma' (west of the Niger), the mytho-historical founder was Odaigbo, who had accidentally committed murder at 'Nshi' (Nri) but was allowed to choose exile and was sent carrying a magic pot on his head to 'find' his new place.[30]

It is clear, therefore, that the word 'Igbo' was known in Africa and used in ways that might be suggestive of 'ethnicity'. But is it possible to see *an* Igbo ethnicity or simply a pluralism of Eboan ethnicities in the region? Is it possible or meaningful to talk of an African-derived collective identity in the diaspora called 'Eboe'?[31]

I would suggest that the answers lie in the historical reality of Nri hegemony in north–central Igboland (Nri-Awka/Isuama),[32] because as late as circa 1900, the Nri were known as 'the first Igbo'. This is one key to understanding the village cultures of people in the area, which was probably the most disrupted during the era of the slave trade (from the late seventeenth to the early nineteenth century) and thus probably an important source of the flow of people to the coast.

The theocratic 'state' or religio-polity known as *Nri* developed in the central heartland of the Igbo region perhaps as early as the tenth century.[33] From his analysis of the *eze* or king lists, M. A. Onwuejeogwu infers that Nri was founded in 948, but this date may be too early as it is based on fifteen 'reigns', and it seems more likely that the *odinani Nri* (Nri culture) founded at Agukwu dates from the fourteenth century.[34] Onwuejeogwu's oral histories indicate that the era of Nri hegemony lasted from the fourth through to the ninth *eze Nri*, that is, in the seventeenth century, 'when Nri was real Nri' (*oge Nri bu Nri*). Indeed, the pattern of the 'troubles' from the tenth through to the fourteenth *eze Nri* (who was installed in 1889) seems to reflect the intrusion of slaving and the slave trade and its essential violence in both the eighteenth and nineteenth centuries.

Ideally, in areas influenced by *odinani Nri*, representatives of the *eze Nri* travelled from village to village to perform rituals to ensure a bountiful harvest and restore harmony in local affairs, and to deal with any other transgressions in a society governed by rules, not rulers. Local men could represent the *eze Nri* by purchasing a series of ranked *ozo* (titles), the highest of which entitled one to ennobling facial scarification and special access to supernatural forces and thus to great influence in village affairs. These *ndi Nri* and *mbreechi* (variant *mgburichi*) dominated the religio-political system by controlling access to the spirit world for collective ritual, material and agricultural ends. In particular, the Nri-men controlled the agricultural calendar and the making of the annual 'yam medicine' (*ifejioku*; variants *njokku, ahonjoku*) and, in their capacity as diviners/shamans, determined guilt in cases that brought to the sacralized Earth force that they represented ritual pollution, which only Nri-men could remove. The threat of refusing to remove such 'abominations' created a state of 'ritual siege' and thereby isolated the particular lineage, village or village-group, so that no one would trade with them until the situation was fixed.[35]

Nri hegemony lasted several hundred years, but it appears to have flourished in the seventeenth century, declined in the eighteenth century and survived in ever more reduced form until 1911, when British troops forced the reigning *eze Nri* to renounce the ritual power of the Nri-men. In the early twentieth century, Nri still retained a special symbolic status in much of 'Igboland' as representative of what may be called 'deep Igbo'.[36] In Nsukka (on the northern borderlands), Nri were thought of as 'the first Igbo'.[37] They may have thought of themselves as the only 'free' people in Igboland, although Nri did sanction slave owning and trading in the eighteenth century.[38] In Agukwu (Nri), status distinctions based on previous conditions of servitude did not exist. There were no *oru* or *ohu* (bought slaves) or *osu* (cult slaves).[39] Indeed, Agukwu may have served as a sanctuary. According to Onwuejeogwu, 'runaway slaves were considered free once they set foot on Nri soil' at least since the time of the tenth *eze Nri*, and in general they 'were completely absorbed into Nri lineage without limitations to their rights as full citizens'.[40]

The Nri were 'the first Igbo' for a number of reasons. They were considered the descendants of the oldest ancestors (the *ndi ichie*), or the elder brothers of Igbo, and thus owned the original ancestral *ofo*. The Nri are associated with the introduction of such essentially 'Eboan' things as *nso* and the ideology of abominations, yam cultivation and *ifejioku/njokku*, the *ofo* itself, the multi-tiered *ozo*-title system, with its *ichi* marks and other insignia of exalted rank, as well as the drum and perhaps even human sacrifice. The Nri, in short, were the arbiters of custom (*omenani*) or 'what the ancestors said was done'.[41]

Igbo people recognized that *omenani* was a function of local arrangements. As one proverb states, 'The bush-fowl of a village cries in the dialect of the village'. Or put another way, 'The hawk of Ezalo catches a fowl of Ezalo and goes to the cotton tree of Ezalo'. Each village or village-group might do things in its own fashion, but often the appearance of particularism merely coloured a more fundamental unity of form and function. As another proverb put it, 'I am a drum; if there is no wedge the drum has no head'.[42]

Foodways were an important method of defining *omenani*. Igbo did not eat just anything, and what was edible was often a function of ancestral tradition. The proverb, 'If vultures were edible birds, our forebears would have eaten them all up', captures this perfectly. Another proverb closely identified folkways with foodways: 'The type of firewood that is native to a village is the one that cooks the food of the people who live there.' In fact, the relationship between the common garden crop okra (from the Igbo word *okro*) and the wisdom of the ancestors as distilled in proverbs was itself proverbial: 'Those who cook okro soup have done [gone?], there remains those who only beat the [empty] plate.'[43] Proverbs themselves were 'the oil for eating speech'.[44]

The staple food throughout Igboland in the era of the slave trade was 'foofoo', or boiled and pounded yam, variously described as 'yams boiled and then beaten into a consistence like dough' or 'pounded until they become like a stiff dough'.[45] Heavily peppered soups served in calabashes, greens 'of the Calilue kind' and stews rounded out the Eboan diet.

One of the oldest recorded proverbs, collected in Igboland in the 1850s, was about how people should respond to new situations. Drawing on the imagery of the *okoko* (guinea fowl) and of the houseyards so common throughout all Igboland, and of the group of fellow *okoko* who surely would be there, the proverb went: 'A new fowl, when brought into the yard, walks gently and looks steadily on the old ones, to see what they do.' Such beings, of course, would learn to crow in the language of that village. This imagery of learned performance, of useful things passed down by the group, undergirds another saying, one that dates from the early years of this century: 'The song I sing, the chorus is not difficult to sing.'[46] In the diaspora, 'Eboe' learned to 'sing' in the languages of their various new settlements.

When Olaudah Equiano (1745–1797) attempted to capture the essential character of what he termed 'Eboan Africans' or 'natives of Eboe', he stressed the importance of group-based performances ('songs') as a metaphor for Igbo community culture. 'We are almost a nation of dancers, musicians, and poets,' he wrote in the 1780s. 'Every great event . . . or other cause of public rejoicing is celebrated in public dances, which are accompanied with songs and music suited to the occasion.'[47] According to Equiano, these group dances always followed general rules of function and arrangement, with the assembly of people divided into four sections by age and sex. In particular forms or details, however, the actual performances often seemed to be newly constructed or *ad hoc*. Equiano wrote that because public dance was meant to convey a narrative, 'and as the subject is generally founded on some recent event, it is therefore ever new'. This topicality gave 'our dances a spirit and variety which I have scarcely seen elsewhere'.[48]

The dances, music and poetry that Equiano believed defined Igbo-speaking people as 'Eboan' demonstrate the existence of a group of people, culturally conversant with each other and bounded by time and space, who would understand the performances. As an Igbo proverb states: 'A new man does not sing' (*onye ofo edekwe*).[49] In other words, 'Eboan' community culture was something that people at the time recognized guided their behaviour in concrete ways. As Equiano understood, in historical Igboland every person belonged to a specific group, and every group had its rituals, its customs, its beliefs, its ways of life – in short, its community culture (*omenani/odinani*).[50]

Eboan African community culture, that is the artifacts, learned behaviour, institutions and beliefs of the people in Igboland in the era of the trans-Atlantic slave trade, had an essential character. As Equiano suggested, this Eboan cultural logic was both universalistic (through general forms of public performance, already in evidence during the period of Nri hegemony) and particularistic ('ever new', as it continued to be in the Americas).

In the era of the trans-Atlantic slave trade, most people throughout Igboland had never heard of whites, much less seen any of those exotic creatures. The Eboan African world remained largely untouched by any direct contact with Europeans until the mid-nineteenth century or later, which underscores the vitality and integrity of Eboan community culture and the dynamism of Igbo peoples. Just as Europeans were struck by the exoticism of the people they saw in Igboland, so Eboan Africans thrown into slavery must have interpreted Europeans as equally exotic Others. Relying on essentially familiar and shared resources, Eboan peoples constantly fashioned new ways of being and doing in Igboland. This cultural dynamism, moreover, may very well have provided an adaptive model (or perhaps a set of interrelated models) for those who went as slaves into the diaspora.

Notes

1 The writing of this paper was helped by the generous kindness and constructive criticism of many people, including Paul E. Lovejoy, Robin Law, Joseph C. Miller and Jerome Handler. Special thanks to the participants at the UNESCO/SSHRCC Summer Institute, 'Identifying Enslaved Africans: The "Nigerian" Hinterland and the African Diaspora' (York University, Toronto, 1997), especially those in the Igbo history workshop, for their support and suggestions; any mistakes are mine, of course. I revised the paper while I was a fellow-in-residence at the Virginia Foundation for the Humanities, Charlottesville, in the fall of 1997.

2 For recent published explorations of these themes, see John K. Thornton, 'African Dimensions of the Stono Rebellion', *American Historical Review* 96, no. 4 (1991), pp. 1101–13; Thornton, *Africa and Africans in the Making of the Atlantic World, 1400–1680* (Cambridge, 1992), part 2; Thornton, '"I Am the Subject of the King of Congo": African Political Ideology and the Haitian Revolution', *Journal of World History* 4, no. 2 (1993), pp. 181–214; Gwendolyn M. Hall, *Africans in Colonial Louisiana: The Development of Afro-Creole Culture in the Eighteenth Century* (Baton Rouge, LA, 1992); João José Reis, *Slave Rebellion in Brazil: The Muslim Uprising of 1835 in Bahia*, trans. Arthur Brakel (Baltimore, 1993); Sandra E. Greene, 'From Whence They Came: A Note on the Influence of West African Ethnic and Gender Relations on the Organizational Character of the 1733 St. John Slave Rebellion', in George Tyson and Arnold Highfield (eds), *The Danish West Indian Slave Trade: Virgin Islands Perspectives* (Virgin Islands, 1994), pp. 47–67; Jean-Pierre Tardieu, 'Origines des esclaves au Pérou: La région de Lima (XVIe et XVIIe siècle)', in *Colloque international: De la traite négrière au défi du développement: Réflexion sur les conditions de la paix mondiale*, vol. 1 (Ouidah, Bénin, 1994); Paul E. Lovejoy, 'Background to Rebellion: The Origins of Muslim Slaves in Bahia', in Paul E. Lovejoy and Nicholas Rogers (eds), *Unfree Labour in the Development of the Atlantic World* (London, 1994), pp. 151–80; Colin A. Palmer, 'From Africa to the Americas: Ethnicity in the Early Black Communities of the Americas', *Journal of World History* 6, no. 2 (1995), pp. 223–36; Maria Ines Cortes de Oliveira, 'Viver e morer no meio dos seus: Nacoes e comunidades africana na Bahia do seculo XIX', *Revista USP* [Brazil] 28 (December 1995–February 1996), pp. 174–93; Douglas B. Chambers, '"My Own Nation": Igbo Exiles in the Diaspora', *Slavery and Abolition* 18, no. 1 (1997), pp. 72–97.

3 Or at least recognized each other as members of a 'nation' once in the diaspora: Olaudah Equiano, *The Interesting Narrative of the Life of Olaudah Equiano, Written by Himself*, ed. Robert J. Allison (Boston, 1995), passim; Revd Sigismund W. Koelle, *Polyglotta Africana* (1854; Graz, Austria, 1963), pp. 7–8; William B. Baikie, *Narrative of an Exploring Voyage up the Rivers Kwora and Binue* (1856; London, 1966), p. 307. Contrast the statement by an ethnographer who did her fieldwork in Agbaja in the 1930s: 'Two men from whatever part of Ibo-speaking country when they meet in Lagos or in London will call themselves brothers . . . At home, however, people will count themselves as belonging to their village-group . . . and will say of the people beyond a radius of about seven miles: "The people of that place are very wicked"'; M. M. Green, *Ibo Village Affairs* (1947; New York, 1964), p. 7.

4 Chambers, '"My Own Nation"', and notes therein. Compare a recent estimate of 75 per cent of '637,500' in J. N. Oriji, 'The Slave Trade, Warfare and Aro Expansion in the Igbo Hinterland', *Transafrican Journal of History* 16 (1987), pp. 151, 164 n. 2.

5 See, for example, the entries for 'Ibo (Nation) – dance' and 'nation-dance' in Richard Allsopp (comp.), *Dictionary of Caribbean English Usage* (Oxford, 1996), pp. 302, 400. See also Douglas B. Chambers, 'Source Material for Studying Igbo in the Diaspora: Problems and Possibilities', in Robin Law (ed.), *Source Material for Studying the Slave Trade and the African Diaspora* (Stirling, UK, 1997), pp. 90–118.

6 For a general discussion of this kind of approach, see Paul E. Lovejoy, 'Identifying Enslaved Africans in the African Diaspora', in this volume. For a systematic counter-argument, though one that recognizes the Africanity of New World slave cultures, see Philip D. Morgan, 'The Cultural Implications of the Atlantic Slave Trade: African Regional Origins, American Destinations and New World Developments', in *Slavery and Abolition* 18, no. 1, pp. 122–45.

7 Throughout the Caribbean, *Dioscorea rotundata* is commonly called 'Guinea-yam'; in Nigeria, and West Africa generally, *D. rotundata* is commonly called 'Eboe-yam'; see Allsopp (comp.), *Dictionary*, p. 274, and D. G. Coursey, *Yams: An Account of the Nature, Origins, Cultivation and Utilisation of the Useful Members of the* Dioscoreaceae (London, 1967), pp. 59–60, 64. A more technical linguistic example of a calque is the general Caribbean term 'mouth-water' (dribble, saliva); cf. Igbo *onu mili* (mouth-water; 'spittle'); see Allsopp, *Dictionary*, p. 392, and examples below on Igbo-Haitian *loa*. Other West African languages include similar constructions, of course, because linguistic calquing is a common process.

8 This, again, underscores the importance of seeing these societies in their historical contexts and in terms of a 'creole continuum', and of applying a 'words and things' methodology. See Mervyn C. Alleyne, 'Continuity versus Creativity in Afro-American Language and Culture', in Salikoko S. Mufwene (ed.), *Africanisms in Afro-American Language Varieties* (Athens, GA, 1991), pp. 167–81; Jan Vansina, *Paths in the Rainforests: Toward a History of Political Tradition in Equatorial Africa* (London and Madison, WI, 1990); Douglas B. Chambers, '"He Is an African but Speaks Plain": Historical Creolization in Eighteenth-Century Virginia', in Joseph E. Harris et al., Alusine Jalloh and Stephen E. Maizlish (eds), *The African Diaspora* (College Station, TX, 1996), pp. 100–33; and Chambers, 'Eboe, Kongo, Mandingo: African Ethnic Groups and the Development of Regional Slave Societies in Mainland North America, 1700–1820', Working Paper no. 96–14, International Seminar on 'The History of the Atlantic World, 1500–1800', Harvard University, 1996.

9 Allsopp, *Dictionary*, p. 400.

10 Harold Courlander, *The Drum and the Hoe: Life and Lore of the Haitian People* (Berkeley and Los Angeles, 1960), p. 328.

11 Maya Deren, *Divine Horsemen: Voodoo Gods of Haiti* (New York, 1970), pp. 68, 83–5, 94, based on fieldwork in 1947–50. See also Alfred Metraux, *Le vaudou Haitien* (1958; reprint, Paris, 1968), pp. 75–6, on how the names of various 'families' (*fanmi*) or 'nations' (*nanchon*) (including 'Ibo') apply equally to the religious character of these ethnic groups in Haiti. Each 'nation' differed in the way they conducted sacrifices and even in the choice of animals they offered (*ibid.*, 151). For discussions of drums and song style differences by ethnicity in early twentieth-century Haiti see Harold Courlander, *Haiti Singing* (Chapel Hill, NC, 1939), and Melville Herskovits, *Life in a Haitian Valley* (New York, 1937).

12 See the documentary evidence assembled in P. Amaury Talbot, *The Peoples of Southern Nigeria*, vol. 1, *Historical Notes* (1926; reprint, London, 1969).

13 For historical references, see Alonso de Sandoval, *De Instauranda Aethiopum Salute: El mundo de la esclavitud negra en América* (Madrid, 1647; Bogotá, 1956), p. 94;

O. Dapper, *Naukeurige Beschrijivinge der Afrikaensche Gewesten* (Amsterdam, 1668), p. 509 (in P. E. H. Hair, 'An Ethnolinguistic Inventory of the Lower Guinea Coast before 1700: Part II', *African Language Review* 8 (1969), p. 251 n. 78); Bryan Edwards, *The History, Civil and Commercial, of the British Colonies in the West Indies*, vol. 2 (London, 1793) (in Roger Abrahams and John Szwed (comps), *After Africa: Extracts from British Travel Accounts* (New Haven, CT, 1983), p. 70); Captain John Adams, *Sketches Taken during Ten Voyages to Africa, between the Years 1786 and 1800* (1823; New York, 1970), pp. 38, 40; Hugh Crow, *Memoirs of the Late Captain Hugh Crow, of Liverpool* (1830; London, 1970), p. 200; Koelle, *Polyglotta Africana*, pp. 11–13. For ethnological references, see M. D. Jeffreys, 'Note', *Africa* 5 (1934), 504 (cited in Hair, 'Ethnolinguistic Inventory', 2:251, n. 82); Herskovits, *Haitian Valley*, p. 18; G. I. Jones, *The Trading States of the Oil Rivers: A Study of Political Development in Eastern Nigeria* (London, 1963), pp. 19–21; Nkparom C. Ejituwu and Songpie Kpone-Tonwe, 'Atlantic Trade', in E. J. Alagoa and Tekena N. Tamuro (eds), *Land and People of Nigeria: Rivers State* (Port Harcourt, Nigeria, 1989), p. 120; John N. Oriji, *Traditions of Igbo Origin: A Study of Pre-Colonial Population Movements in Africa* (New York, 1990), p. 150; and Kenneth O. Dike and Felicia Ekejiuba, *The Aro of South-Eastern Nigeria, 1650–1980: A Study of Socio-Economic Formation and Transformation in Nigeria* (Ibadan, 1990), pp. 176, 178–9, for a possible reference to Cross River Igbo c. 1700.

14 Fernando Ortiz, *Hampa Afro-Cubana: Los negros esclavos; Estudio sociológico y de derecho público* (Havana, 1916); reprinted as *Los negros esclavos* (Havana, 1975), pp. 41, 50 [my translations]. Ortiz also noted about Igbo that 'Little is known in Cuba of these natives, surely by confounding some with the Lucumís and with the Yorubas, and others with Carabalís' (p. 50), but then listed the names of at least seven *cabildos* (half of the fourteen 'Carabalí') with likely Igbo derivations (pp. 41–59).

15 Abrahams and Szwed (comps), *After Africa*, p. 70.

16 For example, on Ejagham, see Robert F. Thompson, *Flash of the Spirit: African and Afro-American Art and Philosophy* (New York, 1983); and see Adriana Perez and Norma Garcia Cabrera (comps and eds), *Abakuá: Una secta secreta; Selección de textos* (Havana, 1993); Ivor Miller, 'Cuban Abakuá History and Contemporary Practice: The Testimony of Andres Flores, Elder' (paper presented at the conference 'West Africa and the Americas: Repercussions of the Slave Trade', University of the West Indies, Mona, Kingston, Jamaica, 1997).

17 Vansina, *Paths in the Rainforests*, is the basic source of these ideas.

18 See Douglas B. Chambers, '"He Gwine Sing He Country": Africans, Afro-Virginians, and the Development of Slave Culture in Virginia, 1690–1810', (PhD thesis, University of Virginia, 1996), part 1; and Chambers, '"My Own Nation"', pp. 72–9.

19 Northcote W. Thomas, *Anthropological Report on the Ibo-Speaking Peoples of Nigeria*, 6 vols (1913; reprint, New York, 1969), 4:191; Talbot, *Peoples*, 2:404; Darryl Forde and G. I. Jones, *The Ibo and Ibibio-Speaking Peoples of South-Eastern Nigeria* (London, 1950), p. 9; Austin J. Shelton, *The Igbo-Igala Borderland: Religion and Social Control in Indigenous African Colonialism* (Albany, NY, 1971), pp. 6–7. See also Philip A. Oguagha, 'Historical and Traditional Evidence', in Philip A. Oguagha and Alex I. Okpoko (eds), *History and Ethnoarchaeology in Eastern Nigeria* (Oxford, 1984), p. 271; T. Uzodinma Nwala, *Igbo Philosophy* (Lagos, 1985), p. 19; Oriji, *Traditions*, p. 4.

20 Oriji, *Traditions*, p. 2; M. A. Onwuejeogwu, 'An Outline Account of the Dawn of Igbo Civilization', *Odinani* 1, no. 1 (1972), p. 40; Shelton, *Igbo-Igala Borderland*, pp. 6, 260, 264.

21 Oriji, *Traditions*, p. 2.

22 They also called him *eze* (Master/Sir), *beke* (whiteman), and in the case of one *ozo*-title holder Taylor was thought of as 'my *moa* [spirit] companion'; John C. Taylor,

'Journal of the Rev. J. C. Taylor at Onitsha', in S. Crowther and J. C. Taylor, *The Gospel on the Banks of the Niger* (1859; reprint, London, 1968), p. 261.

23 R. A. K. Oldfield, 'Mr. Oldfield's Journal', in M. Laird and R. A. K. Oldfield, *Narrative of an Expedition into the Interior of Africa*, vol. 1 (London, 1837), p. 394; Taylor, 'Journal', p. 261; Elizabeth Isichei, *A History of Nigeria* (London, 1983), p. 9.

24 Thomas, *Anthropological Report*, vol. 4, p. 191; vol. 5, p. 36; vol. 2, pp. 195, 200.

25 Baikie, *Narrative*, pp. 308–11.

26 Oriji, *Traditions*, pp. 83–4.

27 Elizabeth Isichei, *A History of the Igbo People* (London, 1976), p. 98.

28 John O. Alutu, *Nnewi History*, 2nd edn (1963; reprint, Enugu, Nigeria, 1985), pp. 101–2.

29 Shelton, *Igbo-Igala Borderland*, p. 270.

30 Alutu, *Nnewi*, pp. 1–2; see also pp. 67–9 for the story of 'Eze Igbo', who would have been sold into slavery to the Aro but for the timely intervention of his eldest brother; for Anioma, see Don C. Ohadike, *Anioma: A Social History of the Western Igbo People* (Athens, OH, 1994), p. 16.

31 See the debate among historians of Yoruba: 'Biodun Adediran, 'Yoruba Ethnic Groups or a Yoruba Ethnic Group? A Review of the Problem of Ethnic Identification', *Africa: Revista do centro do estudos africanos de USP* 7 (1984), pp. 57–70; Robin Law, 'Ethnicity and the Slave Trade: "Lucumí" and "Nago" as Ethnonyms in West Africa', *History in Africa* 24 (1997), pp. 205–19.

32 See, for example, Adiele Afigbo, *Ropes of Sand: Studies in Igbo History and Culture* (Ibadan, 1981), pp. 31–67; M. A. Onwuejeogwu, *An Igbo Civilization: Nri Kingdom and Hegemony* (London, 1981); A. Ikechukwu Okpoko, 'Traditions of Genesis and Historical Reconstruction: The Umueri of Igboland as a Case Study', in B. W. Andah and Ikechukwu Okpoko (eds), *Some Nigerian Peoples* (Ibadan, 1988), pp. 103–25.

33 In the same region, as early as the eighth or ninth century, people had created complex societies with a 'highly ritualized and symbolic culture' and traded local agricultural surpluses for goods that traders brought, including carnelian beads. See Thurstan Shaw, *Igbo-Ukwu: An Account of Archaeological Discoveries in Eastern Nigeria*, vol. 1 (Evanston, IL, 1970); Shaw, *Unearthing Igbo-Ukwu: Archaeological Discoveries in Eastern Nigeria* (Ibadan, 1977).

34 Onwuejeogwu, *Igbo Civilization*, pp. 22–9. These condensed genealogies of the fifteen *eze Nri* in the Agukwu traditions clearly reflect an 'official' Nri perspective, as is to be expected since the extensive fieldwork on which his reconstructions are based was conducted in Agukwu.

35 Afigbo, *Ropes of Sand*, pp. 8–9; Onwuejeogwu, *Igbo Civilization*, pp. 21–22, 31–50; Dike and Ekejiuba, *The Aro*, pp. 109–14. See also Chambers, 'Gwine Sing He Country', part 1.

36 A. G. Leonard, *The Lower Niger and Its Tribes* (London, 1906), pp. 11, 34–5, 37. Afigbo recognizes the profound formative influence of Nri culture for communities within its sphere, but notes that significant swathes of communities (southern Owerri, Ngwa, and east and north-east through Afikpo and Abakaliki) developed in many ways separately. Onwuejeogwu's research and argument for a generally wide influence at an early date is suggestive (see *Igbo Civilization*, p. 27, map), though he recognizes areas and peoples outside of Nri influence (p. 13); patterns of migration and the folk accounts of them recently published by Oriji seem to support Onwuejeogwu on this issue.

37 Oguagha, 'Historical and Traditional Evidence', p. 214. See also M. A. Onwuejeogwu, 'The Igbo Culture Area', in F. C. Ogbalu and E. N. Emenanjo (eds), *Igbo Language and Culture* (Ibadan, 1975), pp. 1–10.

38 Onwuejeogwu, *Igbo Civilization*, pp. 26–8, 30 n. 13.

39 *Ibid.* Cf. Alutu, *Nnewi*, and his condemnation of 'outcast' status still operative in Nnewi. See also Carolyn A. Brown, 'Testing the Boundaries of Marginality: Twentieth-Century Slavery and Emancipation Struggles in Nkanu, Northern Igboland, 1920–9', *Journal of African History* 37, no. 1 (1996), pp. 51–80.

40 Onwuejeogwu, *Igbo Civilization*, pp. 26, 30 n. 13. In the nineteenth century, some village-groups in the area sent 'abominable' persons such as dwarfs and toddlers who cut an upper tooth before a lower one to 'the Oreri people' (Nri) instead of killing them; 'abominable' children became clean on being brought to Nri; Alutu, *Nnewi*, pp. 270, 388 n. 35.

41 Onwuejeogwu, *Igbo Civilization*, pp. 8, 38–40; Afigbo, *Ropes of Sand*, pp. 51–4; Dike and Ekejiuba, *The Aro*, pp. 109–13; C. K. Meek, *Law and Authority in a Nigerian Tribe: A Study in Indirect Rule* (1937; reprint, New York, 1970), p. 166.

42 Thomas, *Anthropological Report*, 2:353, 291.

43 Isichei, *Nigeria*, 28. Okra (*Hibiscus esculentus*) was cultivated throughout Atlantic Africa and called *nkruma* in Twi [Akan], variations of *gombo* in KiKongo, etc. [western Bantu]; see also Lorenzo D. Turner, *Africanisms in the Gullah Dialect* (Chicago, 1949), p. 194. Major Leonard mentioned that okra was considered an aphrodisiac in southern Igboland; Leonard, *Lower Niger*, p. 369. See also Captain Crow's note that around Bonny there 'are also some vegetables of the Calilue kind (which are much like spinach), and there is no want of ocra, well known in the West Indies as a good ingredient in making soup'; Crow, *Memoirs*, p. 258.

44 Thomas, *Anthropological Report*, 1:70. The 'oil for eating speech' proverb is a staple of Igbo oral literature, much of which speaks to the singular value Igbo place on oblique speech (i.e. on 'signifying'). See Joyce Penfield, *Communication with Quotes: The Igbo Case* (Westport, CT, 1983); Gloria Chukukere, 'Analysis of Cultural Reflection in Igbo Proverbs', in R. N. Umeasiegbu (ed.), *The Study of Igbo Culture: Essays in Honour of F. C. Ogbalu* (Enugu, 1988), pp. 13–20; D. Ibe Nwoga, 'Appraisal of Igbo Proverbs and Idioms', in F. C. Ogbalu and E. N. Emenanjo (eds), *Igbo Language*, pp. 186–204; Romanus N. Egudu (trans. and comp.), *The Calabash of Wisdom and Other Igbo Stories* (New York, 1973); Austin J. Shelton, 'Relativism, Pragmatism, and Reciprocity in Igbo Proverbs', *The Conch* 3, no. 2 (1971), pp. 46–62. Compare Isidore Okpewho, *African Oral Literature: Backgrounds, Character, and Continuity* (Bloomington, 1992), esp. pp. 226–52, and Ruth Finnegan, *Oral Literature in Africa* (Oxford, 1970), pp. 389–425.

45 Richard Jackson, *Journal of a Voyage to Bonny River*, ed. Roland Jackson (1825–6; Letchworth, UK, 1934), p. 70; William Allen, *A Narrative of the Expedition Sent by Her Majesty's Government to the River Niger in 1841* (London, 1848), 1:388. For evidence on the recent (twentieth-century) introduction of cassava, see Elizabeth Isichei (comp.), *Igbo Worlds: An Anthology of Oral Histories and Historical Descriptions*, and Isichei, *Nigeria*; see also Susan M. Martin, *Palm Oil and Protest: An Economic History of the Ngwa Region of South Eastern Nigeria, 1800–1980* (Cambridge, 1988).

46 Taylor, 'Journal', p. 255; Thomas, *Anthropological Report*, 2:161.

47 Olaudah Equiano, *The Life of Olaudah Equiano, or Gustavus Vassa, the African*, ed. Paul Edwards (London, 1988), p. 4. The term 'Eboan Africans' is in a section omitted from this edition, but see the text of the first American edition (1791), *Interesting Narrative*, p. 45. The term was included in the excerpt in G. I. Jones, 'Olaudah Equiano of the Niger Ibo', in Philip D. Curtin (ed.), *Africa Remembered: Narratives of West Africans from the Era of the Slave Trade* (Madison, WI, 1968), p. 82.

48 Equiano, *Interesting Narrative*, p. 36. For a general theoretical discussion of the processual nature of public ritual (drawn from African materials), see Victor Turner, *Dramas, Fields, and Metaphors: Symbolic Action in Human Society* (Ithaca, 1974), especially 'Social Dramas and Ritual Metaphors', pp. 23–59. Levi-Strauss termed this

tendency to create structure out of events as 'bricolage': traditional (pre-modern, primitive, 'savage') cultural actors were like 'bricoleurs', or handymen, who made do with what they had at hand in order to make something [cultural as well as physical]; Claude Levi-Strauss, *The Savage Mind* (Chicago, 1966; orig. publ. as *La Pensée sauvage* in Paris, 1962), pp. 1–33, esp. pp. 16–22. One ethnographer in 1930s central Igboland (Owerri province) noted that 'Four with its multiples is the sacred number that runs all through Ibo ritual and belief'; Green, *Ibo Village Affairs*, p. 22. For other examples of the significance of the number 4 in Igbo culture, see P. Amaury Talbot, *Tribes of the Niger Delta: Their Religions and Customs* (London, 1932), p. 286; Sylvia Leith-Ross, *African Women: A Study of the Ibo of Nigeria* (1939; reprint, London, 1965), p. 117.

49 Thomas, *Anthropological Report*, 2:314; see also F. C. Ogbalu, *Ilu Igbo: The Book of Igbo Proverbs* (Ouitsa, Nigeria, 1965), p. 47. In general, 'dance' in northern Igboland was associated with masquerades or 'mask-dramas' (or what one Igbo art historian has called 'performance cults'); see Uche Okeke, 'The Art Culture of the Nsukka Igbo', in G. E. K. Ofomata (ed.), *The Nsukka Environment* (1978; reprint, Enugu, 1985), pp. 271–2, 279–80. See also Chike C. Aniakor, 'The Omabe Cult and Masking Tradition', in *Nsukka Environment*, pp. 286–306; Uche Okeke and C. U. V. Okechukwu, 'Igbodo Art and Culture', in *Nsukka Environment*, pp. 307–14; Herbert M. Cole and Chike C. Aniakor, *Igbo Arts: Community and Cosmos* (Los Angeles, 1984); G. I. Jones, *The Art of Eastern Nigeria* (Cambridge, 1984); G. I. Jones, *Ibo Art* (Aylesbury, UK, 1989). For two examples of such 'plays' or 'masquerades', one (Crow) at New Calabar c. 1791, and the other (Jackson) at Bonny c. 1825, see Crow, *Memoirs*, p. 35, and Jackson, *Journal*, pp. 89–90.

50 I take an explicitly essentialist position here, partly because I assume that culture 'exists' and partly because people in pre-colonial Igboland expressed their understanding of the nature of being (ontology) in essentialist terms, as many Igbo proverbs make clear. My understanding of 'community-culture' includes material culture (the things a group commonly uses) and ideological culture (the ideas that a group commonly believes) as well as institutions and socially ordered behaviour. Compare Robert Fogel's common-sense statement that 'Culture does not exist in a vacuum; it is defined by the behaviour, artifacts, institutions, and beliefs of a society. What frequently differentiates one culture from another is not so much the presence or absence of particular types of behaviour, artefacts, or institutions, but the frequency of their occurrence or their distribution over space and time. And much of what we know, or think we know, about the beliefs of a society is inferential, and turns on the study of the frequency of certain types of practices or artefacts'; Robert W. Fogel, *Without Consent or Contract: The Rise and Fall of American Slavery* (New York, 1989), p. 449 n. 3.

= 4 =

Regla de Ocha-Ifá and the Construction of Cuban Identity

Christine Ayorinde

In discussing the transmission and reconstruction of Yoruba religion and culture in Cuba, Miguel Barnet asserts that Cubans have created 'a cultural complex whose versatility and richness minimizes any African model'.[1] According to Barnet, Yoruba culture, which serves as a model or pattern for some practitioners of the *regla de ocha* (also known as *santería*), awakens in others no more than a feeling of curiosity for the exotic. Instead 'many of the divinities of the Yoruba pantheon . . . serve as the pattern which shapes Cuban idiosyncrasy'.[2]

Thus, the most popular *orisha* in Cuba, Changó (or Shango, originally the principal deity of Oyo in Yorubaland), became a macho womanizer in Cuba, and Ochún is a *mulata*, syncretizing the Yoruba deity Oshun with the Virgin of the Caridad del Cobre, the patron saint of Cuba and symbol of the mestizo nation. Yemayá, the Yoruba goddess Jemoja, became a *'linda negra'*, a pretty, black woman with fine features and long, flowing hair, whose transformation is explained in a myth that says she was originally white but fell into the Black Sea.

Myths of the *orisha*, or *patakín*, whose function, like that of the Yoruba Ifá divination corpus, has been to explain and validate ritual practices and relationships between the deities in the Yoruba pantheon, reflect the influence of other cultures encountered in Cuba. An extreme example of this diverse ethnic mix is the *camino* (avatar) of Changó, called Sanfancón or San Fan Kung, which was invented by Marcos Portillo Domínguez, a *santero* of Cantonese and African descent, and is supposedly based on a Taoist myth. A *pataki* recounts how other *orisha* fail to recognize Changó in this *camino* because of his Chinese appearance.[3]

Adapted forms of the Yoruba religion developed into the Cuban *regla de ocha* despite the cultural losses suffered by slaves in the Middle Passage and the adjustments they had to make to a new social context. Since the Cuban Revolution, the commitment to the atheist (now secular) state and the desire to recognize the African roots of Cuban culture have further tested the adaptability of the *regla de ocha*. Conflicting pressures are only the latest manifestations of the contradictory world in which the *regla de ocha* emerged.

African-derived religions in Cuba are called *reglas*, from the *reglamentos*, or rules, of the *cabildos de nación*, mutual aid societies organized along ethnic lines and encouraged by the Spanish colonial government to keep Africans from uniting against the slave system. The ethnic designations of these *cabildos de nación* were derived from those of the slave trade (e.g. *congo*, *mandinga*, *carabalí*, *lucumí*), although Africans themselves had some power to determine their cultural and religious boundaries, and in practice the *regla de ocha* tended to counteract the colonial policy of ethnic division. Initially, the *regla de ocha* was the religion of the *lucumí* slaves, but by the end of the nineteenth century, the *regla de ocha* became increasingly open to Africans of other ethnic origins and to Cuban-born blacks and whites. Indeed, many famous *santeros*, *santeras* and *babalawos* have been white. The term *lucumí* included all Yoruba speakers as well as some neighbouring groups such as Ewe-Fon and Nupe, and was subdivided accordingly: *lucumí eyó* (Oyo), *lucumí ifé/fee* (Ife), and so forth.[4]

The *regla de Ifá* is the Cuban version of the Ifá divination cult, whose male diviners are called *babalawos*. These *babalawos* provide the ritual and spiritual leadership of santería (from *santo*, i.e. saint), the term that is commonly used to designate both the *regla de ocha* and the *regla de Ifá*. *Santería* also includes the *arará* practices of Ewe-Fon (Gbe) origin. In contrast, the *reglas congas*, also called *palo monte*, are of Bantu origin.

The terminology reflects changing attitudes: *santería* was originally called *brujería*, or witchcraft, by those external to the practice. Spanish clerics used the term to refer to the unorthodox rites whereby African gods were worshipped under the guise of Catholic saints. The term *religión yoruba* is used by some *babalawos* to emphasize its African origin. Those who wish to emphasize its Cuban-ness tend to call it *la santería cubana*.

There is little concrete information on the process of transforming the *orisha* cults into *santería*. Oral tradition refers to meetings and *convenios* (agreements) between *santeros* to reconstruct and regulate religious practices in the nineteenth century. However, according to Lydia Cabrera, a Matanzas *babalocha* (a *santero* who has initiated others) called Lorenzo Samá and a Yoruba woman called Latuán (a daughter of Changó), who arrived in Cuba in 1887, conceived the idea of unifying the different Yoruba *orisha* cults in Cuba into a single liturgical body which was called the *regla de ocha*.[5] The *casas de santo* or *ilé ocha* (literally, 'houses of the *oricha*/saint', usually the private houses of *santeros* and *santeras* where ceremonies are held, now also called *casa templos*) replaced the *cabildos*.

Practitioners of the *regla de ocha* worship a number of deities. For members of the relatively independent local and regional *orisha* cults of Yorubaland, the pantheon is more the concern of *babalawos*.[6] In Cuba, a devotee 'makes' or becomes initiated into the cult of a specific *orisha*, or *santo de cabecera* (saint of the head), but other *orisha*, or *santos de fundamento* (usually Changó, Ochún, Yemayá and Obatalá), are received at the same time. The *santos de addimú* are *orisha* received before or after full initiation to resolve specific problems, or when deemed necessary. Divination becomes more central in Cuba determining which *orisha* (and which *camino* of the *orisha*) is to be the *santo de cabecera*. Outside the *iyesá*, *egguado* and *arará* (Ijesha, Egbado and Ewe-Fon) houses in Matanzas, whose practices differ from that of the Oyo-dominated *santería*, *orisha* have not been inherited within families.

Santería practice, like Yoruba *orisha* worship, is flexible: 'Cada practicante tiene su verdad' (Each practitioner has his/her own truth). Each house inherits its traditions from the *rama*, its ritual line of descent. Membership of other religions also affects practices within houses, as in the use of spiritism for dealing with *egun* (lineal ancestors). Great power and efficacy are attributed to initiation into several different practices, and the divination systems and mythology reflect this multi-religiosity. For example, divination verses refer to, and sometimes recommend, elements from other religions.

Cuban traditions evolved out of the need to adapt to different social conditions and to compensate for gaps in the transmission of religious knowledge, both from Africa to Cuba and from older to younger generations of Cuban-born practitioners. Not all *orisha* were transferred to Cuba, and some that were became less relevant: their cults died out, and their rituals were forgotten. As in Nigeria, an *orisha*'s power depends on having numerous and attentive devotees, but some *orisha* were linked with activities no longer important in a slave society, while others had their functions modified. Ochosi, the hunter, who in Africa represents order in society, became in Cuba the patron of jails and acquired the contrary function of offering protection against the police.

Sometimes *orisha* from different regions in Yorubaland were fused, as in the case of Olokun, an independent deity in Africa, who in Cuba is sometimes a *camino* of Yemayá. *Orisha* also became fragmented into multiple *caminos*, who reflected regional variants or multiple conceptions of an *orisha* as expressed in Yoruba oriki poetry. *Orisha* cults in West Africa also display the merging and fragmentation of *orisha*, as well as a tendency to incorporate new material from other cultures.[7]

Social and economic factors also affected practice, for example when its external expressions were not socially acceptable. For example, new initiates (*iyawó*) normally have to shave their heads and wear white for a year, but those who did not want outsiders to know that they were devotees could arrange a dispensation from these requirements. After the Revolution, when rationing restricted the availability of animals for sacrifice, birds were substituted for four-legged animals. Because fabric and coloured beads needed to represent the different *caminos* of the *orisha* were scarce, only one *camino* was represented in ritual objects. When the required items were again available in the dollar economy, some traditions could be restored.

African-derived religions have a long history as subcultures, and their role as escape mechanisms and forms of cultural *marronage* for those of African descent cannot be discounted. Afro-Cuban religious organizations supported more concrete forms of resistance to both slavery and Spanish colonialism throughout Cuban history, reflecting a pan-African and pan-Caribbean sense of solidarity, especially after the St Domingue Revolution in the 1790s. In 1812, José Antonio Aponte, a free black of Yoruba origin who was a carver of religious statues, an Ogboni, and a member of the famous *cabildo* Changó Teddún, united a number of white Cubans, members of other African ethnicities and Haitian émigrés in a plot against the government. Using religious celebrations to conceal their activities, they planned to abolish slavery and to bring about the downfall of the colonial regime.[8] Others made efforts to maintain or re-establish links with Africa or even to return there, both after the Escalera conspiracy of 1844, when thousands of blacks were massacred, and also after Abolition in 1888. According to Fernando Ortiz, the Unión Africana y sus Descendientes was set up in 1892 in order to unite all Africans in Cuba and to establish a steamship line running between Africa and Cuba. This was not permitted by the governor, who maintained that Africans in Cuba were not foreigners but Spaniards. Lydia Cabrera mentions a letter, brought to her attention by Pierre Verger, which was written by a member of the Baró family of Matanzas province to the king of Dahomey in 1926. Baró's letter points out that his parents were born in Africa, were of *arará* origin and spoke Fon, and it expresses his wish to visit Dahomey.[9]

The fact that African-derived religions provide an alternative set of cultural practices available to *all* Cubans makes for a complex situation. There are multiple possibilities for reconstructing and re-inventing identity and tradition, and various power struggles are taking place at both official and popular levels. Afro-Cuban culture was used to define a national culture in the *Afrocubanismo* movement of the 1920s and 1930s. Nationalist intellectuals (mainly white and middle-class), influenced by international artistic trends, attempted to forge a cultural nationalism that incorporated the black population, or elements of their culture. It was believed that middle-class guidance could help Afro-Cuban forms evolve into a national culture.[10]

Fidel Castro and the leaders of the Revolution were also keen to emphasize the African roots of the population. Cuban foreign policy was committed to military and civilian assistance to Africa, in recognition of the fact that it was the place of origin of many Cubans, and thus it aimed to renew links which had been lost after the ending of the slave trade. Indeed, in 1976, Castro declared Cuba an Afro-Latin country. The government sought legitimacy for the Revolution in Cuba's past, recalling the Independence wars when black troops formed the majority of the forces fighting against Spain. The Conjunto Folklórico Nacional was founded, based on folk dance troupes of eastern Europe, its repertoire consisting of dances and songs from Afro-Cuban religions of Yoruba or Bantu origin. The government also established centres for the study of Afro-Cuban 'folklore'.

Yet European intellectual traditions, of which Marxism is another strand, continued to dominate Cuban politics. Although Afro-Cuban elements were acknowledged to be an important part of national culture, the Marxist emphasis on science and technology disparaged the African past, depicting it as outmoded and dying out, like classical civilization. This attitude also affected views of Cuba's role in contemporary Africa.[11] The agenda was still to refine Afro-Cuban culture, give it respectability and harness it to the political and cultural project. Thus the distinction between 'folklore' (Afro-Cuban forms fell into this category) and 'high culture' was retained.

The revolutionary government may also have used the popular appeal of *santería* in its campaign against the Catholic Church, which, in contrast to Afro-Cuban religions, was heavily involved in counter-revolutionary activities in the early years of the Revolution, and this was seen to represent a political threat. In the 1970s scientific atheism was introduced and the 1976 Constitution declared Cuba an atheist state. In the past, Eurocentric attitudes had described Afro-Cuban religions as backward African superstitions, but now Marxist thinking labelled all religions anachronistic. The ideological struggle against religious obscurantism in the 1970s attempted to discourage religious observance. It followed the pre-Revolutionary practice of placing confiscated Afro-Cuban religious objects in museums, linking them with the past rather than with a living culture.

The Department of Socio-Religious Studies of the Academy of Sciences carried out various studies of what were then called '*cultos sincréticos*' (a term now regarded as pejorative, as all religions are syncretic). This research stressed their utilitarian nature and claimed that they resisted the social project because of their historical marginality. Their links with black market activities (essential to obtain items for ceremonies) were seen as likely to make them refuges for delinquents: 'Initiates who display antisocial behaviour or who have committed crimes turn to religion to evade justice.'[12] Participation in Afro-Cuban religions was thus linked by researchers and officials with pathological behaviour and with marginal groups in society such as homosexuals, criminals and drug addicts.

The difficulty of the project to free the masses from religious beliefs may be a further result of Cuba's incorporative multireligiosity. According to Damián Fernández, traditional Cuban values (including popular religious ones) combined with Castroism and Marxism-Leninism to form a 'political religion' which merged seemingly incompatible beliefs into one world-view.[13] One *babalawo* argued that 'our Marxism is syncretic', not doctrinaire; it was adopted as yet another religion rather than as an ideology. Many practitioners even apply Marxist terminology to religion; e.g. Ifá is described as a dialectical science.

The Revolution's insistence that it had eliminated racism reiterated, with more justification than in the past, the long-standing Cuban perception that race relations were better there than in the United States. Demographically, Cuba has become blacker since the Revolution, as a result of the exodus of predominately white exiles. However, although Afro-Cubans had most to gain from the Revolution and have been among its most ardent supporters, the insistence on national unity has left little room for a black consciousness movement among Afro-Cubans. Such movements in the United States and the English-speaking Caribbean in the 1960s and 1970s stimulated a search for roots in Africa and for cultural forms which could replace the dominant Western culture. But, like Brazil, Cuba already had more overt manifestations of 'Africanisms' which were traceable to specific African cultures. Yet, in contrast to the United States, where *orisha* worship was adopted as the cultural arm of the black consciousness movement in the 1960s, and in contrast to Brazil and Trinidad, where attempts have been made to re-Africanize syncretic versions of *orisha* worship, in Cuba, at least in recent times, African-derived religions have not necessarily been linked with the idea of a return to Africa or with a desire to expunge non-African syncretic elements from them.

In the 1980s, due to social and economic factors, there was a change in official attitudes towards religion. Fidel Castro's meetings with Caribbean and later American church members, published as *Fidel and Religion*, his interviews with the Brazilian priest Frei Betto, and his realization that movements such as liberation theology could combine revolutionary thought and Christianity led to a rapprochement with Christian churches, though the revolutionary project still favoured secularization. The collapse of the Soviet bloc, the economic crisis which followed, and the continuing American embargo, led the government in 1989 to declare a 'special period in peacetime'. Strategies to deal with the economic situation were formulated, such as encouraging tourism, inviting limited foreign investment and making some market reforms.

In the face of increasing international isolation, the government intensified its campaign for national unity. It sanctioned an *apertura* (opening up) in Cuba in order to maintain a broad social base of support for the Revolution. Cuba was declared a secular rather than an atheist state, and known religious practitioners were allowed to become members of the Communist Party. Recognizing the *crísis de valores* (crisis of values) meant acknowledging that the old ideology needed reworking in light of its apparent failure in eastern Europe and that Marxism was conceived in places and times with traditions and histories very different from Cuba's. Material difficulties have also shaken confidence in secular means of solving daily problems. All religions, but especially Afro-Cuban religions, with their history of providing solidarity and material benefits that are no longer guaranteed through hard work or education, are experiencing a resurgence.

This is the first time that *santería*, the most widely practised of all the African-derived religions in Cuba, was not relegated to a subaltern status.

The increasing globalization of *orisha* worship elevated the position of *santería* within Cuban society. The exile community in the United States consults Cuban religious specialists, as do those in many parts of Latin America. The change in status, both as a result of official policies and the expansion of *santería* practice, has led to a power struggle, as practitioners, researchers and officials inside and outside the religion attempt to control it for their own purposes. The increasing numbers of Cuban initiates and foreign visitors have raised the possibility of commercialization. The so-called *diplobabalawos* (from *diplotiendas*, dollar shops previously reserved for diplomats and expatriates) attract foreigners who pay up to 10,000 dollars per *babalawo* initiation. The rate for Cuban initiates is 30,000 to 35,000 pesos, about 1500 dollars.

As local colour, Afro-Cuban culture and religion have been used to promote tourism, with *ocha turs* and academic conferences that feature visits to religious ceremonies. But commercialization and commodification have negative implications: the multiplication of cult groups and the consequent loss of control have weakened the fabric of the religion, and the unscrupulous have admitted performing unnecessary or false initiations of foreigners for money.

Lázara Menéndez suggests that indiscriminate contact may be weakening the cults. This may force a return to the hermeticism which in the past assisted a process of conservation of African elements.[14] Withdrawal underground reflects the belief that, as in Africa, power is linked with secrecy and that if knowledge becomes widely diffused there will be a loss of power. One *babalawo* predicted a potential loss of earnings and status; he believes that if the secrets are sold to foreigners, no one will need to come to Cuba for ceremonies.

Previously, the lack of institutionalization or hierarchy was advantageous for the subculture's survival, but now there is no obvious representative among *santeros* and *babalawos* for dialogue with the state. Attempts to create unifying organizations, such as the Yoruba Cultural Association, have been undermined by jealousy among rival groups of practitioners. The attitude of 'En mi casa mando yo' (I rule in my house) has worked against unity. None the less, educated practitioners and those with status have sought to improve the image of the religion; doctors, engineers and university teachers serve as the 'intellectual recovery team' among the *babalawos*.[15]

The 1987 visit of the Oni of Ife, called by some Cubans the Yoruba 'Pope', and his statement that Cubans have kept 80 per cent of the practice intact, confirmed the legitimacy of the *regla de ocha-Ifá* in relation to the Yoruba traditional religion. The Apena of Ife said that the *babalawos*, who are the guardians of the ritual aspect of Yoruba culture, maintain its essence and that despite 'minor changes', the 'practice remains intact and would be even more so if there was more contact between Nigeria and Cuba'.[16]

Cuba was declared a *subsede* (subsidiary) of Ile-Ife, apparently the only one in the Americas, according to the Yoruba Cultural Association. Nevertheless, some practitioners dismissed the Oni's visit as an exercise in tourism and public relations and complained that he did not meet ordinary religious people. Menéndez claims that the visit attracted little interest, unlike the Pope's visit, which was discussed years in advance and was linked to politics.

According to Menéndez, the International Workshop on Yoruba Culture held in Cuba in 1992 recognized a tendency called 'yorubización de la Santería' which implied a recovery of 'ritual orthodoxy' and a return to Africa and to the 'liturgy' of the Nigerian *orisha* cults and the Ifá corpus. Some practitioners believe that their roots are in Yorubaland and that it is important to reappropriate Yoruba history and language. They also wanted the *regla de ocha-Ifá* to be ruled by the dictates of the Oni of Ife, and declared that recovery of the ritual should eliminate syncretism. This view was shared by the Yoruba Cultural Association. The major cause of disagreement was the refusal of some believers to accept terms like *santería* or 'syncretism' in referring to Yoruba religion.[17] In the same year, at a workshop at the Casa de Africa in Havana, there was a debate about the concept of a return to Africa and fears that ethnic identification would be divisive.

Some Cuban practitioners, while acknowledging the need to fill gaps in Cuban religious knowledge, refuse to accept an implied secondary position in relation to Africa. As one *babalawo* put it: 'The Yoruba king said we were the branches of the great tree of Nigerians, that we have 75 per cent of it, and the 25 per cent lacking we'll be given when we go to Africa, because we maintain the purity of the religion . . . while [the Oni's] people have made changes.'[18] Scholars like Jesús Guanche see the idea of a return to Africa as importing an identity crisis and imposing a false interpretation of Cuban cultural institutions.[19] Menéndez suggests that visitors from the United States and elsewhere who have knowledge of Nigeria have created a new anxiety in Cuban practitioners, because there has hitherto been little information about Africa in Cuba despite the internationalist campaigns. Yet, as far back as the 1940s, anthropological works on the Yoruba were obtained through mail order by practitioners and translated and inserted into religious texts.[20] According to Alberto Pedro, the image of Africa is weak in *santería* itself. Africa is a distant place of origin, and saying that "'my religion is pure because it comes from there" is not the same as saying "I am African"'.[21] There is little reference to Africa in the divination verses. Moreover, the prayers used in ceremonies tend to be spoken in Spanish, which Menéndez believes shows a spontaneous rejection of the *lucumí* language.

Attempts at Africanization seem to have involved only a minority of practitioners, often *babalawos* who discredit the more syncretic and therefore more 'Cuban' *regla de ocha*. Many *babalawos* distinguish the *regla de Ifá* from the *regla de ocha* or *santería* by claiming that they have a purer line of transmission from the 'original' and that *ocha* is more Cuban, in the sense of being less orthodox. They attach greater prestige to Ifá for having remained truer to its roots, which seems to reflect a continuation of the hegemony of Ifá in Yoruba traditional religion. Conversely, some *santeros* claim that there is no need to look to Africa for what was lost: the African tradition has changed over time, and Cuba is now the centre of the *orisha* tradition. Cuban practices reflect archaic ones lost in Africa, just as the surviving *lucumí* language, which has less than 50 per cent of the cognates of the Yoruba language, retains some archaic forms no longer used in Nigeria.[22]

According to Víctor Betancourt Estada,[23] what he calls the Yoruba religion (i.e. Ifá) is distinct from what he calls 'popular religion' (i.e. *santería*). Ifá remained a closed cult immune from the transculturation of *santería*. Betancourt heads the Ifá Iranlowo house, which is 'rescuing' traditional healing methods. According to him, the religion is like a broken doll: the knowledge and secrets are there, but they are scattered and need to be put back together, using practice in Nigeria as the frame of reference. Betancourt opposes the use of syncretic elements such as Catholic baptism for *santería* initiates. He has also returned to the older Cuban custom of *paticabezas*, which introduces initiates to only one *orisha* rather than a number of additional *orisha*, which is also referred to as *santos de ensalada*. According to one source, *oriatés*, who were ritual specialists skilled at *diloggún*, or 16-cowry divination, were initiated to two *orisha*, Eleggúa and a *santo de cabecera*, 'con pie y con cabeza' (with the feet and the head).

Babalawo Lázaro Vidal claims that Yoruba traditional religion is losing ground in Nigeria because it is subject to artificial syncretism which creates a 'disorderly amalgam of things'; yet he also draws on Abimbola, Osamaro Ibiè and Idowu to identify the prayers, stories and verses that he believes have been lost in Cuba which can sometimes explain the rituals passed down by imitation without understanding. Nevertheless, he acknowledges that tradition is not necessarily what is ancient, but rather what is accepted by the community.[24]

Some practitioners debate whether *Ifá* is part of the *regla de ocha*. In some religious houses, divination for certain rituals as well as the killing of four-legged animals had to be performed by *babalawos*, whereas in others these were performed by *oriatés* or *obas*. The dispute reflected competition between the *diloggún* and *Ifá* divination systems, the latter trying to regain the prestige it enjoyed in Africa. In Cuba, Changó became the first owner of the Ifá divining tray, which indicates an Oyo-centrism which presumably emerged after practitioners left Africa.[25] Menéndez suggests that Ifá arrived too late in Cuba to compete with European scientific knowledge, and its closed, male-only status made it less popular. *Santeros* who are *diloggún* diviners and are also able to perform the rituals are seen as more efficacious. This has legitimated their practices: 'Voy adonde me lo dicen y hacen' (I go where they tell me what needs to be done, and do it). There may be historical reasons for this: in the past there were fewer *babalawos*, and they were often reluctant to carry out some ritual roles in *ocha*.

The lack of African cultural studies at Cuban universities has meant that, apart from the efforts of practitioners and some academics, there has been little opportunity to relate the Cuban manifestations of these cultures to the place of origin. Very little linguistic study of Cuban forms derived from West African languages has been carried out. Some enthusiasts and scholars have done some research on Bantu languages in Angola and Zimbabwe, though it has been generally accepted that the rituals of the Cuban *reglas congas* show a greater degree of hispanization than *ocha* rituals.

For practitioners of African-derived religions in Cuba, looking to Africa in order to legitimate Cuban practices challenges creole orthodoxy. The emphasis on African origins has led to changes in Cuban practices, replacing them with contemporary African practices which may be no more 'original' than the Cuban. Claims of legitimacy through closeness to Yoruba traditional practice conflict with assertions of Cuba's role as the main upholder and exporter of the *orisha* tradition.

Often alternative practices become variant traditions. This is evident in the case of a Puerto Rican *santera* who, while visiting the house of the *rama* of her deceased godmother in Havana in 1996, was relieved to find that its practices corresponded to those she had inherited but were regarded by Puerto Rican *santeros* as unorthodox. The American Yoruba Movement was founded by African–Americans who rejected the Spanish and Catholic elements in *santería*. They set up Oyotunji, a 'traditional' Yoruba village in South Carolina, where they could live separately from modern American society. What surprised Cubans to whom I described this movement was not that its proponents rejected syncretism but that anyone living in the United States would deliberately choose a 'primitive' way of life.

For Cuban cultural nationalists, emphasizing cultural elements of African origin can be seen as divisive. Barnet regards the term '*cultura negra*' as both pejorative and divisive, while 'Afro-Cuban' is inappropriate for a culture and a religion that are no longer exclusive to Cubans of African descent. Also, if African-derived cultural practices are to reflect and validate a *national* identity (which they do), then the importance of Africa cannot be allowed to predominate. This could lead to transnational ethnic identification which could be potentially threatening to national unity among Cubans.

The inclusion and exclusion of both people and cultures of African origin in society and national consciousness have been problematic in Latin American nations with large black populations. One way of dealing with the problem has been to emphasize the mixed biological and cultural heritage of the entire population, though, inevitably, the components of the mixture have been given different weights where European culture has had connotations of progress and modernity. The emphasis on biological *mestizaje*, or what Nicolás Guillén terms *mulatez* ('mulatto-ness'), as the key to cultural synthesis and to overcoming racial problems reflects a different approach from the rigidly defined identities or multiculturalism adopted in North America.

In Cuba, ethnic identification is more flexible, though racial boundaries and stereotypes still exist, as continuing experience of racial prejudice reveals. Since the time of José Martí, who promoted the ideology of racial fraternity and equality among Cubans during the independence struggle in the late nineteenth century, there has been an emphasis on integration. Yet Africans and their descendants in Cuba, while fighting for the creation of the Cuban nation, in some cases also remained conscious of their place of origin.

However, it would be unfortunate if ideological concerns discouraged a closer examination of the Yoruba *orisha* cults that developed into the

Cuban *regla de ocha-Ifá*. The cultural dynamism that existed in Africa enabled both the African and diaspora forms of religion to respond to change over time. As Olabiyi Yai points out, the mother continent is not merely at the root of diaspora cultures but is embedded in the very process of their creation.[26] Knowledge and recognition of Yoruba culture and religion give us insights into the processes of the development of the *regla de ocha-Ifá*, just as Cuban rituals, the *lucumí* language and the Cuban Ifá corpus throw light on both regional variants and archaic forms of the Yoruba *orisha* cults.

Notes

1 Miguel Barnet, 'La hora de Yemayá', *Gaceta de Cuba* 34, no. 2 (1996), p. 49 ('un complejo cultural de riqueza proteica que minimiza cualquier modelo africano'). I would like to acknowledge the Humanities Research Board of the British Academy whose support made this research possible.
2 *Ibid.*, p. 48 ('muchas de las divinidades del panteón yoruba . . . sirven de patrón para la conformación de la idiosincrasia cubana').
3 Israel Moliner, personal communication, Matanzas, February 1997.
4 See Rafael López Valdés, 'Notas para el estudio etnohistórico de los esclavos lucumí en Cuba', in L. Menéndez (ed.), *Estudios afrocubanos* (Havana, 1990), 2:311-47.
5 Lydia Cabrera, *Yemayá y Ochún* (Madrid, 1974; Miami, 1980), p. 113.
6 Karin Barber, 'How Man Makes God in West Africa: Yoruba Attitudes towards the Orisa', *Africa* 51, no. 3 (1981), pp. 724–45.
7 See Karin Barber, 'Oriki, Women and the Proliferation and Merging of Orisa', *Africa* 60, no. 3 (1990), pp. 313–37, and Barber, 'Discursive Strategies in the Texts of Ifá and in the "Holy Book of Odù" of the African Church of Òrúnmìlà', in P. F. de Moraes Farias and K. Barber (eds), *Self-Assertion and Brokerage* (Birmingham, 1990), pp. 196–224.
8 See José Luciano Franco, *La conspiración de Aponte* (Havana, 1963).
9 For a history of Cuban returnees to Lagos, see Rodolfo Sarracino, *Los que volvieron a África* (Havana, 1988); Fernando Ortiz, *Los cabildos y la fiesta Afro-Cubanos del Día de Reyes* (Havana, 1992), p. 17; Rogelio Martínez Furé, *Diálogos imaginarios* (Havana, 1979), pp. 127–9; and Lydia Cabrera, *Reglas de congo: palo monte y mayombe* (Miami, FL, 1979), pp. 16–17.
10 See Robin Moore, 'Nationalizing Blackness: Afrocubanismo and Artistic Revolution in Havana, 1920–1940' (PhD thesis, University of Texas at Austin, 1995).
11 See Carlos Moore, *Castro, the Blacks, and Africa* (Los Angeles, 1988), p. 324, on Cuba's 'civilizing' role in Africa.
12 Ana Celia Perera Pintado, 'La regla ocha: Sus valores religiosos en la sociedad cubana contemporánea' (Departamento de Estudios Sociorreligiosos, Havana, 1996, mimeographed), p. 12 ('Iniciados que tienen conductas desaprobadas socialmente o que han cometido delitos y acuden a la religión para evadir la justicia').
13 Damián Fernández, 'Revolution and Religion in Cuba', in L. S. Gustafson and M. C. Moen (eds), *The Religious Challenge to the State* (Philadelphia, 1992), p. 53.
14 Lázara Menéndez, personal communication, February 1997.
15 Babalawo Lázaro Vidal, personal communication, October 1996.
16 'Yoruba Culture Is Alive in Cuba', *Granma Weekly Review*, 5 June 1987.

17 Lázara Menéndez, 'Un cake para Obatalá?', *Temas* 4 (October 1995), pp. 38–51; Menéndez, 'The Freedom of Worship and Respect for All Religious Traditions', *Granma International*, 14 June 1992.
18 *Granma Weekly Review*, 1 May 1988.
19 Jesús Guanche, 'Santería cubana e identidad cultural', *Revolución y cultura*, March 1996, pp. 43–6.
20 See Furé, *Diálogos imaginarios*, p. 212.
21 Alberto Pedro, personal communication, February 1997.
22 I am indebted to Taiwo Abimbola for this information.
23 Víctor Betancourt Estrada, personal communication, Havana, January 1997.
24 Lázaro Vidal, personal communication, October 1996.
25 See Rómulo Lachatañeré, *El sistema religioso de los Afrocubanos* (Havana, 1992), p. 17, and Nicolás Angarica, *Manual de Orihaté: Religión lucumí* (n. p., n. d.), p. 54.
26 Olabiyi Babalola Yai, 'Survivances et dynamismes des cultures africaines dans les Amériques', *Studies in the World History of Slavery, Abolition, and Emancipation* 1, no. 1 (1996).

= 5 =

Cultural Zones in the Era of the Slave Trade: Exploring the Yoruba Connection with the Anlo-Ewe

Sandra E. Greene

The cultural background of enslaved Africans in the Americas has bewildered scholars attempting to link specific cultural traits with their African origins. Following the lead of Melville Herskovits, these African origins are sometimes identified with a single 'cultural zone' in western and West–Central Africa that is believed to be the major source of African–American culture. According to Herskovits,

> The civilizations of the forested coastal belt of West Africa and the Congo are to be regarded as forming one of the major cultural areas of the continent; which means that they resemble each other to a far greater degree than is recognized if local differences alone are taken into account.

Although Herskovits's inclusion of Kongo and coastal West Africa in a single cultural zone has long been criticized, his general assessment that 'in many respects the entire area of slaving may thus be thought as presenting a far greater degree of unity than is ordinarily conceived in the face of New World contact' still has considerable validity as a first approximation in understanding the cultural impact of the African background on the cultures of slavery in the Americas.[1]

In moving beyond the first approximation to take into consideration more recent scholarship, however, we must recognize that Herskovits's concept of 'cultural zones' tends to exaggerate the similarities among African cultures, as Sidney Mintz and Richard Price have argued. According to Mintz and Price, the 'overt or explicit social and cultural forms such as "patrilocality", "hoe agriculture", "corporate ownership of land" and so forth' that Herskovits alleged to have been 'widespread or universal West African cultural "elements", "traits" or "complexes" [were] not at all so widespread as Herskovits supposed'. Instead, Mintz and Price are more inclined to stress 'intercultural variation' and indeed reject the idea that 'a generalized heritage of the sort Herskovits postulated' actually existed historically.[2]

Despite this criticism, the concept of 'cultural zones' still has validity, as John K. Thornton has demonstrated in his reconstruction of cultural/linguistic zones along the Atlantic coast of Africa during the era of the slave trade.[3] In assessing the structure of African societies along the Atlantic coast, he distinguishes three zones, relying heavily on linguistic data: the region of Upper Guinea; the Lower Guinea zone, comprising Akan and Aja groups (the latter including both Ewe and the Yoruba); and finally the Angolan group. Thornton recognizes the obvious linguistic and cultural diversity within these zones, but argues that 'in closely related languages there is a variation in the degree of difference'. Moreover, individuals often spoke more than one language, which made it easier for many people to understand a wider variety of speech than monolingual people were able to do. Besides this linguistic fluidity, economic factors also helped to unify the zones:

> In many parts of western and central Africa people of diverse language groups interacted with each other from day to day as a result of residential proximity or commerce. In the course of these interactions they might exchange many cultural ideas even if they did not exchange languages. Thus, they might share religious ideas or aesthetic principles to such a degree that they possessed a common religious or artistic heritage despite their linguistic diversity.[4]

Hence Thornton reconfigures Herskovits's cultural zones to allow for more complex interactions and a greater number of cultural zones.

A study of historical change among the Anlo has particular relevance in understanding how cultural zones were formed. The location of the Anlo (whose language is linguistically related to the other Ewe and Gbe languages) on the south-eastern edge of the Ewe-speaking communities in southern Ghana and Togo tied their history and culture to their Ga/Adangbe and Akan neighbours to the west, as well as to their Yoruba neighbours to the east. But the form and timing of these influences suggest that Thornton, like Herskovits, telescopes historical change and thereby blurs the process by which cultural zones emerged. Thornton places the Anlo and Ewe closest to the Yoruba in the Lower Guinea cultural zone. According to Thornton, 'Yoruba had emerged as a lingua franca along the coast from the Volta to Benin, though other lingua francas functioned both east and west of this'.[5] He bases this conclusion on a 1630 Portuguese document.

But was Yoruba influence along the western Slave Coast really that significant in the early seventeenth century? Robin Law has noted that,

> the series of coastal lagoons and rivers extending from the River Volta to the delta of the River Niger . . . afforded almost continuous waterborne communication for over 400 miles along the coast, the only serious obstacle to navigation occurring in the vicinity of Godomey, at the western end of Lake Nokue in modern Benin, where during the period of low water in the dry season the passage was blocked by a sandbar.[6]

If Law is correct, were there cultural connections between the Anlo and the Yoruba before the Portuguese arrival in the area or did these connections arise as a result of the economic activity generated by the Atlantic slave trade? Moreover, how did these connections shift over time with the political and economic changes that occurred in the region? Did an Anlo who found himself or herself sold into the Atlantic slave trade during the seventeenth, eighteenth or nineteenth century have enough knowledge of Yoruba language and culture to help maintain that culture in the Americas along with Anlo culture? What does Anlo history tell us about the existence and character of cultural zones in West Africa during the era of the Atlantic slave trade?

Anlo traditions seem to support an ancient link with the Yoruba. According to these traditions, the ancestors of the Anlo were originally residents of the Yoruba kingdom of Oyo. The ancestors are said to have left Oyo for an unknown reason and to have migrated first to Yoruba-speaking Ketu and then to Notsie, in present-day Togo, from where they then migrated to their current homeland in south-eastern Ghana. The analysis of these traditions has focused almost exclusively on the Notsie connection rather than exploring the supposed origins of the Anlo among the Yoruba.

FIGURE 5.1   Lagoon near Anlo, western coast, Bight of Benin, early 20th century. Photo taken by missionaries. *Source: Courtesy of Norddeutsche Mission, Germany.*

FIGURE 5.2   Lagoon near Anlo, western coast, Bight of Benin, early 20th century. Photo taken by missionaries. *Source: Courtesy of Norddeutsche Mission, Germany.*

Hence, the traditions suggest a Anlo–Yoruba connection during the era of the Atlantic slave trade.

Both Law and Thornton comment on the extent to which the Yoruba language was spoken throughout the region. As noted above, Thornton cites a Portuguese traveller's recollection of Yoruba as the lingua franca, while Law remarks that 'there was enormous Yoruba influence throughout the eastern section of the Slave Coast' and that "in Allada in the mid-seventeenth century, '"Lukumí" (i.e. Yoruba) was considered "noble" and commonly spoken by local people in preference to their own [language]'.[7] Although the westernmost coastal Yoruba communities were at Apa and Aklon, situated to the east of Lake Nokoe,[8] the Anlo are known to have had trade contacts with Yoruba communities at Atakpame and Anexo during the eighteenth century and hence Yoruba influence seems to have been important from an early date.[9] But did Anlo and Yoruba traders actually use the routes extensively enough to establish substantial links between these distant cultures?

This essay attempts to answer these questions and tests the extent to which Thornton's description of the Anlo and the Yoruba as sharing a particularly close cultural connection within the Lower Guinea cultural zone captures the complex political, economic and cultural characteristics of the Slave Coast.

Contemporary European accounts about the Anlo area in the seventeenth century are quite limited in number; yet these sources, in combination with oral traditions and recent studies on the Slave Coast economy, indicate that while long-standing and continuous communication may have existed between the Anlo-Ewe on the westernmost Slave Coast and Yoruba-speaking peoples to the east, trade along the Anlo section of this east–west communication system was dominated by a mix of ethnic outsiders who brought little in the way of Yoruba culture to the Anlo. In his description of this east–west trade, Law has argued that the movement of trade goods (most often aggrey beads and cloth) between the Gold Coast ports of Elmina and Accra and the Slave Coast ports of Great Popo, Little Popo (Anexo), Allada and Benin was initiated by the Dutch in 1637. This in turn stimulated an African trade shortly thereafter, beginning at least by 1659. Much of this trade took place by ocean, with only that between Anexo and Ouidah being conducted by lagoon.[10] Those who dominated this trade were Fante and Ga/Adangbes. Law cites a Dutch report of 1659 that 'for "some years" (eenige jaren) the trade in *"akori"* beads had been engrossed by the natives of the Gold Coast, who "go with their canoes to

Lay [Le], Great and Little Popo, and as far as Ardra [Allada] to buy them . . ."'
A French report from Ouidah in 1688 'notes not only that the Europeans
bought cloth there for resale on the Gold Coast, but also that "the Negroes
[i.e. of the Gold Coast] even come with canoes to trade in them, and carry
them off ceaselessly"'. Law adds, 'It is probable in fact that the settlement
of Fante canoemen at Anecho dates back to this period, and was intended
to facilitate the operation of Coast trading activities.'[11]

Involvement by Gold Coast residents in this coastal trade not only
brought Fante residents to the Slave Coast ports of Anexo, Ouidah and
Great Popo, but also brought new residents, traders and bandits to the
towns of Aflao and Keta (communities to the east of Anlo but settled by
Ewe-speaking immigrants related by marriage to the Anlo). In 1698, for
example, Jean Barbot noted that the violent surf prevented inhabitants
from fishing in the sea. This account is consistent with Anlo oral traditions
which indicate that the Ewe-speaking peoples then resident on the coast
did not fish in the ocean at first because they lacked the technological
know-how or materials for building ocean-going vessels. Yet it is clear
from W. Bosman's accounts that Ga/Adangbe traders also lived in Aflao
and in Keta to the east. During his visit to Aflao in 1698, for example,
Bosman noted that 'their language is mostly that of Acra, with a very small
adulteration'.[12] Barbot observed that 'some pretend they were formerly of
a more savage and hottish temper than most of the Blacks are'.[13] Dutch
travellers in the area also noted that between 1675 and 1683, bandits
operating from Keta frequently attacked traders who operated by sea
between the Volta river and Ouidah. Ray Kea noted that one particular
band of brigands 'plundered an English boat and killed many of its crew
at Keta; and at the port of Popo about 80 km to the east, they joined the
slaves aboard the English sloop Charlton and "killed ye commander and
all they could and took all the gold and slaves"'. Law has identified these
bandits as groups that came from Ga and Adangbe communities on the
Gold Coast.[14]

This evidence suggests that during the seventeenth century, Ga and
Adangbe immigrants were the major if not the dominant participants (and
predators) in the west–east coastal trade that passed the Anlo area by sea
on its way to the larger, more prosperous Gold Coast and Slave Coast ports.
The situation was little different in 1717, when Ph. Eytzen reported that
the primary orientation of local traders was the north–south trade in slaves
and ivory. Little commerce was actually conducted, however, because local
demand by Europeans who anchored off the coast was limited, while the

Kwawu and Akwamu supplied the markets at Ouidah and Allada. Significantly, those who hosted Eytzen while he was in Anlo were prominent traders also of Gold Coast origins. One was a man by the name of 'Hannibal', who came from Assine; the other, by the name of 'Offoribiacan', may have been from Anexo but was clearly of Fante origin.[15] It is unlikely, then, that the Anlo had much contact with the Yoruba or Yoruba culture during the seventeenth or early eighteenth centuries.

There is no evidence that political or economic connections existed between Anlo and the Yorubaland or the eastern Slave Coast prior to the beginning of trade contacts between the Gold Coast and the Slave Coast, initiated by the Dutch in 1639 and expanded by the Africans from the Gold Coast by 1657. Even with the development of an African trade in aggrey beads and cloth, Anlo appears to have been relatively isolated from this early trade. The latter was conducted by Fante and Ga/Adangbe using ocean-going canoes to travel between the Gold Coast and Anexo; the Anlo were unable to gain access. It is, of course, possible that goods were conveyed by land and by inland canoe through the Anlo area, but Ga and Adangbe bandits regularly attacked any traders who travelled between Anexo and the Volta river. Because the Anlo had limited access to European traders (who rarely came to Keta or Aflao), we can also assume that they lacked the capital needed to compete effectively in the north–south trade, dominated by the Akwamu and Kwawu, or the east–west trade, dominated by the Ga and Adangbe.[16] Anlo contact with Yoruba culture could have taken place through their limited involvement in the east–west coastal trade, but there is no evidence to support this hypothesis.

There were strong economic connections between the Anlo and their western Ga/Adangbe neighbours. As noted by Bosman, Ga/Adangbe was widely spoken in Aflao and perhaps Keta in the late seventeenth century. Several clans whose members were resident in Anlo, Keta and Aflao trace their origins to the Ga/Adangbe immigrants who moved into the Anlo area in 1679, after Akwamu attacked their communities to the east of the Volta river. And it was these immigrants who introduced new boat-building and salt-making technologies, thus providing the Anlo with the opportunity to become more actively involved in both the north–south trade (exchanging fish and salt for slaves and ivory) and the east–west trade when political conditions in the area shifted in favour of Anlo involvement.[17] In addition, connections with the Akan developed after 1702, when Akwamu invaded Anlo, maintaining control over the area until 1730. Among the cultural consequences of this political domination was the

Anlo adoption of Akan military terminology and organizational structures, the use of Akan-type drums and drum language, the use of Akan swords as symbols of political authority, and changes in the Anlo inheritance system.[18]

If the Ga/Adangbe and Akan served as the Anlo's principal economic and cultural contacts on the coast during the sixteenth and early seventeenth centuries, how do we explain the Portuguese account cited by Thornton which states that Yoruba operated as the major lingua franca on the Slave Coast from the Volta to Lagos? Perhaps the account is simply inaccurate. European traders may have encountered Yoruba as a lingua franca and language of prestige in ports to the east of Anlo, Keta and Aflao and then simply assumed that this language operated in a similar fashion to the west. It is also possible that some of the African traders in Keta and Aflao who also participated in the larger Gold Coast–Slave Coast trade did indeed speak Yoruba but that the European traders with whom they interacted erroneously assumed that this was true for much of the population in these towns. Whatever the situation, data to support the veracity of the Portuguese account is virtually non-existent. Yoruba may have been known by some of the traders in the area, but it was certainly not a lingua franca. Trade connections were simply not that extensive. In addition, those Anlos who were involved in trade during the seventeenth and early eighteenth centuries concentrated most of their efforts on linking the Ewe-speaking hinterland with the Anlo coast and selling a quite limited number of slaves and ivory tusks to African and European buyers in the immediate area.

Anlo interest in Yoruba culture, specifically Ifá divination, developed in the mid-eighteenth century, immediately after Anlo began to expand its associations with the east. As indicated above, Anlo's principal contacts prior to 1730 had been with peoples and communities located to the west and the north. Ga/Adangbe refugees from the west entered and then took control of the east–west trade, and they conducted much of the banditry that preyed on this trade during the seventeenth century. During this period, Akwamu and Kwawu domination of the north–south trade limited Anlo involvement, thus minimizing their economic and cultural connections with communities in the east. All this changed, however, in 1730. In that year, a combined force from Akyem and Akuapem defeated Akwamu, and the Akwamu royal family was forced to relocate to the east side of the Volta river. Freed of Akwamu control, the Anlo immediately launched a series of expansionary campaigns to gain greater access to the fishing grounds on the north side of the Keta lagoon. The purpose of the wars was to increase Anlo production of fish, which could then be used to expand their involvement in the purchase of slaves and ivory in the interior that had previously been dominated by the Akwamu and Kwawu.[19] Anlo interest in the communities to the east of Keta and Aflao appears to have come shortly thereafter. In 1737, Dahomey attacked Anexo and then pursued up to Keta its political leader Ashangmo, who had taken refuge on an island in the Volta. Dahomean troops arrived in Keta in July 1737 and remained for five days. The Anlo participated with the Anexo in the military campaign that eventually led to the capture of the entire Dahomean regiment of about 1300 men.[20] An even more intense association with communities to the east began after Anexo conquered both Keta and Anlo in 1741. During this period, Anexo maintained tight control over the political life of Anlo, installing as *awoamefia* (the polity's spiritual and political leader) an individual who by patrilineal descent was eligible to rule but who had also spent a significant amount of time in Anexo with his mother, who came from that town.[21] Anexo traders also managed Anlo's economic relations with the European traders who were operating in the area.[22] Nine years after their conquest, the Anlo managed to free themselves, but Anexo retained control over Keta and continued to interact (if not always on friendly terms) with Anlo throughout the rest of the eighteenth century as marital ties sustained relations even in the face of military conflict.[23]

This interaction with Dahomey and with Anexo was significant because it opened the Anlo to the cultural world to the east at a time when they were especially interested in taking advantage of practices and beliefs that could enhance their ability to expand their military and economic power in the region. Between 1730 and 1741, for example, the Anlo attacked and gained control over the areas north of the Keta lagoon, in what became known as the Abolo and the Kovenu wars. In 1750 and 1751, after freeing themselves from the Anexo, they came into conflict with the Ada over control of the fishing grounds around the mouth of the Volta. Tension continued to develop, and intermittent clashes occurred throughout the period between 1753 and 1768. In almost all these conflicts, Anlo fisherman found themselves rebuffed in their efforts to dominate the fishing industry in the area, while Anlo traders suffered constant attack from polities that wished to prevent them from supplying their trade partners in Akwamu and Asante with firearms and salt.

During this time, the Anlo began to turn to the deities worshipped by the Hula, the Fon and the Yoruba in the polities to the east with which they had become familiar. Anlo traditions, dated with contemporary European accounts, indicate that at least three gods from areas to the east were introduced into Anlo during the mid- to late eighteenth century, when the Anlo were most interested in improving the success of their military efforts. One of these gods was Da. Acquired from Ouidah by Togbui Honi (a prominent Anlo elder and slave trader) because he believed this deity had given his previously barren wife children, Da quickly became known in Anlo not only for its curative powers but also for its ability to protect its worshippers in war.[24] In the nineteenth century, those who led Anlo to war between 1833 and 1869 consulted Afa/Da regularly before going into battle.[25]

Another deity, Togbui Nyigbla, was also acquired from the middle Slave Coast during the mid-eighteenth century. Introduced by Tsiame clan member Aduadui,[26] Nyigbla proved so popular that in 1769 the Anlo elevated it to the status of war god for the entire Anlo polity and its priest, who by this time had shifted his clan affiliation to the Dzevi hlo.[27]

A third deity associated with the Ifá divination system, known among the Anlo as Afa, appears to have also entered Anlo during the eighteenth century. Oral traditions about the history of this belief system are more difficult to interpret, however. In his 1911 publication on the Ewe religion, for example, J. Spieth cited oral narratives indicating that there were several forms of Afa in Anlo and that at least one of these had existed in Anlo prior to the others. No other details are offered, however.[28] Traditions collected more recently indicate that the earliest form of Afa in Anlo was known as Dzisafa. De Surgy speculates that this belief system came into Anlo with the Nyigbla religious belief system: Afa is at present closely associated with the worship of Nyigbla in the town of Aflao.[29] De Surgy does not consider the fact that Aflao was not part of Anlo during the eighteenth century, however. Afa in Anlo and Aflao may have had very different histories. This is certainly suggested by oral traditions collected in Anloga, the traditional political and religious capital of Anlo. These traditions, dated with the assistance of European documentary sources, indicate that Afa came to Anlo in the mid-eighteenth century through the efforts of an Anlo military leader named Anyramakpa:

> Dzisafa was the first [Afa] to come to Anlo . . . Afa originated as follows:
> It is said that one Togbui Anyramakpa brought Afa from a certain war.
> During this war, Anyramakpa fought fiercely with an enemy. After killing
> the stubborn man, he found Afa [that is the Afa nuts] around his waist . . .
> [Anyramakpa] believed that the Afa gave him both the physical and
> spiritual power to fight so resolutely. So he brought the Afa home.[30]

Given our current knowledge of Anlo history, it is impossible to verify this association between Anyramakpa and the origins of Afa in Anlo, but it is significant that the person who is said to have brought a practitioner of Afa to Anloga after associating this belief system with enhanced fighting capacities gained his military reputation in the Kovenu war between 1732 and 1736 and the Ge-Anexo war in 1741 or 1750.[31] Both were fought during the period when Anlo was seeking to become much more involved in the production of the fish that was used to purchase slaves from the interior for sale to the Europeans on the coast.[32] Equally important is the fact that the reputed father of Afa in Anlo was different from the founder of the Nyigbla religious order in Anlo. This suggests that while Afa and Nyigbla were introduced into Anlo during the same period and became popular for the same reason, the origins of Afa and Nyigbla worship in Anlo are separate. Only after Nyigbla became the national war god of the Anlo in 1769 did they incorporate Afa divination (along with a significant number of other religious systems within their religious practices).[33] Thus, in 1792, when the Anlo leadership consulted their religious leaders to determine whether a military confrontation with their neighbours in Keta would be successful, it is likely this consultation involved the war god Nyigbla, as indicated elsewhere. But it is also likely that Afa was consulted as well.[34]

While Anlo interest in Yoruba religious practices had its origins in the eighteenth century, this interest did not end there. Between the early and mid-nineteenth century, Anlo continued to engage in war to produce slaves for the slave trade. This military activity, in turn, encouraged the Anlo to seek spiritual support to ensure success. Thus, when one Anlo elder discussed this period of Anlo history in 1911, he emphasized that 'We had no money then . . . we [were] fond of war. Kill some and catch some and sell and chop and marry their women'.[35] Between 1831 and 1833, the Anlo accepted an invitation from Akwamu to attack Peki. They did so, in part, to obtain prisoners-of-war who could then be sold to the Brazilians and Cubans who operated on the Anlo coast as the principal buyers of slaves for the Americas. They played the same mercenary role in the 1860 and 1865–6 Agoe wars, when the shipment of slaves across the Atlantic from the Slave Coast was just coming to an end. That this interest in the production of potential slaves (for export up to the late 1860s and for domestic use after this time) supported continued Anlo interest in Yoruba religious practices is most evident in the career of Axolu I, military commander of the Anlo army between the 1840s and the 1870s. When leading the Anlo army to war at Agoe and Agotime, Axolu is said to have used Yoruba priests (associated with unknown deities) to bolster the military efforts and the morale of his troops.[36]

Exactly where the Anlo acquired their knowledge of Yoruba religious practices and beliefs during the eighteenth and nineteenth centuries is unclear, but the most likely explanation indicates that acquisition was indirect. Traditions concerning Anyramakpa's association with Afa indicate that the priest he brought to Anlo came from the town of 'Glefe' (Glehue, modern-day Ouidah[37]) in Dahomey. The priests that accompanied the mid-nineteenth-century Anlo military campaigns in Agoe and Agotime were obtained by Axolu, the military commander of the Anlo army, from his ally Kodjo Landzekpo of Anexo. Direct contact with Yoruba-speaking communities and Yoruba priests may have taken place in Atakpame, which Anlo traders may have visited as early as the eighteenth century, when they began to strengthen and expand their trade connections to the communities in the interior. But oral traditions and the history of Anlo interest in religious forms in the east continually point away from Yorubaland and towards local and/or Yoruba practitioners[38] resident in Ouidah and Anexo.

Perhaps more important is the fact that the history of Yoruba religious practices in Anlo – like their history in the Americas – is intimately connected to the Atlantic slave trade.[39] Prior to 1730, immigrants from the Ga/Adangbe areas to the west and the interests of the Akan of Akwamu and Kwawu dominated Anlo's economic (and sometimes political) relations with others in the region. The Ga/Adangbe dominated the east–west trade by land or inland canoe and trade on the ocean in aggrey beads and cloth. The Akwamu and Kwawu controlled the flow of slaves from the interior to the major ports of Ouidah and Accra. Lack of access to capital, the relative absence of European traders on their own coast, and the inability of the Anlo to resist effectively the political and economic dominance of their western neighbours meant that the Anlo had limited relations with polities to the east. During this period, the language of the Ga and Adangbe came to be spoken so commonly in Keta that Europeans believed this was the principal language of the area. After 1702, Akan as a language and a culture also came to occupy a position of social prestige. Freeing themselves from this situation after 1750, the Anlo embarked on a series of ambitious military campaigns to obtain slaves from the interior for sale to the Europeans (and later the Brazilians and Cubans), who had begun after the early eighteenth century to spend much more time on the Anlo coast purchasing slaves. To support their military activities, the Anlo actively sought out and acquired those belief systems that could facilitate their economic and political interests. It was in this context that the Anlo acquired the Yoruba divination system called, in Anlo, Afa.

This history does more than illuminate a previously obscure connection between the Anlo and the Yoruba, however. It also challenges prevalent notions about the character of life on the Slave Coast. While the inland lagoon system linked the coastal communities between the Volta and Lagos in a way that could have facilitated the easy flow of language and culture within this region, such interaction did not always take place. Moreover, it is clear that Yoruba did not serve as a lingua franca in the seventeenth century among the coastal Ewe, as Thornton has concluded, and hence the use of the Yoruba language cannot be used as an indicator of cultural homogeneity. Yet the lack of direct communication and linguistic unity does not mean that the coastal Ewe never shared anything with the Yoruba. Clearly, the Anlo adopted Yoruba Ifá divination, but they did so, not in the seventeenth century, but during the early to mid-eighteenth century through their association with Ouidah, after they had already begun to incorporate Akan and Ga/Adangbe elements into their culture. The Anlo and Ewe may have existed at the margins of the Akan and Yoruba cultural zones during the era of the Atlantic slave trade, but the boundaries of cultural zones, far from static, were subject to the shifting power within the region. Thus, when examining the history of African, and in this case Yoruba, cultural practices in the Americas, one must consider the historical context in which specific cultures spread within Africa even before people, associated with these cultures, reached the 'New World'. Those enslaved Africans who introduced and/or sustained particular cultural practices in the Americas included those who grew up in those cultures as well as those who were introduced to them later in life. To acknowledge the historical validity of cultural zones, it is necessary for scholars to understand these zones as constantly shifting and changing under the influence of the political and economic forces that shaped both the cultural history of West Africa and the history of African cultural practices in the Americas.

Notes

1 Melville J. Herskovits, *The Myth of the Negro Past* (Boston, 1941), p. 295.
2 Sidney W. Mintz and Richard Price, *The Birth of African-American Culture: An Anthropological Perspective* (1976; Boston, 1992), p. 5.
3 Peter Wood and Gwendolyn Hall have proven in their studies that it is possible to establish specific connections between communities in the United States (e.g. the

coasts of South Carolina and Louisiana) and communities in Africa because they obtained slaves from very specific locations. See Gwendolyn Hall, *Africans in Colonial Louisiana: The Development of Afro-Creole Culture in the Eighteenth Century* (Baton Rouge, LA, 1992), and Peter Wood, *Black Majority: Negroes in Colonial South Carolina from 1670 through the Stono Rebellion* (New York, 1974).

4 John K. Thornton, *Africa and Africans in the Making of the Atlantic World, 1400–1680* (New York, 1992), pp. 186, 188.

5 *Ibid.*, p. 190.

6 Robin Law, 'Trade and Politics behind the Slave Coast: The Lagoon Traffic and the Rise of Lagos, 1500–1800', *Journal of African History* 24 (1983), p. 321. See also Robin Law, *The Slave Coast of West Africa, 1550–1750* (Oxford, 1991), p. 21, and Sharon E. Nicholson, 'Climatic Variations in the Sahel and other African Regions during the Past Five Centuries', *Journal of Arid Environments* 1 (1978), p. 6.

7 Thornton, *Africa and Africans*, p. 190; Law, *Slave Coast*, p. 24.

8 Law, *Slave Coast*, pp. 23–4.

9 See Ray A. Kea, 'Akwamu-Anlo Relations, c. 1750–1813', *Transactions of the Historical Society of Ghana* 10 (1969), pp. 35, 43, 58; Robin Law, *The Oyo Empire, c. 1600–1836* (Oxford, 1977), pp. 169–71; John Igé and Olabiyi Yai, 'The Yoruba-Speaking People of Dahomey and Togo', *Yoruba: Journal of the Yoruba Studies Association of Nigeria* 1, no. 1 (1973), pp. 1–29; G. C. A. Oldendorp, *History of the Mission of the Evangelical Brethren on the Caribbean Islands of St. Thomas, St. Croix and St. John*, ed. Johann Jakob Bossard, trans and eds Arnold R. Highfield and Vladimir Barac (Ann Arbor, MI, 1987), p. 165.

10 Robin Law, 'Between the Sea and the Lagoons: The Interaction of Maritime and Inland Navigation on the Pre-Colonial Slave Coast', *Cahiers d'études africaines*, 29 (1989), p. 232.

11 *Ibid.*, pp. 231–2.

12 William Bosman, *A New and Accurate Description of the Coast of Guinea* (London, 1967; originally published in English in 1705), p. 331.

13 Jean Barbot, *A Description of the Coast of North and South Guinea* (London, 1732), p. 321. For the 1688 version of this account, see P. E. H. Hair, Adam Jones and Robin Law (eds), *Barbot on Guinea: The Writings of Jean Barbot on West Africa, 1678–1712* (London, 1992), 2:619.

14 Law, *Slave Coast*, pp. 226, 243.

15 Albert Van Dantzig, *The Dutch and the Guinea Coast, 1674–1742* (Accra, 1978), pp. 199–200.

16 Barbot, *Description*, p. 321. Fante trade connections and the limitations on Anlo involvement with the east–west and north–south trade are also discussed in Sandra E. Greene, 'The Anlo-Ewe: Their Economy, Society, and External Relations in the Eighteenth Century' (PhD thesis, Northwestern University, 1981), pp. 116–17, and Greene, 'Social Change in Eighteenth-Century Anlo: The Role of Technology, Markets and Military Conflict', *Africa* 58, no. 1 (1988), pp. 73–5.

17 For further discussion, see Greene, 'Social Change'.

18 For a more detailed discussion of these cultural influences, see Sandra E. Greene, *Gender, Ethnicity, and Social Change on the Upper Slave Coast: A History of the Anlo-Ewe* (London and Portsmouth, NH, 1996), pp. 41–2, 124–5, and Greene, 'Anlo-Ewe', pp. 110–13; Daniel Avorgbedor, personal communication, 4 November 1991.

19 For a more detailed discussion of the defeat of Akwamu, see Ivor Wilks, 'Akwamu, 1650–1750: A Study of the Rise and Fall of a West African Empire' (MA diss., University of Wales, 1958), chap. 3; Ray A. Kea, 'Trade, State Formation, and Warfare on the Gold Coast, 1600–1826' (PhD thesis, University of London, 1974), pp. 163,

167, 212. On the subsequent expansionary campaigns launched by the Anlo, see Greene, 'Anlo-Ewe', pp. 97–100.

20 Van Dantzig, *The Dutch and the Guinea Coast, 1674–1742*, Document No. 390–4: NBKG 190, June/September 1737, WIC III, 2 October 1737, 14 April 1737, 4 December 1737, NBKG 8, 19 December 1737, pp. 322–3, 326–32; Furley Collection, 9 July 1731, 17 July 1737, 28 July 1737, 1 August 1737, 5 August 1737 and 25 September 1737. See also Law, *Slave Coast*, pp. 316–17; C. Hornberger, 'Etwas aus der Geschichter der Anloer', *Quartal-Blatt der Norddeutschen Missionsgesellschaft* 82 (1877), pp. 453–4.

21 Carl Spiess, 'Könige der Anloer', in *Weltgeschichte 3: Westasien und Afrika*, ed. H. J. Helmot (Leipzig and Vienna, 1901), p. 574; R. S. Rattray, 'History of the Ewe People', *Études Togolaises* 11, no. 1 (1967), p. 93; Greene, Fieldnote 30: Interview with T. S. A. Togobo, 26 September 1978, Anloga, and Fieldnote 42: Interview with Boko Seke Axovi, 1 November 1978, Anloga.

22 Vestindisk-guineiske Kompagnie (VgK) 883: 13 August 1744, L. F. Roemer, Quita; VgK 887: 21 August 1744, L. F. Roemer, Quita.

23 See Greene, 'Anlo-Ewe', chap. 4, for a complete discussion of Anlo–Anexo relations.

24 The shrine for Nyigbla in Be (Togo) is called *Dangbe vio*, as is Dangbe's sanctuary in Ouidah. Albert de Surgy, *La géomancie et le culte d'Afa chez les Evhe du littoral* (Paris, 1981), p. 21.

25 Some of these military leaders included Gbodzo of Woe, Tamakloe of Whuti, and Tengey and Attipoe of Anyako. Greene, Fieldnote 100: Interview with Ahiaba Bonvedi, 6 April 1988, Anyako; Greene, Fieldnote 72: Interview with Christian Nani Tamaklo, 13 January 1988, Keta; Greene, Fieldnote 101: Interview with Midawo Alowu Attitpoe, 6 April 1988, Anyako; Greene, Fieldnote 24: Interview with Boko Seke Axovi, 5 September 1978, Anloga; and Greene, Fieldnote 76: Interview with Togbui Anthonio Gbodzo II and his councillors, 20 January 1988, Woe. For additional information on Togbui Honi, see Dzigbodi Kodzo Fiawoo, 'The Influence of Contemporary Social Changes on the Magico-Religious Concepts and Organization of the Southern Ewe-Speaking Peoples of Ghana' (PhD thesis, Edinburgh University, 1959), p. 68, and Richard Tetteh Togby, 'The Origin and Organization of the Yewe Cult' (BA essay, Department for the Study of Religions, University of Ghana, 1977), pp. ii–iii. For additional information on Da and Dangbe worship in Dahomey and Ouidah, respectively, see Melville J. Herskovits, *Dahomey: An Ancient West African Kingdom* (Evanston, IL, 1967), 2:248, and Law, *Slave Coast*, pp. 109–10, 332–3.

26 See Greene, Fieldnote 53: Interview with Togbui Alex Afatsao Awadzi, 16 December 1987, Anloga, for a discussion of how the Nyigbla god came to be adopted by the Dzevi clan rather than the Tsiame clan.

27 For additional information on the history of Nyigbla, see Greene, *Gender, Ethnicity and Social Change*, pp. 55–9, 81–93, 112–13.

28 J. Spieth, *Die Religion der Eweer in Sud Togo* (Leipzig, 1911), p. 189.

29 De Surgy, *Géomancie*, pp. 26–9.

30 Greene, Fieldnote 112: Interview with Toboko Daniel Kwasi Afedo, Anloga, c. March 1988.

31 Anlo Traditional Council Questionnaire on Nomination, Election, Installation and Outdooring of Chiefs: Anyramakpa 3, 19 May 1949, Anlo Traditional Council, Volta Region, Ghana; E. K. Aduamah, *Ewe Traditions* 3 (n.d.), no. 13 (Institute of African Studies, University of Ghana, Legon).

32 Europeans had begun to frequent Anlo during this period because of disruptions in the trade to the east and west. For additional information on fluctuation in trade relations between the Anlo area and Europeans, see Greene, 'Social Change', pp. 75–6.

33 See Greene, *Gender, Ethnicity and Social Change*, pp. 86–90, for a discussion of how the Nyigbla priest reordered the religious life of the Anlo.

34 *Ibid.*, pp. 85–6. For information on Sakpata (Sokponno), yet another deity acquired directly or indirectly from the Yoruba, see A. B. Ellis, *The Yoruba-Speaking Peoples of the Slave Coast of West Africa* (1894; New York, 1970), pp. 73–4; Anthony Buckley, *Yoruba Medicine* (Oxford, 1985), pp. 98–102; and Greene, Fieldnote 203: Interview with Aklorbortu Efia and Zanviedor Kwawukume, 16 May 1996, Anloga.

35 Ghana National Archives, ADM 11/1661: Notes of Evidence – Commission of Inquiry, 1912, Awuna, Addah and Akwamu, by Francis Crowther (National Archives of Ghana, Accra), p. 35.

36 Anlo State Council Minute Book, 9 January 1935: 'Chiefs Kata, Adaku, Avege and Agblevo per Samuel Nutsuga for themselves and on behalf the Tsiame Tribe of Anloga, Atokor, Atsiavie and others vs. Chiefs Zewu, Agbozo, Anakoo Attipoe and Zioklui, Davordji Banini and others for themselves and on behalf of Agave Tribe of Anloga, Djelukopwe, Anyako, et cetera', pp. 391–2; Kue Agbota Gaba, 'The History of Anecho, Ancient and Modern' (unpublished manuscript, Balme Library, University of Ghana, Legon, c. 1942), chap. 18. For a discussion of Axolu's career, see L. P. Tosu, 'A Short Account of the Awada-da Stool of Anlo' (unpublished manuscript, Anlo Traditional Council Archives, Anloga, Ghana, n. d.).

37 See Law, *Slave Coast*, pp. 15–16, on the distinction between the port and kingdom of Ouidah.

38 Anlo conceptions of the area east of Cotonou associate it with the land of the dead. The name 'Cotonu' means 'the shore of the dead', that is, the place at which the Anlo dead pay to cross the river to the land of the dead. In nineteenth-century Anlo, the citizens of this polity referred to Yorubaland as Noli, 'ghost', 'the land of the dead'. See Greene, Fieldnote 56: Interview with William Tiodo Anum, 22 December 1987, Anloga; Spieth, *Religion*, p. 189 n. 2. It is possible that Dahomey intentionally encouraged the belief that the area east of Ouidah was the land of the dead to discourage Ewe-speakers from taking their slaves to Lagos instead of selling them at Ouidah. See Law, 'Trade and Politics', pp. 345–7, which discusses Dahomey's attempts to limit the extent to which Lagos successfully competed with Ouidah as the principal port for the export of slaves.

39 This was not true elsewhere on the Slave Coast. According to Law (*Slave Coast*, pp. 106, 333), Afa was present in Allada by the mid-seventeenth century and was adopted as an official religion in Dahomey in order 'to discredit and supersede the indigenous divinatory system which had been employed to forge "alliances . . . against [the king]"'. For a history of Yoruba religious practices, and Yoruba divination in particular, in Cuba, see George Brandon, *Santería from Africa to the New World: The Dead Sell Memories* (Bloomington, IN, 1993).

= 6 =

Texts of Enslavement: Fon and Yoruba Vocabularies from Eighteenth- and Nineteenth-century Brazil

Olabiyi Yai

This paper examines two unjustly neglected documents of the African diaspora that are in languages from the hinterland of the Bight of Benin, the first a Fon (Gbe) vocabulary and sentence book and the second a Yoruba word list. Documents of this kind did not abound in the Americas during the years of the slave trade, so these represent a rare species in the corpus of diaspora literature and therefore deserve special attention. Although they differ in length, both are equally important. They are, in chronological order, *Obra Nova de Lingua Geral de Mina,* by Antonio da Costa Peixoto, published in 1741,[1] and *Vocabulario Nago,* written some time during the first half of the nineteenth century by an unknown author.[2]

Before considering the issues arising from an examination of the two documents, some methodological and epistemological considerations are in order. In the scientific imagination of most scholars engaged in African diaspora studies, vocabularies are not ordinarily associated with the challenge of identifying enslaved Africans. Vocabularies are usually viewed as documents of essentially linguistic interest. Analysts tend to conceive of them as documents reflecting the state of a language in the past, useful for making comparisons in historical linguistic or dialectological studies with the state of the language spoken today by groups that descend or claim to descend from its speakers. Sometimes, particularly when they are extensive or self-contained, or when they are explicitly teleological, they are assessed in pursuit of an analyst's special interests. A catechism, for example, will be read primarily as a religious document, while a conversation manual will receive treatment with a linguistic slant.

Despite the useful information that is derived from specialized study, we need also to reconceptualize vocabularies and similar documents. In my opinion, each of them constitutes an instance of what I would like to call 'dialogic performance in the Atlantic world'. Such texts should be recontextualized, as fully as possible, in their remote as well as immediate ecologies. Viewed from these perspectives, they can then be pressed by various disciplines to speak loudly about their real and complete nature.

Reconceptualizing vocabularies as dialogic performances in the Atlantic world enables us to distinguish two types within the genre, namely those performed on the east bank of the Atlantic and those performed in the New World. Rare exceptions notwithstanding, vocabularies were forced dialogic performances. The European participant, who almost invariably took the initiative in the dialogue, cared little about the interests of the African participant and seldom exposed his real intentions. Yet, the degree, perhaps the nature, of the violence involved in this forced dialogue differed from one shore of the Atlantic to the other. It is easy to imagine that, although the initiative was his, the European traveller in Africa was not, for obvious reasons, always able to choose his informants. For example, he rarely had access to women informants. Conversely, the dynamics of slavery invested the slave owner with virtually absolute power in the Americas. Different ecologies determined different products. More importantly, different ecologies determined different vocabulary production processes. We cannot approach a vocabulary by Bosman or Barbot as we would one by Peixoto or Nina Rodrigues.[3]

Since the two vocabularies under analysis were produced in Brazil, we should investigate the ecology of forced dialogic performance in the conditions existing in Brazil. If the economic and social system of slavery was characterized by violence, the production of a vocabulary was perhaps the locus, in this essentially violent system, where confrontation was 'softest'. It is not far-fetched to surmise that an enslaved African who found herself/himself in the position of a participant in an imposed dialogue saw this as a window of opportunity, an unexpected space of freedom which s/he would naturally seek to widen. As a forced dialogic performance, a vocabulary was almost invariably a *quid pro quo*. The freedom space thus opened was also a negotiation space, though a narrow one, since the African participant did not find herself/himself in the privileged position of a question setter. S/he always responded. But in some cases, s/he could orientate her/his answers in such a fashion as to register her/his voice and traces of issues s/he cherished. As we would put it in Yoruba, '*Oran to ndun babalawo ko dun Ife*' (The agenda of the diviner is at variance with that of the god of divination). It is with these considerations in mind that I examine the two known vocabularies of two important languages of West Africa – Fon and Yoruba – spoken in eighteenth- and nineteenth-century Brazil.

Obra Nova de Lingua Geral de Mina (*New Book of the Common Language of Mina*) languished for two centuries in Portuguese archives in Evora and Lisbon and was rediscovered and published in 1945 by Luis Silveira, with philological commentary by Edmundo Correia Lopes. The manuscript contains a word list and a conversation manual in Fon, with translations into Portuguese. Historical reasons account for the two centuries of total oblivion. Had the area then called Mina (today's Ghana, Togo and Benin) been colonized by the Portuguese, as were, for instance, Guinea-Bissau and Angola, the manuscript might have attracted linguistic interest and might well have become a classic of African historical linguistics like Koelle's *Polyglotta Africana*, which it predates.[4]

The author of the vocabulary was Antonio da Costa Peixoto, who hailed, as he tells us in his preface, from 'entre-Douro-e-Minho' (the country between the Douro and the Minho). From his style in Portuguese, he does not seem to have been a highly educated person, certainly not of the calibre of the missionaries who worked on indigenous languages in Brazil or worked with Pedro Claver and Alonso de Sandoval, author of *De Instauranda Aethiopum Salute,* in Cartagena de Indias in the seventeenth century.[5] One significant feature of Peixoto, for our purpose, is that he seems to have attained a comfortable degree of proficiency in the African target language. He was able, for instance, to formulate his questions in Fon, even though his sentences were sometimes ungrammatical. Thus, in the conversation sections of his manual, we have the recurrence of the Portuguese word '*pregunto*' (I ask), followed by a sentence in Fon. The implication of Peixoto's relative proficiency in the African target language is that he must have studied it, through interaction and familiarization techniques, over many years. Presumably, he asked his questions in Fon because his Fon was better than the Portuguese of his informants. Peixoto wrote what appears as a first, much shorter draft of his œuvre in 1731, with the title *Alguns Aapontamentos da Lingoa Minna com as Palavras correspondentes* (*Some Notes on the Language of Minna with Corresponding Words in Portuguese*). If ten years separate the two manuscripts, we can surmise that he acquired the language over twelve to fifteen years.

But, regardless of the proficiency of the official authors of African vocabularies in the Atlantic world, the fact remains that such works were, by necessity, the result of collaboration between Europeans and Africans, even though the Europeans did not acknowledge the Africans' contribution. We therefore have to determine as accurately as possible the collective identity of the anonymous African authors. The issue here is not to look for individual names to match the European names. Even if that were feasible, the information would still have relevance beyond the perspective of the contemporary informants/co-authors themselves. Rather than attempt to identify the individuals who served as informants, we should try to ascertain the identity of the ethnic groups on behalf of whom the informants/co-authors participated in the forced dialogue, their genders, their importance in the demographics of the colony, and so on.

The very idea of a vocabulary in a language called *lingua geral de Mina* stems from the conviction, based on daily experiential observation, of Peixoto and the Portuguese colonists in Brazil, that Africans communicated among themselves in what we would term today a *lingua franca*. As Edmundo Correia Lopes observed,[6] Peixoto's contemporaries knew perfectly well that it was not the mother tongue of all enslaved Africans who spoke it in the Minas Gerais area in Brazil. What then was this language? Lopes, perhaps influenced by the writings of Westermann available to him, suggested that it was 'Gu or Alada, a dialect of the Ewe language'.[7] But in fact the language of *Obra Nova* is overwhelmingly Fon. To be sure, any lingua franca, particularly in the context of the New World, is likely to have been, to a certain degree, a mixture. As is well known, the Americas provide a fertile linguistic ground for creolization. From the list of words and, even more, from the conversation section of *Obra Nova*, it can be seen that the language is Fon, but with a beginning of creolization by absorption of lexical and grammatical features of other Gbe languages. There are many instances of Alada words and expressions, and a finer analysis will certainly reveal instances of words from other members of the Gbe continuum.

Since Dahomey conquered Alada in 1724, many *Aladagbe*-speaking men and women must have been enslaved and sent to Brazil through the port of Whydah. This explains the occurrence in the manuscript of such unmistakably *Aladagbe* words and expressions as *hehunhe* [éuniɛ̃] (here it is); *jale* [jàlé] (please); *hedem* [édɛ̃] (it is far); *hedomogui* [édɔmɔ̃ji] (s/he said that). Besides, on various occasions, the African informant/co-authors referred to themselves as Guno (Peixoto's spelling for Gunnu, a Gun-speaking person),[8] and to their country as Gutume (his spelling for Guntome, the country of the Gun-speaking people).[9]

Peixoto's last sentence, the only one with a hint of his methodology, is a revelation: '*Em alguns nomes onde ouverem estas letras juntas /ch/ he necess.o [necessario] tomar parecer com algũ [algum] negro, ou negra mina porq.to [porquanto] tem diferente pernuncia*', that is 'In certain nouns where these letters /ch/ are found, I had to ask the opinion of a Mina man or woman because each has a different pronunciation'. If Peixoto's untrained Portuguese ears could detect differences in the pronunciation of the 'Mina' *lingua franca*, we are comforted in our assumption of a Gbe creolization process at work, with Fongbe as the main dialect. In this sentence, we also have, for the first time, the candid admission that women were involved in the process.

Besides this perfunctory recognition of women's participation in the forced dialogue, there are other indications here and there in the vocabulary of contributions by women. In what looks like a *malentendu bien entendu*, Peixoto apparently asked his informant to translate the following sentence: 'I am going to visit/see my wife or concubine' (*Vou ver a minha mulher ou amiga*). The informant, no doubt a woman, translated his sentence as 'I am going to visit my husband' (*Mahipomasuhe*). Various entries in the vocabulary refer to market or street activities. Almost two pages of entries beginning with the phrase *Mahisa* (I am selling/I go to sell) are followed by such items as beans, bread, okra, etc. Given that this activity was almost exclusively the preserve of women, one can hypothesize that women co-authored this section with Peixoto.

The vocabulary also mentions another African ethnic group, the Angolans (Aglono in Peixoto's transcription of the Fon rendition of the ethnonym). We can infer that the 'Mina', i.e. people of southern Benin and Togo, and Africans from the Kongo kingdom and vicinity, constituted the majority of enslaved Africans in eighteenth-century Minas Gerais. But how important was the African population *vis-à-vis* the European? Peixoto's vocabulary and conversation manual reveal what we would today call 'functional literacy'. But, unlike today's primers in Africa, his manual was not directed to enslaved Africans. Slavocratic Brazil obviously did not intend to conduct a literacy programme among enslaved Africans. Peixoto's targeted audience was explicitly the slave owners, actual and potential. In his prologue to the reader, he says, '*se todos os senhores de escravos, e hinda os que hinda os nao tem, souvecem esta lingoage nao sucedariao tantos insultos, ruhinas, estragos, roubos, mortes e finalmente cazos atrozes, como mutos mizeraveis tem experementado'*, i.e. 'If all slave owners and also those who are yet to own them had known this language, many of them would not have suffered so many cases of insult, devastation, loss, theft, death and, finally, atrocities as many unfortunates have'.[10] From this statement and from many others in the same vein in the dialogue section of the manuscript, Peixoto appears to be reflecting the general anxiety of the white population. Enslaved Africans outnumbered their masters in such proportions as to constitute a constant threat, a *péril noir* (black peril). While the interests of European travellers in African languages were obviously motivated in Africa by commercial and, later, missionary objectives, learning a slave language was meaningless in the Americas except for espionage and as a preventive strategy.

The master–slave relationship was characterized by suspicion and frequent acts of violence including assassination, poisoning and marronage. The following examples from the vocabulary provide graphic indications of the situation:

hihabouthome manhoha = the country of the white man is infernal (p. 32)
maguhi hi habouno = let us kill this white man (p. 34)
mabata nim = let me break his head (p. 34)
inhono hutu naguhi = I will kill him because of a woman (p. 35)
jale jale mamagume ha = please, please, don't kill me (p. 35)[11]

Here, it appears, Peixoto reports actual cases and imagines situations in which a white man who was proficient in the African language could plead for his head.

The vocabulary in the section dealing with religion and the African community's *Weltanschauung* in general also records the early presence of *vodun* in the Americas. As early as 1658, in the *Doctrina Christiana* in the Alada language, the concept of God was rendered as *vodun*.[12] In the *Obra Nova*, *vodun* is given a similar meaning:

Avoduno = reverend father (literally, *vodun* man)
Avoduchuhe = church (literally, house of *vodun*)
Avodumge = rosary (literally, *vodun* necklace)
Avodumzambe = Sunday (literally, *vodun*'s day)
Mahipomvodum = I am going to church (literally, I am going to see *vodun*)

These Africans, however, distinguished between their deities and those of their masters. Thus, Jesus Christ is translated as *hihavouvodum* (literally, white man's *vodun*). This is an interesting departure from the *Doctrina Christiana* (1658), where Jesus was rendered as Lisa, a local deity.

A few new concepts also emerged, as a consequence of the forced contact between the two cultures and worldviews. Examples include:

'hell', translated as *zoume* = in the fire
'baptism', rendered as *duge* = to eat salt
'marriage' (Christian), translated as *gulialo* = to take the hand
'surgeon', translated as *boko* = diviner
'the Devil', rendered as *Leba* = Legba, a deity of the Fon/Yoruba pantheon

The intellectual identity of the African participants in the construction of these texts becomes clearer through a comparison of the translation ecologies and strategies that underpin the *Doctrina Christiana* (1658) and the *Obra Nova* (1741) with respect to the Christian concepts of Jesus and the Devil. In 1658, Jesus was translated as Lisa because the Africans from the Bight of Benin were still unfamiliar with Christian concepts, although a handful of African notables were being sent to Spain to serve as informants/co-translators with the Capuchins by 1658. In 1741, many enslaved Africans in Brazil were involved in Christian practices, and they definitely had sufficient knowledge and understanding of Christianity to avoid gross mistranslation of the name of such a central concept/figure as Jesus Christ. In other words, they knew that if Jesus was a *vodun*, he was a *vodun* with a qualification, hence *hihavou vodum*, i.e. white man's *vodun*, quite different from an African *vodun*. The concept of Jesus fitted into preconceived notions of the *vodun*. By contrast, the concept of Satan as an agent of absolute evil was not only strange but indeed was incompatible with the African worldview, and hence does not seem to have been fully grasped in 1741. Peixoto's informants translated Satan as Leba (Legba in Fon), basing their translation on the 'trickster attribute' common to Satan and Legba, on which Peixoto must have insisted, as did other Christian missionaries before and after him. In both Brazil and Cuba, Leba was often identified with various Catholic saints and not with Satan. This early syncretism did not prevail once the enslaved population had a better understanding of the Christian doctrine and the Judaeo-Christian worldview in general.

Although there is an extensive literature on the phenomenon of syncretism in African religions in the New World, it is essential, in my view, to reconstruct these intellectual *démarches* painstakingly. Syncretisms emerge at interfaces, and they are the creation of potentially identifiable agents as translators. Candomblè, Santería and Haitian *vodun*, as syncretic religions, could not have come into being without African translators and cultural interpreters, and they were certainly not the products of Christian European theologians. Africans in the Americas are rarely recognized as astute translators. This trend must be reversed through a systematic investigation of their translation strategies and achievements, especially if by 'identifying Africans', we mean recognizing their deeds.

The second document examined in this paper is *Vocabulario Nago*. Its author is unknown. This document was brought to the attention of the scholarly world at the first Congress of Afro-Brazilian studies in 1934 by Rodolfo Garcia with a perfunctory (half-page) introduction. To my knowledge, no scholar in Afro-Brazilian studies has examined it ever since. Garcia was 'unable to verify who he [the author] was', although he must have been 'an intelligent and learned individual', a citizen of Pernambuco who lived in the first half of the nineteenth century.[13] Was this anonymous European author a Brazilian abolitionist? Was his motivation the Christianization of enslaved Africans? Was he an inquisitive intellectual, simply interested in an African language for its own sake? Had he had time to publish his manuscript, he might have claimed any of these personae.

In contrast to Peixoto's work, *Vocabulario Nago* is a word list with entries arranged in alphabetical order from A to V, which suggests that its author consulted a Portuguese dictionary. The few 'grammatical observations' suggest that the author was familiar with the grammatical terminology of his time. However, here, as in the case of Peixoto's vocabulary, we are in the presence of a dialogic performance.

Although Garcia uses the masculine pronoun consistently in describing the manuscript, which suggests that he took it for granted that the author of *Vocabulario Nago* was a man, an analysis of certain features in the corpus of the manuscript leads to the hypothesis that the author was a woman. For example, contrary to standard lexicographic practice, in which the masculine form is assumed to be the base form (surely an unexamined male chauvinistic assumption), the unidentified author almost invariably used the feminine form of nouns as the base form and the masculine form as a derivative. For example:

dona, dono = queen, king
escrava, escravo = female slave, male slave
filha, filho = daughter, son
menina, menino = girl, boy

Sometimes, only the feminine form appears, as in:

amiga = girlfriend
esposa = spouse

These frequent 'lapses' are too consistent to be insignificant, especially given the notoriously patriarchal context of colonial Brazil. Although conjecture, it is even possible that the reason the manuscript was never published was precisely because its author was a woman, with the implication that her informants/co-authors would have been predominantly women too. Yoruba women in nineteenth-century Brazil were reputed for being 'good' domestic slaves and 'excellent' *negras de ganho*, increasing the likelihood that innumerable women served as linguists. Men, after all, were needed in the sugar fields.

The language in *Vocabulario Nago* helps to establish the identity of its authors. Short though it is, the vocabulary represents various Yoruba dialects. Since it is unlikely that one Yoruba informant was fluent in so many dialects, the source of information must have been from several individuals. The reasons for dialect shift from one word to another cannot easily be accounted for in any other way. The entries for 'animal' (animal) and 'flesh' (carne), rendered in Yoruba by the same word, are transcribed in Portuguese as *ero* and *eran* respectively. The contrast between the half-open nasal vowel [on] and open nasal vowel [an] here suggests that two informants, speaking, say, a central Yoruba dialect (Oyo) and a southern Yoruba dialect, were the sources of the two words. So far, the following Yoruba dialects or dialect clusters have been identified:

1. Ekiti/Ijesa, including the following examples:
   ule = house
   ulu = town, country
   una = fire
   ucu = belly
   eure = goat

2. Oyo, including the following examples:
   echo = fruit
   sure = to run
   eran = flesh

3. Egba/Ijebu, including the following examples:
   fu = give
   ero = animal
   monobere = I have a wife
   anon = yesterday

4. Ketu/Anago, including the following examples:
   amon = milk
   cossum = it is ugly
   sinca = gold

The last example is a loanword from Twi and is found only in the westernmost dialects of Yoruba, where there was some influence from the adjacent Akan states, especially Asante, from whom some cultural features have been borrowed.

Hence, this vocabulary incorporates several dialects and therefore is pan-Yoruba. Moreover, Yoruba co-authors/informants from Ijesha/Ekiti were probably in the majority, judging from the number of entries in these dialect clusters. Unfortunately, the conversation aspect of this vocabulary is not sufficient, comprising only seven short sentences, to warrant any meaningful assessment of the degree of standardization reached by Brazilian Yoruba (Nago) in the first half of the nineteenth century. What we can safely hypothesize is that, here too, a Yoruba *lingua geral* or *lingua franca* existed and that the process of standardization involving the various dialects of Yorubaland was at work. The vocabulary makes little incursion into the Yoruba worldview or the interface with Christianity. It contains only two entries that can be characterized as belonging to the Christian vocabulary, and both belong to the Islamic semantic field as well and could have been given Yoruba equivalents by a Yoruba Muslim ('angel' is translated as *omode orun* [a child in heaven], although a loanword from Arabic, *maleka*, existed in Yoruba); 'the one God, king of Heaven' is translated as *oba-ol-orun* (king/owner of the heaven).

Despite the paucity of examples, it can be suggested that Euro-Brazilian masters were intent on converting their Yoruba slaves by emphasizing what in their eyes were the distinctive features of Christianity which were lacking in Yoruba 'paganism'. First, there was recognition of only one God as opposed to many 'idols', and second there was the contrast between a heaven and the hell which was the inevitable retribution for African pagans.

The choice of Yoruba as the common language among Africans in Pernambuco reflected the demography of the slave population. Warfare in Yorubaland and repeated razzias by Dahomey into Anago and other Yoruba kingdoms accounted for the large number of Yoruba in Pernambuco at the end of the eighteenth century and the beginning of the nineteenth. Slave owners were probably interested in Yoruba as a language for this reason and also because of the frequent slave revolts in Bahia[14] that were blamed on the notoriously dangerous Nago as a pre-emptive strategy. Although a century separates the two vocabularies, it would thus appear that, by and large, the same motivations of controlling the slave population inspired the Euro-Brazilians who compiled them.

Notes

1 Antonio da Costa Peixoto (ed.), *Obra Nova de Lingua Geral de Mina* [1741] (Manuscrito da Biblioteca Publica de Evora e da Biblioteca Nacional de Lisboa, Publicado e apresentado por Luis Silveira e acompanhado de comentario filologico de Edmundo Correia Lopes, Lisbon, 1945).

2 Rodolfo Garcia, 'Vocabulario Nago', in *Estudos Brasileiros* [1935] (Trabalhos apresentados ao 1o Congresso Afro-Brasileiro reunido em Recife em 1934, Apresentação de Jose Antonio Gonsalves de Mello (Recife, 1988), pp. 21–7.

3 Jean Barbot, *A Description of the Coast of North and South Guinea* (London, 1732); William Bosman, *A New and Accurate Description of the Coast of Guinea* (1705; London, 1967); Raymundo Nina Rodrigues, *Os Africanos no Brasil* (São Paulo, 1932).

4 Sigismund W. Koelle, *Polyglotta Africana* (1854; Graz, Austria, 1963).

5 Alonso de Sandoval, *De Instauranda Aethiopum Salute: El mundo de la esclavitud negra en América* (Madrid, 1647; Bogotá, 1956).

6 Edmundo Correia Lopes, 'Os trabalhos de Costa Peixoto e a Lingua Evoe no Brasil', in Peixoto (ed.), *Obra Nova de Lingua Geral de Mina*, p. 46.

7 Lopes, 'Linqua Evoe no Brasil', p. 45.

8 *Obra Nova*, p. 20.

9 *Ibid.*, p. 29.

10 *Ibid.*, p. 15.

11 Peixoto, *Obra Nova*, pp. 32, 34–5.

12 See Henri Labouret and Paul Rivet, *Le Royaume d'Arda et son evangelisation au XVIIe siècle* (Paris, 1929) and Olabiyi Babalola Yai, 'From Vodun to Mawu: Monotheism and History in the Fon Cultural Area', in Jean-Pierre Chretien *et al.* (eds), *L'Invention religieuse en Afrique: Histoire et religion en Afrique noire* (Paris, 1993).

13 Garcia, 'Vocabulario Nago', p. 21.

14 João José Reis, *Slave Rebellion in Brazil: The Muslim Uprising of 1835 in Bahia* (1986; Baltimore, MD, 1993).

= 7 =

Ethnic and Religious Plurality among Yoruba Immigrants in Trinidad in the Nineteenth Century

Maureen Warner-Lewis

Gaps and inconsistencies are not unusual in the genealogical information gleaned from second- and third-generation African descendants in Trinidad; they have not only lost contact with their homeland but also fluency in their ancestral tongue has significantly declined. None the less, in the case of the descendants of Yoruba settlers who arrived in Trinidad during the nineteenth century, their residual language texts in the form of songs, phrases and vocabulary, and their remembered traditions of ethnic and settlement origins enable a reconstruction of the processes of historical change and the political milieux that produced the Yoruba exodus.

The first Yoruba-speakers to arrive in Trinidad appear to have come as slaves before British abolition of the trans-Atlantic slave trade in 1808, but Yoruba immigration was heavily concentrated in the period after the 1838 British abolition of slavery itself. Many in this latter category had been released in Sierra Leone and at Caribbean ports, having been freed from captured slave ships. Some of these were settled in villages in Freetown, Sierra Leone, and on the outskirts, while others were hired almost immediately as labourers and re-shipped to the West Indies under indentureship arrangements which lasted for varying periods, between three and seven years. Yet others were recruited into the British-led West India regiments to prosecute colonial battles in Africa itself as well as in the Caribbean.[1] Thus while most Yoruba came to Trinidad as free immigrants, their migration still took place within the period of trans-Atlantic slavery and under conditions that might well replicate some of the conditions of slavery.[2]

An examination of family traditions, surviving songs and religious practices demonstrates that some of the Trinidad Yoruba migrants had complex cultural and ethnic backgrounds which reflected ongoing processes of change within Africa itself, as well as the further accommodations and renegotiations of self-identity precipitated by relocations in foreign sites within Africa, even further migration across the Atlantic, and inter-island resettlements in the Caribbean.

Yoruba identification in Trinidad reflects the complexities of at least three periods of Oyo imperial rule. The town of Oyo, also called Oyo-Ile (Oyole) and Katunga, was the political centre of the Oyo state in the savanna hinterland of the Bight of Benin. In the first period, beginning in the late seventeenth century, Oyo began to exploit economically the Atlantic slave market. Its victims included not only adjacent non-Yoruba-speaking peoples such as the Nupe, Borgu and Hausa, but also Yoruba sub-groups such as the Yagba, Ekiti and Akoko. Such slaves were exiled through ports on the Bight of Benin to the south of Oyo, particularly Ouidah, and later through Porto Novo and other ports.[3] The second period began in the closing decade of the eighteenth century, after the death of Alafin Abiodun, when opposition to central authority threatened to undermine Oyo's imperial rule. By the early nineteenth century, the head of the Oyo military, Afonja, had established a powerful militarized base at Ilorin, which seems to have been accompanied by unrest among other chiefs in outlying provinces and a breakdown in law and order, with accompanying population shifts within the northern belt of the state. Afonja's base came under the influence of a Muslim faction, primarily because Muslim slaves from further north had been incorporated into the army.[4] This Muslim influence culminated in a military uprising in 1817 and further unrest in the 1820s, as the Muslim faction became allied with the *jihad* of the Sokoto caliphate, further inland. The spread of the Muslim uprising and the collapse of the Oyo state marked the third phase of Oyo's involvement in the slave trade. An already destabilized Oyo collapsed in the early 1830s, sending a flood of refugees into the forested southern Yoruba regions to escape the new and militaristic dispensations, and in their wake, the displaced groups left further unrest and destruction. The spread of Yoruba-speaking peoples in connection with their trading activities also complicated the linguistic and cultural background of

FIGURE 7.1   Lucy Charles. *Source: Photo by the author.*

the peoples who physically experienced Middle Passage dispersal. As S. A. Akintoye observes,

> Probably more than ever before, the nineteenth century witnessed a great deal of mixing of Yoruba peoples. Fragments of the various Yoruba subgroups were thrown all over the Yoruba homeland, most getting absorbed into their new homes.[5]

The effects of this unsettled situation are evident in various accounts and songs.[6]

Various Trinidad accounts, autobiographical in form, describe the ways in which the Yoruba homeland was recalled and interpreted from across the seas. The accounts are based on family memories, as recorded in Trinidad in the late twentieth century.

Lucy Charles, née Greenidge, learned her family history from her paternal grandfather, Farode, who belonged to one of the royal families of Oyo, either perhaps to one of the noble families from whom kings were elected in rotation, or one of the families who negotiated the election of Oyo's kings. Lucy and her drum group recorded the connection with Oyo through praise of a loyal vassal, the king of Ikoyi:

> *Subjects of the King of Ikoyi!*
> *This song identifies the origins of a people*
> *Subjects of the Archer!*
> *We women are hailing you with the greeting*
> *'Yoruba nation'.*[7]

Farode's Oyo connection was also signalled by Lucy's indication that certain Yoruba words she herself normally pronounced with a *sh* sound, like 'Shango', were properly said with an *s* instead. This confirmed her ancestor's Oyo dialect affiliation. In addition, Farode had taught Lucy a lengthy praise song to Oya, Shango's most faithful wife, a chant which is singular in my collection.[8] Certain deities she saluted were particularly revered by the Oyo, such as Oranyan – son of Oduduwa, founder of the Yoruba and reputedly Shango's father, Banyanni – Shango's senior sister, and Aganju – Shango's successor, but also Shango's emblematic knife. Her own family's dedication to the god Ifa formed part of a chant 'to Creation', as she classified it. But the fact that Lucy did not practise Ifa divination or know its verses or *odu* suggests either that Farode (who arrived in Trinidad in his late teens) had left Oyo before he himself could master the complex system, or that that segment of Yoruba religious ritual, traditionally controlled by males, was sequestered from Lucy, a female. The chant specifies Ejigbo as the creation site of the Yoruba people, a town sacred to Obatala who was sent by Olodumare, the Supreme Deity, to establish the earthly sphere, so that Ejigbo is cited as one of the most ancient towns in Yoruba sacred literature. The song begins with the assertion:

Aféfé rúrú lórèrè	God Almighty in the distant heavens
Ọ́ kan dudu lÉjìgbò	Established himself in majesty at Ejigbo
Ilé Ifa mo ti wá	My lineage belongs to the house of Ifa
Èjìgbò rere ará ti bọ̀	My family comes from sacred Ejigbo[9]

As a result of a palace coup or some civil disorder, Farode's family had to leave Oyo. They may have sojourned in Owu to the south, as Farode identified a war begun between two women traders at an Owu market as responsible for his own enslavement. This seemingly private dispute in fact

FIGURE 7.2   Alphonsine Williams. *Source: Photo by the author.*

brought to a head power conflicts between the towns of Ijebu, Ife and Owu over economic control of the important market town of Apomu.[10] The Ijebu destroyed Owu and Farode must have been one of the war captive casualties. He then appears to have spent some time in Ijebuland, probably as a domestic slave.[11] Ijebu's active involvement in political conflicts and the slave trade was reflected in the following song which was widely known by Trinidad Yoruba descendants:

> *The Ijebu are coming*
> *Run, hide*
> *People are hatching conspiracies*
> *Against each other*[12]

All the same, in his favourite chant, Farode identified himself as an Ijebu person. This chant showered praise on his personal deity, Shango, among whose sobriquets is Arira:

> King of the deities,
> Arira the thunderer,
> Pillar of the brotherhood of worshippers,
> You will see him
> You will see the Father

Then the chant continued, with the singer apparently identifying himself as a devotee of Shango among whose symbols was the elaborate *bata* drum, an instrument not otherwise recorded in either oral or written documentation as having been used in Trinidad:

> The old Ijebu man dances to the bata *drum*
> On his way to greet the king
> King of the deities![13]

The multiplication of ethnic identities caused by civil strife, southward overland migration and overseas exile is replicated in the family histories of Alphonsine 'Nanin' Williams. Her father was born on the Caribbean island of St Lucia to parents described as from both Ijesha and Abeokuta. Similarly, her mother's parents were both referred to as Ijesha, but she further identified her maternal grandfather, Afologba Aone 'who uses money profitably', as an Egba from Abeokuta! When singing and playing on the drum Afolo would interject salutations such as '*O ku 'luwu, ọmọ ọdọ Abẹokuta/ọdọ ọkuta*' or '*O ku 'luwu, ọmọ are Afrika*'. These were greetings to citizens of Abeokuta, the principal town of Egbaland, distinguished by its location around a massive inselberg, and to Africans in exile, while the acclamation to Oluwu was to the King of Owu. This town and small kingdom had been a staunch ally of Oyo, but after its destruction, many refugees had been absorbed into the Egba confederacy.

These political and family dislocations were enmeshed in religious realignments as well. It is instructive that Farode sang the chant to Shango as he was dying. At this moment, as on so many occasions before, he was expressing a longing to see the principal deity of the Oyo people, an *orisha* they believed had once ruled over Oyo and never died, but had been drawn from earth to heaven by a supernatural chain. Obviously in conformity with the political and religious sympathies of his family, Farode held Islam in deep suspicion. He believed it to be one of the divisive factors that had destroyed the ethnic unity and identity of the Yooba (Yoruba) people and of African people as a whole.[14]

FIGURE 7.3   Octavia Henry. *Source: Photo by the author.*

On the other hand, another descendant, Octavia Henry, declared with pride that her maternal grandfather was a 'Yoruba Muslim'. His name was Agiya 'one who demolished suffering'. He did not have facial scarifications and had wavy hair which was plaited in three: these details may suggest a Nupe or Fulani blood connection, further confirming the Muslim link. Perhaps her grandfather had lived in Ilorin, with its strong Muslim allegiance. Its population was largely Yoruba, but it also accommodated Hausa and Fulani allies. From the second decade of the nineteenth century and well into mid-century, Ilorin had replaced Oyo as a savannah-based entrepôt slave market; but it also amassed captives by conducting raids on areas such as Igboho to its north-west and Igbomina, Ekiti and Akoko to its immediate east and south-east.[15] Iseyin was to become its political and military surrogate to its south-west and, interestingly, one of Octavia's songs uses a distinctive term, *fa*, from the Ilorin and Iseyin districts. The song in question laments the loss of a particular faction in the plots and counter-plots which constituted the defections and changing power centres of the period:

Èèmọ̀ dé o!	Disaster has come!
Ìró gèè o	The news has spread far and wide
Kò mà sóge ni	Confidence has been shattered
Lẹ́hìn ọ̀tẹ́, fa	Following the revolt, alas!
'Mo gbóge lọ	Failure has demolished pride[16]

Unfortunately Octavia could not recall the names of the towns from which her ancestors came, but she remembered that her grandmother's town was famous for cloth weaving and that the family employed people in their business. One wonders whether her family sold cloths to Hausa and Ilorin weaver–traders further north of their home district.[17] The facial marks of her grandmother are thought to resemble Yagba sub-ethnic scarification. Certainly, Octavia's songs contained grammatical peculiarities of the Ijesha sub-group, and one song identified the singer–composer as belonging to the Ijogun clan from Ilesha, the capital of Ijesha.[18] But one cannot be certain that this song was necessarily her own family's signature statement.

Octavia's grandmother also bore a Muslim name, Jerifo, which appears to be the Yoruba version of the Muslim 'Sherifat'. Is it then that she, perhaps an Ijesha or Yagba native, was also a Muslim? Or had she converted to Islam and then taken this Muslim name? Or was this Agiya's way of re-engineering her identity with a name more acceptable to his religious and political allegiances? It might be significant that Islam, the chief marker of Agiya's identity in Octavia's consciousness, was not invoked for Jerifo. And yet Agiya's name was not of Muslim derivation! Perhaps Jerifo called Agiya by his Yoruba name rather than his acquired Muslim one as a means of insisting on her preferred religious loyalties.

In fact, the names given to Octavia's mother's generation are strongly associated with the *orisha*. They indicate names given in recognition of the help secured in successful childbirth through parental devotion to one or more *orisha*, or names dedicating the child to the service of a particular deity. Octavia's mother's Yoruba name was Orishabiyi 'the deities allowed this child to be born', Octavia's own name was Orishatoyi 'the deities are worthy of pride', and the name of either her brother or father was Oguntusi 'Ogun is worthy of being worshipped'. How then does one explain both the Muslim and *orisha* connections of this family? It may have been that Octavia was brought up in a matrifocal setting in which Agiya did not share the same residence as Jerifo and her children. This would have tended to make his cultural influence marginal. Another scenario allows us to make a connection between the fact that Agiya and Jerifo had lived in St Lucia before relocating to Trinidad. In St Lucia Jerifo may have come under the influence of Oyo Yoruba and their *orisha* religion, remnants of which appear in *kele*, a near-extinct religious ritual.[19] Octavia herself had belonged to several religions during her lifetime, a very common occurrence in the Caribbean. Among these was the *orisha* religion. She had not, to my knowledge, ever been a Muslim, but immediately before singing the lament about the failed coup, she sang a chant with likely Muslim connections. It began with a phrase which on the surface signified an honorific of Shango, that is, *alado*, juxtaposing this with an honorific to Eshu, *alaroye*. The seeming contradiction is resolved when one listens to her explanation of the song's meaning. She attributed the chant to God, with the attributive praises: 'He is the first, He is the last, He is the onliest [only] one.' The last phrase echoes the first Muslim credo: *La ilaha Billallah* 'there is no God but Allah'. The previous two phrases are among the attributes of Allah: the First – *al-Awwal*, and the Last – *al-Akhir*. Octavia then exclaimed: *Ye*[20] *Ala o! Ala o! Baba!* meaning, she said in inverted order, '*My* Father, my God!' On singing the chant, its end line diverted from the Yoruba language with the words *zali balaka*. An attempt is made here to render a plausible Hausa interpretation for this final phrase:[21]

Allah dó	Allah stands firm/endures
A-là-àròyé	He who cures grievances (the Compassionate)
Allah rí òye	Allah is intelligent (Allah the All-knowing)
Allah dó	Allah the everlasting
Baba zali balaka	
< Baba yasa albarka	Father pronounces/grants blessings

Thus interpreted, the chant is an affirmation of the attributes of Allah: He is great – *Allahu akbar*; is All-knowing – *al-Hadid*, in addition to being beneficent and merciful – *ar-Rahman ar-Rahim*.

The chant demonstrates not only the influence of Islam in the then largely non-Islamic Yoruba religious environment, but also one of the processes by which the practices of an antecedent religion or culture – in this case a Yoruba-language artistic artifact – come to be appropriated by a subsequent religion or cultural apport.

Lexical loans and bilingualism are significant indices of cultural and ethnic contact. The extent of Lucy Charles' use of Fon terminology in her religious lore may have some bearing on her maternal background. Her maternal great-grandmother lived in Ondo and traded between there and

Ibadan to the west. Her name was Oshunbunmi and at least one of her children was born in Ibadan, but a daughter came from Ajase (Porto Novo), which might suggest that Oshunbunmi stayed there for a time.[22]

The use of Fon vocabulary in Trinidad *orisha* worship is not however unique to Lucy. Trinidad Yoruba descendants admit to a relatively amicable relationship between *orisha* worshippers and the *vodun*-practising Rada (Allada/Fon) and there was interaction between members of the different shrines, with *orisha* shrines being considerably more numerous. But interchange between the two religions did not begin in Trinidad, having been fostered by the proximity of Yoruba-speaking peoples and Gbe-speakers on the Slave Coast.[23] The Fon names of some of the principal deities shared by both religions are still used interchangeably by several members of *orisha* congregations, and some Fon-based chants are also part of the *orisha* song repertoire. Various terms among Lucy's own Fon vocabulary are listed in Table 7.1.[24]

The overlap in Yoruba and Fon religious and cultural vocabulary makes it difficult to determine what aspects of language and religious contact had taken place in West Africa before practices influenced each other in Trinidad. This historically based interaction is similarly evident in the 1837 war song of the West India Regiment mutineers stationed at St Joseph in Trinidad. It yields a Yoruba-based interpretation although the mutiny was led by a Popo or Gun called Daaga. But at least one of his chief aides was Yoruba, underscoring the multiethnic linkages among the Ewe, Fon/Gbe and Yoruba of the Slave Coast. The song, rendered in historical documents in a partially French-based orthography, reads:

> *Dangkaree*
> *Au fey*
> *Olu weree*
> *Au ley*

But not only does the phrase *ida n kare* recur in a 1939 recorded Yoruba song from Trinidad, but the whole text coherently translates as:[25]

Idà ń kárí	The sword is sufficient
Idà ńkà ré	Behold the cruel sword!
Ó fé	It slices
Ó lù wéré	It strikes without mercy
Ó lé	It is strong

FIGURE 7.4   Joseph Zampty. *Source: Photo by the author.*

FIGURE 7.5   Wood stencil by Joseph Zampty. *Source: Photo by the author.*

The practice of long-distance trading has surfaced in Lucy Charles' genealogical profile, and the issue of religious loyalties and strife affected the ancestors of Lucy and Octavia. These two motifs return in the maternal genealogy of Joseph Zampty. He traced his maternal genealogy through his grandmother, who had been born in Asante, far to the west of the Yoruba-speaking heartland. Although there were communities of Yoruba traders and residents in Dahomey and Togo, there were probably not many Yoruba in Asante, and hence it may be that his grandmother was actually enslaved and taken to Asante. Or did this account relate to the presence of Yoruba, Hausa and other recruits into the British regiments that fought Asante during the 1870s? The name of Zampty's grandmother was Ashetola, meaning 'commerce deserves wealth', and indicated her (and her family's) association with trading. It is therefore possible that her family traded out of the partially Yoruba-populated areas of Dahomey, going as far west as Asante to sell, by Zampty's account, dried meat, honey, *agidi* or steamed corn bread. Already a 'big breasted' girl, she perhaps was responsible for her own trading, or accompanied her parents on long journeys in trade caravans. But she was seized by bandits while on her way to market to sell oil and corn. She and others were bound in twos, hand and ankle, with what Zampty described as 'bracelets'. They were taken first to a camp and then to a waiting ship. By the early nineteenth century Hausa and Yoruba slave traders operating out of Ilorin routed some of their slave captives through Borgu, Dahomey and even Asante, down to Ouidah and other coastal ports.[26]

Zampty was very hostile to the *orisha* religion. His people had not heard of Shango, which suggests that his family were not Oyo or subjects of a Yoruba sub-group allied to that imperial capital. It also appears that his maternal grandfather may have arrived in Trinidad during slavery, i.e. prior to 1838. It is likely then that his sub-group followed local religious practices that bore little if any resemblance to the official (*orisha*) religion of Oyo which was centred on the cult of Shango. Such persons might have tended to be more receptive to a Christianization divorced from *orisha* belief, a tendency which Zampty himself reflected in his religious attitudes. By contrast, Yoruba and their descendants who retained *orisha* beliefs integrated these with Christian concepts and ritual.

These family histories and historical events have been selected in order to demonstrate the complexity of sub-ethnic identity among Trinidad enslaved and indentured persons who could generally be called 'Yoruba'. Some of the immigrants/enslaved identified themselves unequivocally by ethnic categories such as Yaraba,[27] Jesha/Ijesha, Egba, Egbado, Yagba, Ondo, Jebu/Ijebu, or by the name of the towns from which they came: Oye, Ado, Arigidi and Igosi in Ekitiland, Ikole in Ijesha, and Owu, Ota, Abeokuta and Ibadan further south. But the family histories isolated here indicate that some individuals regarded themselves as belonging to – or at least closely associated with – more than one of these regions. Apart from this sense of plural regional origin or allegiance, conflicts in religious loyalties and belief emerge among the persons discussed here, and in some instances also there appear to have been multiple religious practices involving some of the individuals themselves. These factors nuance the vexed and difficult issue of ethnic labelling, which was usually done by persons other than the enslaved themselves. The examples also point to some of the multifaceted religious negotiations which result when cultures anywhere come into contact, and which also take shape as personal and communal strategies in situations of social and political pressure.

It should be noted that in this study only marginal reference is made to the role of Christian religions and European cultural identity in the self-concept of African descendants, not because these were unimportant, but because the ethnographic literature has so far not recognized the interplay of African-based issues: ethnicities and sub-ethnicities, the convergences and syncretisms among African cultural forms, and the hegemonic forces in contention among neighbouring ethnic groups in Africa and in the commingling of African ethnic groups overseas. These produced processes which have worked in complex ways to create the African-based cultural configurations of the Caribbean.

Table 7.1   Fon vocabulary

ababo ~ lababo ~ sababo ~ kobabo: to yodel; yodelling to welcome an *orisha* < *awobobo*: ululation to welcome or express joy

Adangbe ~ Adangwe: serpent god < *Dangbwe*: serpent god

Adosoji: Banyanni, St Anthony < *Da Zoji*: god of smallpox

Aflɛgdɛ ~ Aflegede: Oya < *Avlekete*: goddess of wind and lightning

akakun: guinea pepper < *atakun*: guinea pepper

Awoyo: honorific for Yemanja < *Awoyo*: honorific for the sea

Bo Zewɔn ~ Ba Zewa: a healing deity, Shakpana, St Jerome < *Bo Zuon*: a deity with control over sickness and evil spirits *desunu ~ desuni ~ deshɔne*: sacred ceremony in which priest makes incisions on devotee's head and body, anointing head with palm oil, leaves and salts < *desunu < desu*: atonement or purification + *-nu*: matters pertaining to

Dɔmbala: St Dominic < *Dambala*: serpent god, St Dominic

drazɔ: vigil to start *orisha* ceremony < *dro zan*: to keep a vigil

hubunu: divinely appointed slayer of sacrificial animals < *hobonu*: sacred slayer of sacrificial animals

hunsi ~ usi ~ osi: devotee < *hunsi*: initiate able to assist in priestly functions

huto: lead drummer in *orisha* ceremony < *hunto*: lead drummer in *vodun* ceremony

kwe: earthen *orisha* altar < *kpe*: earthen *vodun* altar

Naite: Virgin Mary < *Naetɛ*: a water goddess, St Philomen

Ologbo: a healing deity < *Oloko*: god of trees

Osokbo: Shango < *Sogbo*: thunder deity

Parada: Orunmila, St Joseph < *Parada*: god of smallpox and disease

-si: indicator of spiritual affiliation < *-si*: wife of

vudunu: worship ceremony for the *orisha* < *vudunu*: ceremony in which the *vodun* (deities) are worshipped

vudunsi: person possessed by the *orisha* < *vudunsi*: person possessed by the *vodun*

Notes

1 Maureen Warner-Lewis, *Guinea's Other Suns: The African Dynamic in Trinidad Culture* (Dover, MA, 1991), pp. 9–15; Maureen Warner-Lewis, *Trinidad Yoruba: From Mother Tongue to Memory* (Tuscaloosa, AL, 1996; Kingston, 1997), pp. 28–31.
2 As Francine Shields demonstrates in her study of enslaved Yoruba women in this volume, these conditions also prevailed in Yorubaland itself; also see Shields, 'Palm Oil and Power: Women in an Era of Economic and Social Transition in 19th-Century Yorubaland (South-Western Nigeria)' (PhD thesis, University of Stirling, UK 1997), pp. 33–113.
3 See Peter Morton-Williams, 'The Oyo Yoruba and the Atlantic Trade, 1670–1830', in J. E. Inikori (ed.), *Forced Migration: The Impact of the Export Slave Trade on African Societies* (New York, 1982), pp. 167–86.
4 See Abdullahi Smith, 'A Little New Light on the Collapse of the Alafinate of Yoruba', in G. O. Olusanya (ed.), *Studies in Yoruba History and Culture: Essays in Honour of Professor S.O. Biobaku* (Ibadan, 1983), pp. 50–1.
5 S. A. Akintoye, *Revolution and Power Politics in Yorubaland, 1840–1893: Ibadan Expansion and the Rise of Ekiti Parapo* (London, 1971), p. xviii.
6 See songs 99–116 in Maureen Warner-Lewis, *Yoruba Songs of Trinidad* (London, 1994).
7 Warner-Lewis, *Yoruba Songs of Trinidad*, p. 134.
8 *Ibid.*, pp. 62–3.

9 *Ibid.*, p. 27. An interesting but by no means unusual case of variant legends occurs when another informant, Alphonsine Williams, in her version of this chant includes the same information about Ejigbo, but by a change of vowel from Ifa to Ife, asserts Ile-Ife as the source of humankind:

> *Aféfẹ́ rúrú lórèré* God Almighty in the heavens
> *Ó tẹdo lÉjìgbò* He established (his) city at Ejigbo
> *Ilé-Ifẹ̀ ọmọ ti wá* Humankind originated from Ile-Ife

10 See 'Clues from Oral History', in Warner-Lewis, *Guinea's Other Suns*, pp. 1–6; Akin Mabogunje and J. Omer-Cooper, *Owu in Yoruba History* (Ibadan, 1971).

11 For comparable experiences of domestic slavery, see Shields, 'Palm Oil and Power' and J. F. Ade Ajayi, 'Samuel Ajayi Crowther of Oyo', in Philip D. Curtin (ed.), *Africa Remembered: Narratives by West Africans from the Era of the Slave Trade* (Madison, WI, 1967), pp. 289–316.

12 Warner-Lewis, *Yoruba Songs of Trinidad*, pp. 122–3.

13 *Ibid.*, p. 55.

14 Smith ('New Light', pp. 55–9) points to the presence of Muslim traders, accountants, religious instructors and court advisors in Oyo at least from the closing decades of the eighteenth century and to the religious and political repercussions of their influence on palace officials.

15 See Ann O'Hear, 'Ilorin as a Slaving and Slave-Trading State', paper presented at UNESCO/SSHRCC Summer Institute, 'Identifying Enslaved Africans: The "Nigerian" Hinterland and the African Diaspora', York University, Toronto, July 1997, pp. 3–4.

16 Warner-Lewis, *Yoruba Songs of Trinidad*, p. 124.

17 O'Hear, 'Ilorin', p. 3.

18 Warner-Lewis, *Yoruba Songs of Trinidad*, p. 142.

19 See Manfred Kremser, 'The African Heritage in the "Kele" Tradition of the "Djine" in St. Lucia', in Manfred Kremser and Karl R. Wernhart (eds), *Research in Ethnography and Ethnohistory of St. Lucia: A Preliminary Report* (Horn-Wien, Vienna, 1986), pp. 77–101; Annita Montoute, 'The Search for Kele: A Dying Religion', Caribbean Studies essay, Department of History, University of the West Indies, Jamaica, 1996.

20 Yoruba, meaning 'hear, listen', and a frequent device at the start of songs.

21 I am grateful to John Hunwick for help in identifying the Arabic source of the name *Jerifo* and the final word of the song, and to Ibrahim Jumare for help in deciphering a plausible interpretation of the song's last line.

22 Ajase, the Yoruba name for Porto Novo, was also the name of a town to the east of Ikoyi and Ogbomosho. Ajase occurs in at least two of Lucy's songs. Its occurrence in a chant to Dada, Shango's deified brother, might indicate that its reference in that context is to the northerly town, closer to Oyo itself.

23 See chapter by Sandra E. Greene, in this volume. In keeping with the recommendations espoused by Hounkpati Capo, *A Comparative Phonology of Gbe* (Berlin, 1991), Gbe is treated as a dialect cluster comprising, among others, Ewe, Fon, Gun, Aja.

24 See Warner-Lewis, *Trinidad Yoruba*, pp. 93–4.

25 *Ibid.*, pp. 178–9. The 1939 recording of Margaret Buckley singing '*Ye! Iwo*', in which the phrase occurs, was identified in the fieldnotes as a war song. See *Peter Was a Fisherman: The 1939 Trinidad Field Recordings of Melville and Frances Herskovits*, vol. 1, produced by Donald Hill, Rounder Records Corp., CD 1114 (Cambridge, MA, 1998), song 25.

26 O'Hear, 'Ilorin', p. 3.

27 This pronunciation reflects the Hausa origin of the term (*Yarba*). But the frequency in the use of this term among Trinidad Yoruba and other African descendants may in fact lend support to Smith's contention that Islamic influences among the northern-based Yoruba were more significant than has been thought.

8

Portraits of African Royalty in Brazil

Alberto da Costa e Silva

Often during the time of slavery, Africans crossed the Atlantic – but not always as slaves and sometimes for reasons that are at odds with the stereotypical enslaved black in the Americas. The life stories, as far as is known, of several individuals in eighteenth- and nineteenth-century Brazil provide case studies of African royalty in exile, whether forced or voluntary. The links between Salvador, Bahia and the Bight of Benin were particularly close, and hence it is not surprising that the cases examined here reflect these connections. There were formal diplomatic missions, as recorded by Pierre Verger, with official visits from Dahomey to the capital of Brazil at Salvador da Bahia in 1750–1, 1795, 1805 and 1811; from Porto Novo to Bahia in 1810; and from Lagos in 1770, 1807 and 1823.[1] And there is knowledge of other connections, including the education of the sons of Dahomean kings in Bahia, and the commercial activities of Pierra Tamata of Porto Novo, the Hausa slave boy educated in France and the leading merchant at Porto Novo when Oyo decided to make the place its leading outlet to the Atlantic trade, thereby bypassing Ouidah in importance.[2] As Verger has demonstrated, Africans from the Bight of Benin came to Bahia to study, to trade or to escape political persecution, not just as slaves destined for the sugar and tobacco fields of north-eastern Brazil or the mines of Minas Gerais.

Among the political exiles were members of African royal families who arrived as slaves. Several who had been sold as slaves kept their identities secret in order to protect themselves. Only their own countrymen or women knew their regal identities, and those who made efforts to buy their freedom were bound to secrecy. However, although some of the royal exiles tried to conceal their origins, it is possible to trace the lives of a few, while others did not take such precautions, but revealed their real identities and the ranks they held. This paper sketches the lives of several enslaved, exiled princes, an enslaved, exiled queen (who tried to keep her real identity secret for unknown reasons) and a free, exiled (rather flamboyant) prince.

In the late eighteenth century, Archibald Dalzel, the notorious slave trader, reported that he had met the former Jengen (Guinguin) of Badagry.[3] The Jengen was the chief of Awhanjigo ward, and at times the most powerful official at Badagry. The man whom Dalzel met had lived in Bahia in two different periods. He had been educated in Brazil as a young man, probably during the reign of his father, who held the same title. The succession was disputed by another chief called 'Sessou', but the Jengen emerged supreme in 1776, according to Law, but was in turn deposed and exiled to Brazil in 1782, whereupon the Akran, the chief of Ijegba ward, became dominant.[4] Twenty slaves were sent in the same ship for the subsistence of the Jengen, which confirms his status as a political prisoner. Free Africans who went to Brazil often took with them a number of slaves instead of money. The slaves could be sold one by one, according to their owner's needs, as if they were traveller's cheques or letters of exchange. The fate of the twenty slaves who accompanied the Jengen into exile is unknown, however.

Fruku, the son of King Agaja (1708–32) of Dahomey, had been sold into slavery and sent to Brazil by King Tegbesu (1732–74), along with several others of Agaja's line. Fruku lived in Brazil for twenty-four years, until he was recalled by his childhood friend, Tegbesu's successor, Kpengla (1774–89). Upon Kpengla's death in 1789, Fruku (now using his Brazilian name, Dom Jeronimo) made a bid for the throne, but Agonglo secured the appointment and ruled until 1797.[5] It is not clear what happened to Fruku.

King Adandozan (1797–1818) also used slavery in the Americas as a means of banishing his political enemies. He sold Nan Agotimé, the mother of the future King Gezo (1818–58), together with many of her retainers, to the slave traders. According to Verger, Nan Agotimé founded the Querebetam de Zonadonu, or Casa das Minas (the Minas House), in São Luis do Maranhão, in north-eastern Brazil, where all the royal *vodun* of Abomey, including ones for each of the kings down to Agonglo, were (and still are) worshipped.[6] If Verger's hypothesis is correct, Nan Agotimé must have changed her name to María Jesuína, for this was the name of the founder of the Minas House, according to oral tradition. However, anthropologist Sérgio Ferretti, who spent many years studying the Querebetam de Zonadounu, states that the old *vodunsi* never mention the founder's name, and he considers it to be one of the lost secrets of the Minas House.[7] Nevertheless, the old *vodunsi* do say that the founders were all Africans and were brought to Maranhão in the same ship. Ferretti suggests that if *Mãe* (Mother, or *Nochê*) María Jesuína was not Nan Agotimé, the queen could have been the person who initiated *Mãe* Jesuína into the religion. It is also possible that *Mãe* Jesuína was one of Nan Agotimé's relatives or retainers and was placed in charge of the Minas House in order to permit the queen to keep her identity secret.

Two princes who flaunted their identities were Benvindo da Fonseca Galvão and his son, Cândido, alias Prince Obá II of Africa. 'Benvindo' was the Brazilian name of an alleged son (or grandson) of Alafin Abiodun (1774–89) of Oyo who was sold into slavery at the beginning of the nineteenth century. Manumitted by his owner, Benvindo tried his fortune as a freedman in Bahia's diamond fields, where his son Cândido was born. In his biography of Cândido da Fonseca Galvão, Eduardo Silva describes him as an intelligent and outstanding man.[8] Tall and strong, Cândido distinguished himself as a soldier during Brazil's war against Paraguay in the 1860s, and he returned from the battlefield a lieutenant. He settled in Rio de Janeiro, where he became known as a prince – a prince-in-exile – not only of the Yoruba (the black settlers from Bahia who congregated in a quarter known as 'Little Africa') but of all the African slaves and freedmen. In one of the articles he wrote for various newspapers on the problems of the country, the town and the poor people, he claimed that he 'had the right of God, entrusted to [his] Abiodun grandfathers', for, he explained, '*Omo-obaa me je oba*, which means: the son of a king is king.'[9]

In the view of some contemporaries, Cândido was a megalomaniac drunkard, but Emperor Dom Pedro II did not hesitate to receive him in São Cristovão palace. Every Saturday, Prince Obá II (his father, Benvindo, was Obá I) dressed in military uniform with the medals and decorations to which he was entitled, perched his pince-nez on his nose, above a thick moustache and pointed goatee, and presented himself at the hand-kissing ceremony. During the rest of the week, he wore a black frock-coat, top hat and white gloves, and carried a cane and an umbrella – the cane a sign of rank among the Brazilian élite, and the umbrella a prerogative of the Alafin. Mello Moraes Filho, who knew Cândido personally, wrote that as the prince walked along the streets, many blacks would go down on their knees at his passage, and that he was supported by tribute paid by those who considered themselves his subjects.[10]

The Brazilian emperor's fall and exile in 1889 represented a blow to Prince Obá II; he suffered pain and humiliation, and less than eight months after the proclamation of the republic, he died penniless and forlorn. 'Surprisingly,' writes Eduardo Silva, 'his death made the front pages of Rio's newspapers, and nearly every article about him emphasized the prince's "enormous tribe of followers" or "his immense popularity"'.[11]

Entirely different were the life and death of another prince, who adopted the Brazilian name of José Custódio Joaquim de Almeida.[12] He arrived in Brazil around 1864, not as a slave but as a free man and an exiled chief. It is not known why Custódio Joaquim went to Brazil. Had he been expelled by political strife? Was he a fugitive? Or had he been sent by the British? Custódio Joaquim used to say that the British consul in Porto Alegre paid him a monthly stipend in pounds sterling to ensure that he stayed away from Africa. But where was he from? His contemporaries were convinced that he had come from the Mina coast, but this does not explain much, because 'Costa da Mina' was a very vague term in eighteenth- and nineteenth-century Brazil; it included the Bight of Benin and the Gold Coast. A Mina man could be Fante, Ga, Asante, Gun, Fon, Mahi or Yoruba. In some places, as in Rio de Janeiro, any African who was not from West–Central Africa might be called Mina.

All that we know about Custódio Joaquim comes from what was printed in newspapers in Rio Grande do Sul during the first decades of the twentieth century. According to these reports, Custódio Joaquim left his homeland in 1862, when he was thirty-one years old. He was known by the African people in Porto Alegre, the capital city of Rio Grande do Sul, as *o Príncipe* (the prince) or *Príncipe de Ajudá* (Prince of Ouidah), but he probably had little or no connection with that town. The title could have been given to him in Brazil because he had embarked from Ouidah. It is possible that he was one of the chiefs involved in the dispute between the British and the French for the control of the trade of the Bight of Benin, which led to the annexation of Lagos in 1861.

Two years after Custódio Joaquim left West Africa, he arrived in the port of Rio Grande, which means that he did not travel directly from the African coast to Brazil. He may have gone first to Britain and even to

Montevideo or Buenos Aires, for both cities had strong connections with the British. If so, it is easy to explain why he chose to live in Rio Grande do Sul: he had only to cross the border. He lived in Rio Grande for many years, and then moved to Bagé, in the interior of the province. In both Rio Grande and Bagé he opened sanctuaries for the practice of traditional African religion; he was a devotee of the *orisha* Ogun (the Gun *vodun*). He also became well known as a herbalist.

In 1901, Custódio Joaquim settled in Porto Alegre. He bought a house in Lopo Gonçalves Street, number 496. It was a mansion, and he lived there with his five daughters and three sons (no mention of a wife or wives has ever been found in the press). The neighbourhood of Lopo Gonçalves Street was mostly inhabited by Italian immigrants and their descendants. Little by little, old Africans and black Brazilians began to settle around the prince's house, probably because they wanted to be near the man they considered their leader. As the years passed, the number of people living in the house increased to twenty-five (not including servants) and formed a kind of small royal court.

Behind the house, Custódio Joaquim kept a stud of several racehorses. He considered himself a great expert on horses and took personal care of his animals. Every Sunday, one or more of his horses took part in the official races of the city's jockey club. His knowledge of horses may be an indication that he was not a native of the African coast, where horses were very few because of the deadly tsetse fly, but of the savannah. It must be recalled, however, that when he arrived in Porto Alegre, he had already lived for thirty-seven years in a Brazilian region famous for its love for horses and horse breeding, and he may have acquired the tastes and abilities of a *gaucho* in Brazil.

Custódio Joaquim also had a coach house for his landau that was later used as a garage for his Chevrolet car. At this time, one could see only one or two dozen cars circulating the streets of Porto Alegre, because only well-to-do people could afford them. Custódio Joaquim most certainly belonged to this group. He owned a second house – a beach house in Praia da Cidreira – where he used to spend part of the summer, always surrounded by an enormous number of guests.

In his house in Porto Alegre he not only received many guests and visitors but also sheltered people with financial or health problems. He continued his practice of treating sick people with herbs, drawing on traditional medicine. In this practice he had the assistance, for many years, of the son of a German immigrant; the son came to his door as a pauper asking for help and stayed on as a more or less permanent member of the household.

Each year, during the week of his birthday, the prince threw a three-day party in the African manner. The governor of the state, Borges de Medeiros, was always present for the celebrations. After slavery was abolished in Brazil in 1888 and Brazil became a republic, men like Custódio Joaquim assumed electoral importance. The governor knew that a favourable word from the prince of Ouidah meant a large number of votes from Brazilians of African descent.

More than six feet tall, strong, outgoing and full of energy, Custódio Joaquim was fluent in both English and French, although, curiously, his Portuguese was never perfect. Most of the time he dressed in black, according to the European fashion, but on special occasions he wore African garments or a *mélange* of African and nineteenth-century European clothes, never omitting his British decorations. He frequently wore a red fez or a white cap with lateral flaps covering both ears, similar to a leather Akan cap, and in most photographs he appears smoking a big cigar and wearing a pocket watch with a heavy gold chain.

The prince of Ouidah died on 28 May 1935, supposedly more than 100 years old. He took pride in boasting of his old age. He commemorated his centenary with a party that was considered by one newspaper as the most fantastic ever held in Porto Alegre.[13] On that day he mounted one of his horses without any help to show that he was still a strong man. He had a traditional West African funeral: to the amazement of his white, Catholic friends, it lasted for several days, with music, dancing and banquets.

Custódio Joaquim applied his prestige and wealth to improving the conditions of Africans and their community in a state where there was strong discrimination against blacks. Thanks to his flamboyant and charismatic personality, and perhaps also to the fact that he presented himself as a member of the aristocracy, he was not merely accepted but appreciated and even admired by white society. Nobody knew the origin of his wealth, for he had no visible occupation other than being the undoubted leader of his community. It is possible that he received a substantial allowance from the British government, but we do not know why it was given to him or how it was paid. So far, there is no evidence that the British consul in Porto Alegre or the British legations in Montevideo, Buenos Aires or Rio de Janeiro, supported him. Nor do the Foreign Office Archives in London mention Custódio Joaquim or any payments to an African personality in Porto Alegre.

It is a pity that during the seventy-one years that Custódio Joaquim lived in Brazil, nobody seems to have had enough curiosity to ask him to narrate his life story or to commit it to writing. Although Nina Rodrigues and Manuel Querino, in Bahia, and Sílvio Romero, in Rio de Janeiro, were exceptions, most of the prince's contemporaries believed that Africans had no history. As Romero wrote, it was a shame that Brazilians of the time did not study the Africans they had living side by side with them and working in their houses.[14] As Romero was collecting Brazilian popular songs and tales of African, Amerindian and European origin, he urged linguists, historians and other specialists to learn from ex-slaves before they died what they knew and remembered of their people and native land. Unfortunately for us, his advice was not followed with respect to José Custódio Joaquim de Almeida or other distinguished, or not so distinguished, Africans in Brazil.

Notes

1 Pierre Verger, *Trade Relations between the Bight of Benin and Bahia, 17th-19th Century* (Ibadan, 1976), pp. 179–249; first published as *Flux et reflux de la traite des nègres entre le golfe de Bénin et Bahia de Todos os Santos du dix-septième au dix-neuvième siècle* (Paris, 1968), pp. 199, 218–49.
2 John Adams met Pierra Tamata, apparently in the 1790s; see *Remarks on the Country Extending from Cape Palmas to the River Congo* (1823; London, 1996), pp. 82–7. Also see Verger, *Trade Relations*, pp. 186–8; A. Akindele and C. Aguessy, *Contribution à l'étude de l'histoire de l'ancien royaume de Porto-Novo* (Dakar, 1968), pp. 73, 137; and Alain Sinou and Bachir Oloude, *Porto Novo, Ville d'Afrique noire* (Marseille, 1988), p. 73.
3 Robin Law, 'A Lagoonside Port on the Eighteenth-Century Slave Coast: The Early History of Badagry', *Canadian Journal of African Studies*, 28, no. 1 (1994); Verger, *Trade Relations*, p. 188.
4 Archibald Dalzel, *History of Dahomey* (1793; London, 1967), pp. 181, 184–5. See the discussion in Law, 'Early History of Badagry', pp. 42–3. Also see I. A. Akinjogbin, *Dahomey and Its Neighbours, 1708–1818* (Cambridge, 1967), p. 165; and Caroline Sorensen, 'Badagry 1784–1863: The Political and Commercial History of a Pre-Colonial Lagoonside Community in South West Nigeria' (PhD thesis, unpublished, University of Stirling, UK, 1995).
5 Dalzel, *History of Dahomey*, p. 223; and Akinjogbin, *Dahomey*, pp. 116, 171, 178.
6 Pierre Verger, 'Le culte des vodoun d'Abomey aurait-il été apporté à Saint-Louis de Maranhon par la mère du Roi Ghézo?' *Les afro-américains*, Mémoires de l'Institut français d'Afrique noire, no. 27 (Dakar, 1953), pp. 157–60.
7 Sérgio Ferretti, *Querebetam de Zonadounu: Um estudo de antropologia da religião da Casa das Minas*, tese de mestrado apresentada a Universidade Federal do Rio Grande do Norte, Natal, 1983, p. 44.
8 Eduardo Silva, *Prince of the People: The Life and Times of a Brazilian Free Man of Colour*, trans. Moyra Ashford (London, 1993).
9 *O Carbonário*, 21 June 1886, cited in Silva, *Prince of the People*, p. 110.

10 Mello Moraes Filho, *Festas e tradições populares do Brasil* (Rio de Janeiro, 1901), p. 536.

11 *Ibid.*, p. 2.

12 I owe my interest in José Custódio Joaquim de Almeida and the basic information on his life to a very informative two-part article by Amaro Júnior, 'Um príncipe africano morou na Lopo Gonçalves . . .,' published in an unidentified Porto Alegre newspaper. Undated clippings were sent to me by Álvaro da Costa Franco.

13 *A Federação*, Porto Alegre, 30 março 1935.

14 Sílvio Romero, *Estudos sobre a poesia popular do Brasil* (Rio de Janeiro, 1888), pp. 10–11.

Slavery, Marriage and Kinship in Rural Rio de Janeiro, 1790–1830

Manolo Garcia Florentino and José Roberto Góes

Kinship relations contributed to the maintenance of slavery in early nineteenth-century Brazil, despite the large number of newly arrived Africans in the slave population who lacked such connections. The plantation regime of rural Rio de Janeiro, at least, required the forced importation of individuals who were variously identified as Mozambiques, Cabindas, Minas, Rebolos, Congos or Benguelas, but who otherwise lacked ties of kinship with their compatriots in slavery. Brazilian slave society relied upon the market to maintain its labour supply, and because the reproduction of labour was structured through the market, which ceaselessly introduced uprooted foreigners, the society was characterized by a high degree of social dislocation. Relationships based on kinship among African-born slaves were therefore almost non-existent. Slave masters who might have wanted to act as paternalistic overlords and dissolve the dissimilarities among their slaves were limited in what they could achieve in turning slaves into their 'offspring'. Slavery in Brazil did not find stability in paternalism, as Gilberto Freyre has argued, and hence was not like the United States, as analysed by Eugene Genovese.[1] In the first three decades of the nineteenth century at least, slave masters in Rio de Janeiro could not run their businesses without the slave market, nor could they overcome the fact that they were as much foreigners as the enslaved Africans whom they bought.

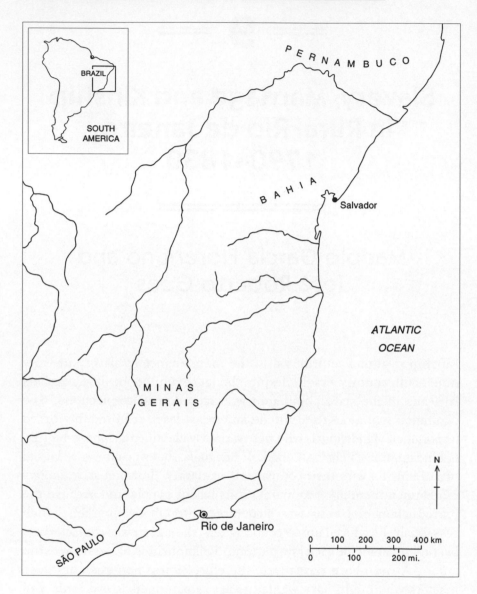

FIGURE 9.1   Map of Brazil in the early 19th century. *Source: Drawn by the Cartographic Office, Department of Geography, York University, Canada.*

Pacification of the enslaved Africans was indispensable to the stability of the slave system. Hence laws and rules were imposed on the enslaved population, and because slaves were the objects of greed, masters resorted to coercion and arbitrary action. Naturally, slaves responded to these conditions by establishing liaisons among themselves, developing a sense of solidarity and establishing means of mutual aid to help them live in bondage. Benguelas had to co-operate with Minas, Minas with Quilimanes, and Quilimanes with Benguelas. Slaves had to maintain peace among themselves. They created a community by building kinship ties, even as the market repeatedly introduced foreigners into their midst.

The sense of community that emerged in the slave quarters was indispensable for both slaves and masters. For the captives, it conjured away chaos by establishing rules through which a specific kind of socially produced worker could live; kinship and marriage (whether legally recognized or not) helped create a new sense of identity in the wake of the collapse of the cultural particularities they had inherited. Such ties were indispensable for masters, who wanted to weave peaceful interaction into the fabric of slave life. Kinship relationships among captives made it easier for masters to maintain a pacified population, which guaranteed them a political income based on subordination and allowed them to purchase new slaves in the market to expand production.

In this study, we examine family relations among slaves in rural Rio de Janeiro from 1790 to 1830 in order to show how slave owners were able to turn both the market for new slaves and the desire of slaves to maintain personal relationships to their advantage. The study draws on 374 post-mortem wills from *fluminense*, the countryside in the state of Rio de Janeiro that was opened to plantation development between 1790 and 1835. Documents from the rural areas around Rio de Janeiro are particularly useful for analysing the plantation economy during a period of rapid expansion. This expansion was characterized by a high degree of integration with the international market and depended on the continued import of new captives across the Atlantic for the physical reproduction of its labour force; however, for slaves, expansion affected their ability to consolidate family connections.

Between 1790 and 1830, approximately 700,000 Africans were landed in the *carioca*, the various landing points in and near the city of Rio de Janeiro. From a low of 6000 slaves in 1790, the trade peaked at 47,000 slaves disembarked in 1829, which represented an average annual increase of about 5 per cent for the period as a whole (see Figure 9.2). In the absence

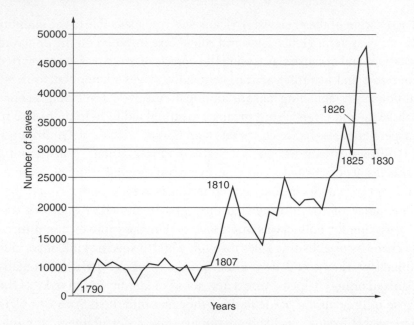

FIGURE 9.2 Number of enslaved Africans landed at Rio de Janeiro, 1790–1830. *Source: Manolo Florentino*, Em costas negras: Uma História do Tráfico de escravos entre a Africa e o Rio de Janeiro (séculos XVIII e XIX). *São Paulo, Companhia das Letras, 1997, p. 51.*

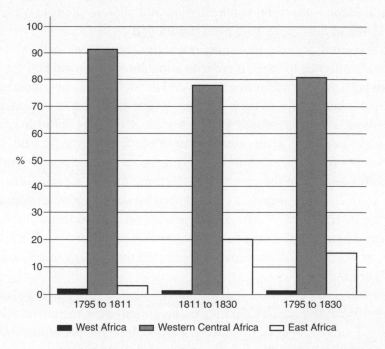

FIGURE 9.3 African origins of slave ships arriving at Rio de Janeiro, 1795–1830. *Source: Manolo Florentino*, Em costas negras: Uma História do Tráfico de escravos entre a Africa e o Rio de Janeiro (séculos XVIII e XIX). *São Paulo, Companhia das Letras, 1997, p. 80.*

Table 9.1 Size of slave holdings, kinship among slaves and variations in the trans-Atlantic slave trade to Rio de Janeiro, 1790–1830

Sources: Manolo Florentino, Em costas negras: Uma história do tráfico de escravos entre a Africa e o Rio de Janeiro (séculos XVIII e XIX) São Paulo, 1997, p. 51; and Post-Mortem Wills (1790–1830), Arquivo Nacional, Rio de Janeiro.

	1790–1807			1810–25			1826–30		
	2 to 9 slaves	10 to 19 slaves	+20 slaves	2 to 9 slaves	10 to 19 slaves	+20 slaves	2 to 9 slaves	10 to 19 slaves	+20 slaves
Average annual increase of slave trade	0.4			2.5			3.5		
Size of slave holding									
Number of slaves	228	313	680	199	356	1716	38	102	481
Percentage of first-degree relatives	31.1	23.6	42.4	25.1	20.2	25.1	23.7	7.8	36.8
Percentage total first-degree relatives	35.5			24.7			31.2		

of severe mortality, such an increase would have meant a doubling of the African population every fifteen years. In fact, however, between 1790 and 1808, the trade was relatively stable, averaging just under 10,000 slaves in most years, with most growth occurring after 1807. Hence, the slave population did not increase substantially as a result of newly arrived Africans between 1790 and 1807, but thereafter the scale of forced immigration was so substantial that the population more than doubled between 1807 and the late 1820s. The arrival of the Portuguese royal family in 1808 and the concomitant opening of colonial ports to international trade increased the volume of landings. The number of slaves imported increased from 10,000 in 1807 to 35,000 in 1826, despite a slump in exports between 1811 and 1813. After 1826, in anticipation of the end of the slave trade, the slave-owning élite of south-eastern Brazil demonstrated a great capacity for gathering resources to purchase as many slaves as possible before British-imposed abolition took effect. An agreement to end the traffic within three years was ratified on 13 March 1827. Approximately 45,000 enslaved Africans were landed in 1828, another 47,000 in 1829, and 31,000 in 1830.

As Figure 9.3 indicates, the overwhelming majority of newly imported slaves arriving between 1795 and 1830 came from West–Central Africa; slaves originating there constituted 92 per cent of new arrivals in the period 1795 to 1811 and almost 80 per cent thereafter. Mozambique became a significant supplier after 1808, providing 20 per cent of new arrivals between 1811 and 1830. A relatively small number of slaves came from West Africa throughout the period under study, never amounting to more than 2 per cent of disembarkations. The overwhelming majority of newly arrived slaves came from West–Central and south-eastern Africa, therefore, and since people in these areas spoke closely related Bantu languages and came mostly from matrilineal societies, it can be expected that some of the adjustments to the slave regime in rural Rio de Janeiro were thereby affected.

It is plausible to suppose that reproduction of kinship relationships, family arrangements and corresponding social and cultural patterns changed over time at the whim of slave-trade movements. The figures given above make it possible to analyse the relationship between kinship and traffic during three long intervals: a period of stability (1790–1807), a period of expansion (1808–25), and a period of crisis in African supply (1826–30). In order to examine the frequency of kinship relationships among the slave population, we have selected those wills that present the most complete information on the ages, physical conditions, aptitude for work, and kinship and marital ties of slaves, being careful to exclude cases that had only information on kinship but provided no other context for analysis. Our universe consists of 4,113 slaves for the years between 1790 and 1830. It should be noted, however, that these sources recorded only what may be described as first-degree family ties, i.e. those uniting mothers and children, husbands and wives, or couples and their offspring.

As shown in Table 9.1, kinship bonds appear to have been most frequent during the period of stability in the slave trade between 1790 and 1807. At a time when the average annual increase in the number of slaves being imported was only 0.4 per cent, about 35.5 per cent of the slave population recorded in the wills are shown to have had first-degree relatives, although certainly not all such relationships were recorded. Such relationships appear to have been most common on estates with twenty or more slaves, accounting for 42.4 per cent of the slave population. The number of recorded first-degree relationships declined to less than a quarter (24.7 per cent) between 1810 and 1825, apparently reflecting the increased proportion of African-born slaves in the population at a time when the average annual increase of the slave trade approached 2.5 per cent. In this period, there appears to have been little difference in the proportion of slaves identified as having first-degree relatives on either large or small estates. The last surge in imported African slaves between 1826 and 1830, when the average annual increase in the number of imports rose to 3.5 per cent, was matched by an increase in first-degree relatives recorded in the sample of wills. Overall, the proportion of slaves reported to have relations rose from 24.7 per cent to 31.2 per cent. However, the decline in the percentage of first-degree relatives from 35.5 per cent to 24.7 per cent between 1790 and 1807 and 1810 and 1825 and the increase to 31.2 per cent between 1826 and 1830 disguise other trends. For the whole period, the proportion of slaves on small holdings of 2 to 9 slaves who were reported to have near relatives declined from 31.1 per cent to 25.1 per cent, dropping to 23.7 per cent between 1826 and 1830. A similar decline characterized holdings of 10 to 19 slaves, falling from 23.6 per cent between 1790 and 1807 to 20.2 per cent between 1810 and 1825, and hitting a low of 7.8 per cent between 1826 and 1830. By contrast, holdings of 20 slaves or more experienced a precipitous drop from 42.4 per cent between 1790 and 1807 to 25.1 per cent during the period of large-scale importation of slaves, but rebounding to 36.8 per cent between 1826 and 1830.

These fluctuations seem to indicate that the frequency of kinship relations follows a cycle over the three periods and was most fully reflected in holdings of 20 slaves or more. First, there was a period of low slave imports that corresponded with a high incidence of family connections. Then an influx of new arrivals lowered the frequency of kinship. This trend was then reversed as the number of children born to those who had arrived from Africa between 1810 and 1825 had the effect of increasing the incidence of kinship. This increase is reflected in the frequency of kinship connections in the period 1826 to 1830, which reflected the general growth in population, even though the number of African-born slaves was at an all-time high. In any case, at least one in four and perhaps one in three slaves had primary kinship ties that were recorded in the wills.

Perhaps more significant than the increase in the number of births, the imminent abolition of the slave trade led to the restructuring of the trade so that more women were purchased. We have considerable evidence for the increased preference for women. An analysis of post-mortem wills shows that the average price of adult *crioulas* (Brazilian-born captive women) increased 10.2 per cent between 1810 and 1825 and 1826 and 1830, from £28.93 in the 1810 and 1825 period to £31.89 between 1826 and 1830, while the price of adult *crioulos* (Brazilian-born captive men) increased 8.5 per cent, from £34.14 to £37.03. The price of adult slave women from Africa rose 11.9 per cent, from £28.14 to £31.49, while adult slave men from Africa increased in price from £33.36 to £35.01 (a 5 per cent increase). The prices for all women rose by 10.9 per cent; in contrast the average prices for all men increased by only 6.1 per cent. These relative prices suggest that the reproductive potential of slave women had now become a major factor in the determination of slave prices.

As Figure 9.4 reveals, the newly arrived Africans sold in Rio de Janeiro market between 1822 and 1833 tended to be adults and also male. Three out of four new slaves were men, four out of five were adult (from 15 to 40 years old), and among these there were 3.4 men for every woman. Children under the age of 10 or so were a small proportion (4.1 per cent) of the total number of new arrivals; this low number is comparable to the pattern of the slave trade from Luanda and Benguela to Rio de Janeiro in the second half of the eighteenth century, as analysed by Herbert Klein.[2] About 16 per cent of imported slaves were 10 to 14 years old; that is about one in five of the new Africans was under 14 years of age. These figures suggest that slave children were almost always Brazilian born. Our analysis of the

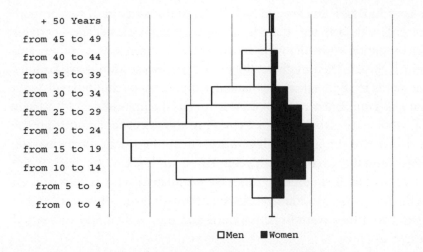

FIGURE 9.4   Age and gender of enslaved Africans arriving in Rio de Janeiro, 1822–33. *Source:* Códice 425 (Registro da Polícia de Saída de Escravos). *Arquivo Nacional, Rio de Janeiro.*

sample of wills allows us to glimpse certain structures that indicate a tendency for slaves to procreate. In the first instance, slave women gave birth earlier than free colonial women, and indeed we suggest that slaves married or lived together to generate children.

Unfortunately, little is known about past Brazilian matrimonial habits, although Maria Bassanezzi has recently tried to systematize the demographic study of this matter.[3] Current research indicates that there were a great number of single people in colonial times. Colonial matrimonial practices were subject to a high degree of segmentation according to colour, ethnic group, national origin and considerable population mobility, which had the combined effect of limiting the frequency of marriage. With respect to the age of marriage, various studies indicate that élite girls tended to marry young. Sheila Faria has shown that such girls married when they were about 16 years old,[4] but other studies suggest that the more common age of marriage was 19 or 20, and even as high as 22 or 24. Whatever the average age, marriage at 19 or 20 (with birth soon after) was earlier than among modern Western Europeans.[5]

Post-mortem wills do not allow us to accurately determine the age when slaves married. However, slave families were established very early, with or without church approval. Wills indicate (by the oldest son's age) that slave women under 29 years of age became pregnant around 20 if they had been born in Brazil and around 22 if brought from Africa. If we compare our records with birth registrations, we obtain a slightly lower age – perhaps closer to reality, since the wills record only children who survived and remained close to their mothers. Robert Slenes, in a study of slave families in Campinas in 1872, calculated that only 50 per cent of children registered in that year's enrolment as firstborn were in fact the first child and it is likely that firstborn are also underrepresented in the documentation from the early decades of the nineteenth century. Given the infant mortality rate, parents probably married between three and six years before the registration of their children's births.[6] We postulate that the captive women from the Rio de Janeiro countryside began to give birth between 14 and 17 years of age if they were Brazilian born and between 16 and 19 years if African born.

It should be noted that an average age at marriage of 19 years for slave women from Africa and 17 years for those born in Brazil indicates that African and Brazilian-born slave women both began to give birth early: six to eight years earlier than English women of the seventeenth and eighteenth centuries, seven to ten years before French women of the eighteenth century, four to six years before white North American women of the mid-nineteenth century, and one to three years before slave women in the 'Old South'.[7] African and *crioula* women gave birth earlier than free Brazilian women, one year earlier on average in the case of African-born women and three years earlier than *crioula* women. Our figures indicate that initial procreation patterns among Rio de Janeiro slaves were similar to those in traditional Africa. Many women married and gave birth soon after puberty – around 15 years of age – in both the African and Brazilian contexts of the early nineteenth century.[8] Thus, it is logically and historically reasonable to deduce that the slave procreation pattern was to a great extent the result of the transplantation and further adjustment of an African cultural pattern.

The post-mortem wills suggest that slaves became pregnant at intervals of about three years (for African-born slaves, there was an additional half year). This period between pregnancies suggests that there was some effort to control procreation, although the source materials do not record children who were stillborn or otherwise died between the births of surviving children. Although the actual incidence of conception may have been less than three years, maybe two years, African-born slaves took longer to become pregnant than Brazilian slave women. This difference indicates that the nursing period may have been extended in Brazil and thereby helped to postpone new pregnancies for three or four years.[9] The pattern appears to be similar to that described by Herbert Klein and Stanley Engerman for Caribbean slave societies (and unlike the North American situation): Brazilian slave women (including *crioulas*) appear to have followed traditional African practices, which would in theory have had negative consequences for general fertility.[10] Thus, we have before us seemingly contradictory patterns: from the young age when reproduction was possible and seems to have begun, we infer an effort or at least a willingness to have children as early as possible, but there were long periods between births, which suggests an effort to avoid procreation. Under these sociological conditions, any urgency to have children would only be manifested through late procreation, reaching the upper limit of women's biological capacity.

Unlike early procreation and long reproduction intervals, which may have been influenced by strong African practices, the age of last conception appears to have diverged from African practices. Sexual abstinence when women became grandmothers may have been common in Africa, apparently lowering the general level of fertility, despite evidence that a few women had children late in their reproductive life.[11] The wills show that the age at which Brazilian slave women last gave birth increased from about 38 between 1790 and 1807 to about 42 between 1810 and 1825 and almost 44 years of age between 1826 and 1830 (see Figure 9.5). Assuming that women in Africa began having children around 15 or 16 years of age, it was possible that a woman could become a grandmother by the time she was 30 or so, and normally her last conception occurred at about this time. The upper limit for the age of reproduction among slaves in Brazil which we have found in our research appears to be higher than was usual in Africa, and moreover seems to have increased.[12]

The variation in ages of last conception seem to reflect phases in the Atlantic slave trade. Slaves gave birth as soon as they reached puberty, avoiding new pregnancies for close to three years. Given this pattern, the sole way of increasing fertility, therefore, was to postpone the time of last conception. This trend became pronounced during the rapid expansion in the Atlantic slave trade after 1807. As Figure 9.5 shows, the variation in age at last conception was a function of the increase of slave imports at Rio de Janeiro. The upward trend in age appears to mirror the anticipated effects of abolition.

One could argue that the propensity to procreate was simply an expression of the atrocious imbalance between the numbers of males and

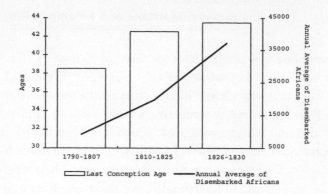

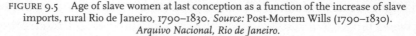

FIGURE 9.5   Age of slave women at last conception as a function of the increase of slave imports, rural Rio de Janeiro, 1790–1830. *Source:* Post-Mortem Wills (1790–1830). *Arquivo Nacional, Rio de Janeiro.*

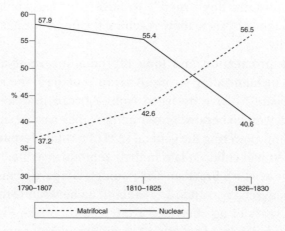

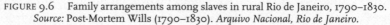

FIGURE 9.6   Family arrangements among slaves in rural Rio de Janeiro, 1790–1830. *Source:* Post-Mortem Wills (1790–1830). *Arquivo Nacional, Rio de Janeiro.*

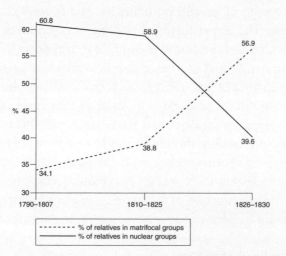

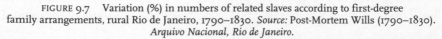

FIGURE 9.7   Variation (%) in numbers of related slaves according to first-degree family arrangements, rural Rio de Janeiro, 1790–1830. *Source:* Post-Mortem Wills (1790–1830). *Arquivo Nacional, Rio de Janeiro.*

females. There is no doubt that this disproportion was one of the most important problems slaves had to cope with when seeking ways to make their lives less painful. In the absence of other evidence we would probably take this imbalance as the best explanation of early reproduction: given the relative scarcity of women, girls should have been available for marriage as soon as they were biologically able to conceive. We think that the sexual imbalance encouraged a certain way of thinking, in which procreation may have been assigned some urgency. The situation of slavery may have been interpreted in ways not dissimilar to those observed for small, isolated communities where the risk of annihilation has sometimes required the establishment of rules to maximize the possibility of reproduction.[13] There is no reason why slave communities too might not have developed mechanisms to achieve the same goal. Procreation was an investment, and its full achievement depended on putting into action many practices arising from the slave experience. Unlike the difficulties facing people in isolated societies, slaves could aim to recreate kinship structures that established their social space in the larger society.

As demonstrated in Figures 9.6 and 9.7, family arrangements of the first degree were either nuclear or matrifocal in almost 95 per cent of cases. The families include legally married couples with or without children (nuclear), and single mothers and their children (matrifocal). Although some mothers were widows or women whose husbands had been sold, most women in the matrifocal category can only be described as being single. Data contained in the wills indicate that between 1790 and 1807, when slave imports were low and the population therefore relatively stable, the nuclear family was dominant. At that period, six in ten family arrangements and six in ten slave relatives lived in nuclear families. However, as the slave traffic boomed after 1807, matrifocal groups increasingly came to form the majority of family arrangements, rising from 37.1 per cent of family units between 1790 and 1807 to 56.5 per cent between 1826 and 1830, while nuclear families declined from 57.9 per cent of family units between 1790 and 1807 to 40.6 per cent between 1826 and 1830. This pattern was mirrored in the numbers of related slaves in nuclear and matrifocal groups (see Figure 9.7).

The increase in matrifocal family units suggests that many children were 'illegitimate', which was not only a characteristic of the slave community but was common even among the free population. In the second half of the eighteenth century in Vila Rica (Minas Gerais), illegitimacy rates were very high. Approximately 65 per cent of the free

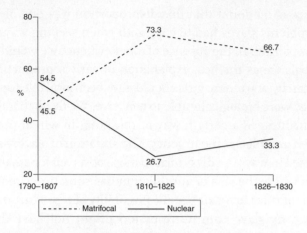

FIGURE 9.8   Family arrangements among slaves on plantations of fewer than 20 slaves, rural Rio de Janeiro, 1790–1830. *Source:* Post-Mortem Wills (1790–1830).
Arquivo Nacional, Rio de Janeiro.

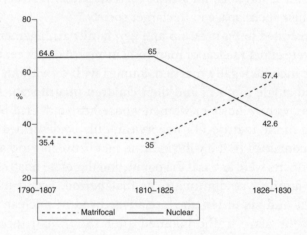

FIGURE 9.9   Family arrangements among slaves on plantations of 20 or more slaves, rural Rio de Janeiro, 1790–1830. *Source:* Post-Mortem Wills (1790–1830).
Arquivo Nacional, Rio de Janeiro.

population were involved in unstable relationships that did not involve marriage and hence resulted in high levels of illegitimacy.[14] However, illegitimacy is a social construct, and in reality there were high levels of illegitimacy during almost all periods in rural Rio de Janeiro. Slave girls became pregnant, and only then, if ever, was there a search for church approval.[15] Hence any evidence for the existence of slave families is remarkable and probably does not fully capture the extent to which enslaved Africans and their descendants were able to establish lasting relationships.

However, if high rates of illegitimacy were not peculiar to slaves, the particular forms assumed by their family arrangements according to the fluctuations of the Atlantic slave trade allow us to examine the problem of family socialization within and outside the colonial norm. The mechanisms of maintaining and reproducing political stability in this slave society are often underestimated; almost always the focus is on the generic violence underpinning the slave regime. Slavery, based on the imprisonment of foreigners, demanded countless tools for integrating and managing the servile outsiders, who none the less were still human. Legal marriage was one of the methods of managing assimilation. Of course, slaves who sought Catholic marriage not only united themselves before God, but recognized their own servility. Slave society had to integrate the foreigners culturally, and matrimonial consecration was suitable for that purpose. In this way the enslaved gave a new meaning to their bondage within the cultural heritage of the Christian world.[16] Marriage was a powerful tool for thinning the thick coat of attitudes inappropriate to the slave condition. In brief, marriage gave rules to life.

As our sources reveal, the institution of marriage seems to have operated reasonably well during the stable period when the slave trade was relatively small. Most family groups then were made up of legally married couples (with or without children). During the period of economic expansion and the massive introduction of newly enslaved Africans, however, matrifocal groups became more common and even prevailed. The mechanisms of reproduction during the period after 1807 were fragile, although family groups continued to function.

As seen in Figures 9.8 and 9.9, first-degree family arrangements and how these changed over time varied according to the size of plantation. Considering the phases of the slave trade, and noticing that between 1826 and 1830 imports of Africans attained their peak, it can be seen that large and small plantations reacted to the increase in disembarkations in the same way: in both, matrifocal groups became more common than nuclear families, suggesting that fewer men were able to remain with the mothers of their children but that families continued to stay together otherwise. On small plantations (with fewer than 20 slaves), at the first sign of expansion in the slave trade, matrifocal groups began to predominate, which may indicate that these plantations contributed to the expansion in the first instance through the sale of male slaves, which would have been important in liquidating debts. Thus matrifocal arrangements increased from 45.5 per cent of all families on estates with fewer than 20 slaves between 1790 and 1807 to 73.3 per cent of all families between 1810 and 1825, before declining slightly to 66.7 per cent between 1826 and 1830. This increase in matrifocal families probably indicates that small groupings of slaves, which had been subject to manorial attitudes, were under severe pressure, as reflected in the increasing absence of males in family units, who appear to have been sold off.

On large plantations, matrifocal arrangements remained secondary much longer than on small estates; 35.4 per cent of family arrangements were matrifocal between 1790 and 1807, and this proportion remained virtually the same from 1810 to 1825, increasing to 57.4 per cent of family arrangements only between 1826 and 1830. The resilence of nuclear families on the large estates seems to reflect the fact that men were retained on these plantations during the period of expansion. Hence changes in family patterns seem to reflect an internal slave trade that responded in tandem with the increased import of new slaves from Africa. Presumably, smaller slave holdings could do without legal marriage more easily than larger estates, where the church was more likely to concentrate its efforts and there was a greater need to find mechanisms for controlling the slave population. Indeed, among the slaves belonging to great estates, only when the Atlantic trade reached high levels did the matrifocal arrangements become predominant, revealing the limits of matrimony as a tool for integrating the mass of slaves but none the less demonstrating the importance of gender ratios in understanding how the slave regime had changed over time.

Marriages were the most frequent family ties among slaves. About 30 to 40 per cent of all relationships of any age involved married people. If children are excluded from the sample of related slaves, the range among adult slaves who were married varied from 50 to 57 per cent of total adult relationships.[17] Because of their preponderance in the population, there were more African-born slaves who married than Brazilian-born slaves, especially in the rural areas of Rio, where Africans were the majority of the population over age 15 in the early nineteenth century. Because a large portion of this population was male, moreover, women were in great demand and greatly courted. Mixed marriages across various ethnic and regional boundaries appear to have been common. Because of the high proportion of men, we might assume that mixed marriages tended to increase as the number of landings rose, but as shown in Figure 9.10, the

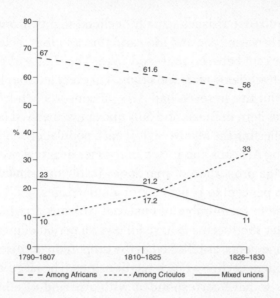

FIGURE 9.10   Slave marriages according to spouses' origin, rural Rio de Janeiro, 1790–1830.
Source: Post-Mortem Wills (1790–1830). *Arquivo Nacional, Rio de Janeiro.*

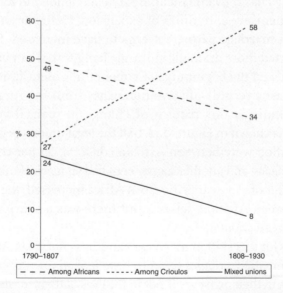

FIGURE 9.11   Slave marriages according to spouses' origin, Freguesia de Jacarepaguá,
1790–1830. *Source:* Livro de casamentos de escravos da freguesia de Nossa Senhora do Loreto de
Jacarepaguá, 1790–1830. *Arquivo da Cúria Metropolitana do Rio de Janeiro.*

percentage of mixed marriages actually declined slightly from 23 per cent to 21.2 per cent between 1790 and 1807 and 1810 and 1825, before dropping in half to 11 per cent between 1826 and 1830. The choice of partners was guided by selective criteria related to origin. For every ten couples identified in the wills, from five to seven had African consorts, while one, two or three were slaves born in Brazil, and only one or two involved both Africans and *crioulos*, reflecting the relative size of each population.[18] Whereas both marriage among Africans and mixed marriages declined over the period 1790 to 1830, the proportion of marriages involving *crioulos* more than tripled from 10 per cent to 33 per cent of all marriages.

The increase in the number of enslaved Africans arriving in the Rio countryside after 1807 seems to have followed a period of great fluidity in marriage arrangements, as reflected in the proportion of mixed marriages and the subsequent decline in such relationships. The large influx of new arrivals seems to have corresponded with a period of ethnic mixing, whereas periods of low imports may have encouraged the retention of African survivals in relation to the choice of marriage partner. We have already seen a feature of this change in the variation in the types of first-degree family arrangements. The decrease in both purely African and mixed marriages has only one meaning: *crioulos* tended to form a closed circle among themselves. In times of expansion, rivalry among Africans and *crioulos* for marriage partners seems to have increased. Exogamous marriage reflected more dramatic cultural changes that can be described as 'creolization' and the beginnings of super-ethnic identifications.

The ecclesiastic records of slave marriages from the rural parish of Jacarepaguá confirms this pattern of change in marital and kinship relationships. As shown in Figure 9.11, half the legal unions between slaves from 1790 to 1807 were between African consorts, 27 per cent of them were among *crioulos*, and another 24 per cent had spouses of mixed origins. After the number of slaves arriving from Africa increased, the number of marriages between Africans fell off, but there was a sharp increase in marriages between *crioulos*.

The reasons for this shift in marriage patterns is not clear. As the arrival of Africans intensified, *crioulos* seem to have looked for ways to establish their legitimacy, in their own eyes if not in the eyes of their masters, through legal means. At least formal marriage required official recognition and thereby helped distinguish *crioulos* from African-born slaves whose patterns of sexual partnership and cohabitation reflected customs that originated in Africa. The relative increase in the increment of marriages among *crioulos* occurred at the same time that there was a decline in mixed unions. Whereas between 1790 and 1807, *crioulos* were likely to seek partners from the African-born population, and Jacarepaguá *crioulos* were just as likely to marry Africans as other *crioulos*, by the 1820s *crioulos* were likely to marry their own at least seven times more often than an African. This trend suggests that *crioulos* may have been seeking a haven from the slave system within a network of kinship. The marked increase in African arrivals may have threatened the customary world of the *crioulo* population and the limited rights and privileges which they thought they may have had in more stable times. Legalized matrimony provided another means of safeguarding their security and hence confirming their identity within Brazilian slave society. After all, *crioulos*, since they were born in bondage, were not obliged to marry, but they could do so without causing any damage to the slave order, and indeed thereby could benefit from the supposedly Christian commitment of the Catholic Church to tend to the spiritual needs of the enslaved.

Crioulos responded in a hostile way to the increasing presence of Africans. The fracturing of family structures, as reflected in the increase in matrifocal families, may have been a factor. Africans had to adjust to the special interests and relatively greater power and influence of both whites and *crioulos*. In the period of low slave imports, new arrivals had tended to find partners from the same ethnic group or region of origin. Only one in five unions among Africans united people from different communities such as Congo and Mina or Caçanje and Mozambican. The same pattern of ethnic intermarriage was in effect in Bahia in the second half of the eighteenth century, according to Stuart Schwartz.[19] Intermarriage among different ethnic groups may have been the norm during periods of few slave imports. In the time of many disembarkations, however, the situation was inverted. From 1808 to 1825, for example, when many Africans arrived, almost four in five unions linked different ethnic groups. In fact, this was the time when 'the African' emerged as a social figure and the ethnic boundaries among African-born slaves were softened.

As a matter of fact, many slaves were identified as Cabinda, Angola, Rebolo, Ambaca, Moange, Benguela, Congo, Monjolo, Caçanje, Macua, Mozambican, Quilimane and Mina, terms which identified the port of embarkation in Africa or the coastal region from where the slaves came. There is no doubt these are inaccurate designations of ethnicity or place of origin. Indeed they hid from their masters, because of their vast ethnographic ignorance, a mosaic of ethnic differences. None of the captives was properly 'African', nor did they see each other that way, as we can infer from their choices of partners of the same origin in times of stable imports. But they had been forcibly drawn from many different communities, perhaps selectively distributed among various slave holdings in order to suppress old solidarities. With a hunger for women, the predominantely male slave population from Africa was less interested in maintaining inherited cultural singularities than in finding spouses. The resulting relationships, often severed through sale, were destined to disappear as matrimonial unions, therefore reinforcing the tendency towards a new identity based in Brazil. The expansion in the slave trade elevated social tensions to high levels among the slaves, sometimes reinforcing nascent family ties but also promoting ethnic barriers that can be traced back to Africa.

The analysis of average differences in spouses' ages, considering age groups and origins, allows us to verify some other norms by which the slave matrimonial customs were ruled. They are full of lessons about slavery. But first, consider some further data about slave families collected by Stuart Schwartz on the Santana sugar plantation, located in Bahia, in the second quarter of the eighteenth century. Schwartz found two slave population enrolments at the plantation, the first dated 1731 and the second 1752. In 1731, the estate was managed by Father Manuel de Figueiredo, who thought it was unnecessary to legalize slave matrimonial relationships, despite his supposed clerical commitments and as shocking as it was to the subsequent managers of the property. According to Schwartz, however, the priest acted in a manner not unlike other masters who also ignored the religion of their slaves and felt no compulsion to convert them. As a consequence, unfortunately, there are no records of family relationships.

In 1731 there were 57 dwellings serving as slave quarters and 178 slaves, of whom only 26 were officially married. Few had received the Christian sacrament, but most 'lived in units including a man and a woman declared as sexual partners or with ages that make this relationship probable'.[20] What existed on the Santana plantation, therefore, was very similar to what we found in Rio de Janeiro during stable times: slave matrimonial unions tended to assume the shape of nuclear family groups – father, mother and children. Schwartz noticed that some dwelling arrangements had a strange shape, and he was not wrong when he assumed that this was a consequence of slavery. There were, he found, 'residential groups composed of one or more elderly women and a young single man . . . Those units seem to have involved arrangements in which aged, less productive women were designated to cook and clean for newly arrived single men.'[21] That the elderly slave women were there for that purpose is questionable, as we will see. But there is another notable feature of the first enrolment: there were considerable age differences between partners. One man, for instance, was twenty years older than his wife; another, thirty years. One woman was seventeen years older than her husband. As a general rule, the older partner was male.

By 1752 many things had changed since the 1731 enrolment. Santana management was now religious. A policy to encourage legal matrimony had produced notable results – considering both frequency and form. Before, there had been ten dwellings headed only by women; twenty-one years later, there were barely three, presumably widows. The average age difference between partners resembled a 'typical European standard', according to Schwartz; that is, it had fallen from 7.2 to 4.1 years.[22] There were no more old men married to young women, or women more than five years older than their partners.

Figures 9.12 to 9.17 show the differences in the ages of spouses, both African and *crioulo*, in rural Rio in three periods, 1790 to 1807, 1810 to 1825 and 1826 to 1830. A comparison of these charts reveals that during stable times, both African and Brazilian male slaves 24 years of age or more tended to be older than their wives. From 1790 to 1807, wives, from 15 to 44 years of age, were generally not much younger than their partners, although the older the male partner, the greater the age difference between the man and his wife. We see this asymmetrical movement as a trend: the age difference rose as men grew older, especially among *crioulos*. Men tended to marry younger women, and during the period of large-scale immigration after 1807, elder men tended to control access to the fertile women. At this time, competition seemed to favour the oldest slaves born in Brazil.

We found a similar age asymmetry between elder women (above 45 years of age) and very young men (from 15 to 25 years): the older the women, the bigger the age difference between them and their partners, and the younger the men, the older their wives tended to be. The monopoly of the elder men over fertile women was so strong that young slaves could never access such women. The resemblance to what happened on the Santana sugar plantation (even when managed by a religious man with little concern for the souls of slaves) is not, of course, a coincidence. According to Schwartz, the special tasks assigned to older slave women

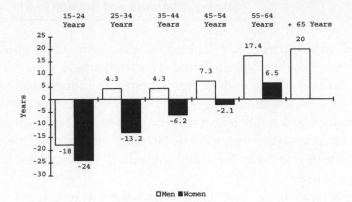

FIGURE 9.12   Differences in ages of African spouses, rural Rio de Janeiro, 1790–1807.
Source: Post-Mortem Wills (1790–1830). *Arquivo Nacional, Rio de Janeiro.*

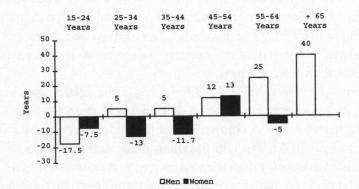

FIGURE 9.13   Differences in ages of *crioulo* spouses, rural Rio de Janeiro, 1790–1807.
Source: Post-Mortem Wills (1790–1830). *Arquivo Nacional, Rio de Janeiro.*

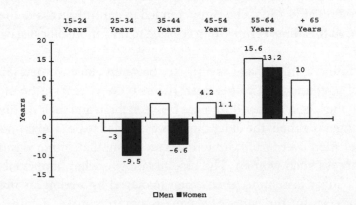

FIGURE 9.14   Differences in ages of African spouses, rural Rio de Janeiro, 1810–1825.
Source: Post-Mortem Wills (1790–1830). *Arquivo Nacional, Rio de Janeiro.*

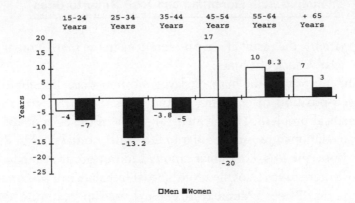

FIGURE 9.15   Differences in ages of *crioulo* spouses. rural Rio de Janeiro, 1810–1825.
Source: Post-Mortem Wills (1790–1830). *Arquivo Nacional, Rio de Janeiro.*

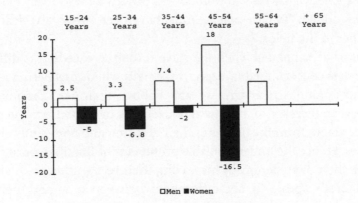

FIGURE 9.16   Differences in ages of African spouses, rural Rio de Janeiro, 1826–1830.
Source: Post-Mortem Wills (1790–1830). *Arquivo Nacional, Rio de Janeiro.*

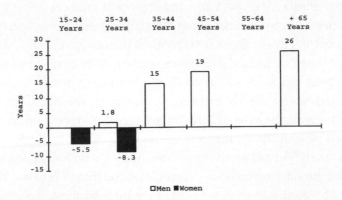

FIGURE 9.17   Differences in ages of *crioulo* spouses, rural Rio de Janeiro, 1826–1830.
Source: Post-Mortem Wills (1790–1830). *Arquivo Nacional, Rio de Janeiro.*

were apparently the result of slave preferences in the matrimonial market and the relative lack of women.

As the minority in the mass of slaves, women were thought to be in a privileged position in choosing partners, as if mating was merely a mathematical problem. The asymetrical shape of the ages of spouses in marriage relationships was peculiar to the matrimonial pool in Rio slave society. None the less, connubial unions did not occur at random; they were not a mere function of the severe sexual imbalance or some culturally accepted rules. Esteban Montejo (an ex-slave who spent his life hidden in the Cuban forests in order to avoid re-enslavement) probably referred to such rules: 'The elders themselves did not want the youngest to get to know women. They said that only when a man was twenty-five would he have experience.' Access to women was otherwise effectively denied. As Montejo added: 'To have one, he must have been twenty-five years old or catch her in the fields.'[23]

But what happened when the slave trade increased? It is difficult to obtain data concerning this impact, especially when considering marriage patterns among Africans. As we stated above, their demographic profile suggests an increase in matrifocal households in response to the removal of male slaves from the homes of their children and apparently also their spouses. Hence the understandable propensity of Brazilian-born slaves to tighten their own identity by increasing their recognition of kinship.

Generally speaking, age differences between men and their wives decreased with the intensity of the slave trade. Young African men reported married between 1826 and 1830 were older than their wives, whereas earlier they tended to be married to older women or not at all. Because the increase in landings meant the absorption of young Africans, it weakened the control of elders over the matrimonial market. Previously, the importance of elders in sanctioning marriage arrangements had reinforced kinship connections. Their intervention in relationships probably also mediated potential friction over scarce women. At its best, elders had served as a pacifying influence within the slave community, but when the number of new arrivals swelled to significant numbers, the decisions of elders failed to check the rise of tension within the slave community. The expanded slave trade seems to have exacerbated the struggle by men to find a woman. The old matrimonial mechanisms no longer worked all the time, and the slave community entered a period that effectively constituted a state of social war over women, in which women, as a rule, were increasingly forced into unions after being trapped in the fields. There was increasing competition between African and Brazilian-born slaves, and hence fewer marriages between these two groups. Some slaves certainly escaped from the contradictions in the slave system that are revealed in the changing patterns of family and kin relationships by running away, but our sources are not able to reveal anything about such individuals. None the less, this exploration of social relationships among slaves demonstrates the complex ways in which slaves reacted to their bondage, and the ways in which kinship and marriage patterns reflected the changing conditions of the slave regime of rural Rio de Janeiro.

Notes

1 Gilberto Freyre, *Casa-grande e senzala* (Rio de Janeiro, 1989); Eugene D. Genovese, *A terra prometida (o mundo que os escravos criaram)* (Rio de Janeiro, 1988); originally published in English, 1972, *The World the Slaves Made* (New York).
2 Herbert S. Klein, *The Middle Passage* (Princeton, NJ, 1978), pp. 254–6.
3 Maria S. C. B. Bassanezzi, 'Considerações sobre os estudos do celibato e da idade de casar no passado brasileiro', in *Anais do IX encontro de estudos populacionais*, 3 vols (Caxambú, Brazil, 1994), 1:381–96.
4 Sheila de Castro Faria, 'A colônia em movimento: Fortuna e família no cotidiano colonial' (PhD thesis, Universidade Federal Fluminense, Brazil, 1994).
5 Herbert G. Gutman, *The Black Family in Slavery and Freedom, 1750–1925* (New York, 1976), pp. 50ff; Maria L. Marcílio, 'Sistemas demográficos no Brasil do século XIX', in Marcílio (ed.), *População e sociedade* (Petrópolis, Brazil, 1984), p. 195 (hereafter cited as *População*).
6 Robert W. Slenes, 'Escravidão e família: Padrões de casamento e estabilidade familiar numa comunidade escrava (Campinas, século XIX)', *Estudos Econômicos* 17 (1987), p. 220.
7 Gutman, *Black Family*, p. 50.
8 Patrick Manning, *Slavery and African Life: Occidental, Oriental, and African Slave Trade* (Cambridge and New York, 1990), p. 55; David Eltis, *Economic Growth and the Ending of the Transatlantic Slave Trade* (New York, 1987), p. 65.
9 *Ibid.*
10 Herbert S. Klein and Stanley L. Engerman, 'A demografia dos escravos americanos', in *População*, pp. 208–27.
11 Manning, *Slavery*, p. 55; Eltis, *Economic Growth*, p. 65.
12 See Michael Anderson, *Aproximaciones a la historia de la familia occidental (1500–1914)* (Madrid, 1988), p. 10.
13 See Claude Meillassoux, *Mulheres, celeiros e capitais* (Porto, 1977), part 1; also published in English, *Maidens, Meal and Money* (Cambridge, 1981).
14 Iraci del Nero Costa, *Vila Rica: População (1729–1826)* (São Paulo, 1979), p. 227; see also Renato P. Venâncio, 'Nos limites da sagrada família: Ilegitimidade e casamento no Brasil colonial', in Ronaldo Vainfas (ed.), *História da sexualidade no Brasil* (Rio de Janeiro, 1986), pp. 107–23; and Luiz Mott, *Escravidão, homossexualidade e demonologia* (São Paulo, 1988), pp. 52ff.
15 See José R. Góes, *O cativeiro imperfeito* (Vitória, 1993), pp. 184–5. See also Manolo Garcia Florentino and José R. Goés, *A Paz das Senzalas* (Rio de Janeiro, 1997).

16 Robert W. Slenes, 'Malungu, ngoma vem! África coberta e descoberta no Brasil', *Revista USP* 12 (1991–2), pp. 48–67.

17 *Post-Mortem Wills* (1790–1830), Arquivo Nacional, Rio de Janeiro.

18 *Ibid.*

19 Stuart B. Schwartz, *Segredos internos* (São Paulo, 1988), pp. 319ff.

20 *Ibid.*, p. 323.

21 *Ibid.*

22 *Ibid.*

23 Miguel Barnet, *Memórias de um cimarrón* (São Paulo, 1986), p. 40.

= 10 =

Female Enslavement and Gender Ideologies in the Caribbean

Hilary McD. Beckles

'Modern' slave societies in the Caribbean facilitated a revolutionary restructuring of traditional gender representations and produced some unique features of their own.[1] The institutional design of Caribbean slavery, particularly its cultural specificities, significantly affected the (re)making of gender identities of males and females. Individuals evolved self-identities within the context of the gender orders they encountered – and often contested – and a wide range of strikingly unstable circumstances gave rise to an organized ideology of gender. With the constant reordering and redefinition of conditions and terms of social living – and dying – gender representations were oftentimes perceived as paradoxical and contradictory. This indicates the considerable fluidity of ideological readings of slavery and constitutes a barometer of the turbulence in the construction of the gender order.[2]

The methodological approach chosen here explores the changes in gender identities and representations, and their ideological effects, by visiting three historical sites where gender discourses seem to have been particularly effective in determining social relations and popular perceptions of identity. First, the gender order of West Africa in the period when enslaved Africans were forcibly removed to the Americas is contextualized in terms of pressures exerted upon it by forces endemic to the wider Atlantic political economy. Second, the effects on work and reproduction of the ideological constitution of gender identities within the Caribbean plantation complex are examined. Third, the instability of gender representations in the increasingly adverse circumstances of sugar production and the global political challenge to the legitimacy of slavery in the early nineteenth century is presented as a consequence of changes in women's relations to production and reproduction.

Sex distribution patterns within the Atlantic slave complex were as much the result of gender divisions in traditional West African societies as of modernist discourses of work, gender and social life in colonizing Europe. Most persons used as slaves in West Africa during the period from 1500 to 1800 were female.[3] This was also the case in the older sugar plantation colonies of the West Indies between 1800 and 1833. Before 1800, however, the overwhelming majority of slaves in the West Indies had been male. The mid-eighteenth century witnessed a major transition in demographic structure brought about by a new focus on the female in the conception, design and reproduction of the slave systems in the West Indies, which was the result of discernible social and managerial imperatives.[4] After the 1750s, the established Caribbean custom of purchasing and retaining male slaves gave way to a trend toward females that transformed sex structures and modified gender discourses.

Barbados had attained the unique status of having a female majority in its slave population by the end of the seventeenth century. The Leeward Islands came to share this characteristic by the end of the eighteenth. Sugar planters in these colonies gradually moved towards privileging females through a strategic plan to promote the natural reproduction of the labour force, and the effects of the demographic shift on gender representations and identities were considerable. Obtaining insight into the causes and nature of the conflict and instability in these slave societies therefore requires the application of gender-derived forms of knowledge.

New World slavery represented something altogether unfamiliar to African males and females. It rejected and restructured the gender attitudes and identities legitimized by their traditions. Labour ideologies in most West African societies distinctly gendered certain types of work and relations of power, but these were reconfigured within the Caribbean context. It is therefore problematical to suppose that there was a fundamental continuity between the forms of slavery and legitimization encountered by Africans in their traditional societies and in the New World. The gender implications of West Indian plantation slavery were culturally transformative. Hence, it is important to identify the nature of the changes and to explain their implications for gender roles and identities.[5]

Analyses of varieties of Atlantic slavery have tended to focus on criteria like degree of intensity or type of involuntary servitude. Differences in property relations in particular have been used to differentiate between modernist Caribbean chattel slavery and traditional forms of slavery in Africa. But notions of kinlessness, marginalization, exclusion and subjection to others have been privileged by cultural anthropologists engaged in comparative studies of slavery in societies in different regions in Africa or in African societies at different times. Neither approach, however, has claimed that these criteria produce mutually exclusive categories. Rather, they have sought to identify what may reasonably be described as 'principal' and 'secondary' characteristics of this mode of production.[6]

In West African societies during the period of Atlantic slavery, the majority of persons described as slaves were female. The reason for this circumstance lies in the functions performed by women within the gender order of these mostly patriarchal societies. In the large internal slave market, demand was mostly for women and children. Women were also traded through the Sahara into the North African Muslim labour markets. In contrast, the non-African Atlantic market was supplied mostly with males. One compelling explanation for this pattern is that West African societies did not easily absorb male slaves. Many males captured in internecine warfare were executed by the state; limited numbers of men were retained for military rather than agricultural or industrial purposes. The majority of captives in war and other forms of political conflict who were retained and integrated into local socio-economic systems were woman and children.[7]

The greater local demand for female slaves was reflected in the prices paid for them in coastal and interior societies. Philip Curtin has shown, for example, that whereas in Senegambia African traders supplied men and women to European buyers at the same price, in the interior agricultural belt women slaves were sold for twice the price of male slaves. It is often stated that women slaves were preferred because of their biological reproductive functions, but this is only a minor part of the explanation. African men with property did demand wives and concubines who were kinless within their immediate social space and whose progeny had little or no claim to property rights or status within the inheritance system. But such kinless women and their children were secured by patriarchal élites primarily as workers, and they were marginalized mainly because of their alienability as marketable labour.[8]

The ability of the patriarchal system to absorb, assimilate and subjugate greater numbers of kinless women is the critical part of a more systemic explanation. The more expansive the economic system, civil society and state apparatus were, the greater was the demand for female slaves. The wide range of possible forms of absorption of kinless women magnified the numbers any society could carry. In most West African societies wealth was accumulated by the state and by individuals principally through the recruitment and retention of such labour. Consequently, women in these societies had an enormous need to maintain their 'free' status. Even within the kinship system there was significant pressure to alienate women for social offences and thus create situations that could easily lead to their enslavement. While it was possible for some slave women to gain their freedom through gradual assimilation into a kinship system, a greater tendency existed, on account of the demand for female slaves, for free women to be denied kinship rights and to be marginalized into the pool of transferable slaves.

The principal objective was to generate servile female labour for productive functions. Slavery, concubinage and patriarchal dominance assured that women were centred as the principal productive agency within the gender order. Women worked, and the majority of their labour hours were dedicated to agriculture, as they are now. A recent survey shows that in the sub-Saharan region women still contribute between 60 and 70 per cent of the labour within the agricultural sector.[9] Women planted and harvested crops, looked after animals and engaged in all labour-intensive work such as crafts and domestic service. They were expected to perform agricultural labour, which was understood within the dominant gendered division of labour as 'woman work'.

As well as supplying their owners with socio-sexual benefits, female slaves were used in economic activities as traders, cultivators, craft workers, domestics and were also expected by male and female élites to reduce the demand for the intensive-labour services of free women. Hard labour, intensive and of low status, became considered by West Africans as 'woman work', beneath men's social standing within the gender order. With respect to agricultural labour, free West African men considered themselves privileged, with female slaves the 'lowest creatures on God's earth'.[10]

Since material development in most West African societies was based upon agricultural activity, production and productivity expansion required the aggressive integration and engagement of women slaves. Meillassoux has shown that in these societies 'women were valued above all as workers'. Claire Robertson and Martin A. Klein have argued that since 'women's work in Africa was generally the less desirable labor-intensive, low status work', increasing production depended on acquiring female labour. Hence, 'the value of women slaves was based on a sexual division of labor which assigned much of the productive labor to women'.[11]

In these societies the progeny of female slaves were claimed by their owners. Slave owners could also secure the right to the labour of slaves' children when the fathers were outside their sphere of legal influence, although the situation was not so clear when the father was himself a slave owner and a man of influence within the society. The biological reproduction of slavery that centred around women was as complicated a process as its ideological reproduction within the gender order.

Caribbean slavery launched a direct assault on traditional West African gender orders. To begin with, significantly fewer black women than black men entered the Atlantic slave trade. The available records of European slave traders demonstrate this point forcefully. Klein's comprehensive analysis of the records of Dutch slave traders, who in the seventeenth century also supplied French, Spanish and English colonies, shows that only 38 per cent of Africans shipped were female. The adult sex ratio for Dutch traders was 187 men for every 100 women, and the child sex ratio was 193 boys for every 100 girls. Danish records reveal a similarly gendered cargo (36 per cent female); these comprised sex ratios of 186 men to 100 women and 145 boys to 100 girls. Using a more broadly based sample of British slave-trade records, Klein found a similar preference for males and hence discrimination against females is discernible (see Table 10.1).[12]

Table 10.1 Average sex ratios of adults shipped in the English slave trade to the West Indies 1791–98[13]

Region in West Africa	Sex ratio (males per 100 females)	Number of shipments
Senegambia	210	5
Sierra Leone	210	29
Windward Coast	208	15
Gold Coast	184	26
Bight of Benin	187	2
Bight of Biafra	138	79
Congo-Angola	217	60
Unknown	188	56
Average	183	272

The general pattern is clear. With only slight variations from Senegambia to Angola, between 65 and 75 per cent of all slaves shipped from the western African coast were males. This pattern indicates the tendency of western African societies to retain their traditional commitments to the dominant gender order, in which men were considered more dispensable from internal processes of social and economic activity than women.

The Atlantic slave trade, however, carried to West Indian plantations not only measurable units of labour but also gender identities and ways of thinking about gender. Early in the West Indies, enslaved African men formed the social majority on plantations, but many were pressed into forms of labour which were gendered as woman work. The social implication of this development was that the Caribbean became the site of an early modern clash between two formally contradictory gender orders – European and West African – in which the potency of African gender ideologies was tested against the production needs of colonial capitalism. Managerial power was held by European males, who had views on gender and the sexual division of labour that differed from those of African males. Both, however, shared many attitudes towards masculinity and the relation of 'woman' to patriarchal power.

Englishmen, in particular, sought a coherent articulation of gender representation, sharply distinguishing between different categories of women and work. White women described as 'ladies' were not expected to labour in the fields or to perform any 'demeaning' physical tasks. 'Ladies' were identified by class, for the thousands of white female indentured servants imported from the British Isles between 1624 and 1680 worked in gangs on the cotton, tobacco and sugar plantations alongside their male counterparts and enslaved Africans. It was not until the late seventeenth century that English planters, beginning to add race to their thinking about gender, finally implemented the policy that no white woman was to work in plantation labour gangs. This ideologically driven initiative to isolate white womanhood from plantation field work reflected the social needs of patriarchy to idealize the white woman as a symbol of white supremacy, moral authority and sexual purity. The patriarchal ideology of white supremacy required the social isolation of all white women, irrespective of class, from black men in order to minimize the dreaded possibility of miscegenation.

The space thus vacated within the labour ranks had to be filled. White men believed that black men were best equipped for the physical task of constructing frontier plantations but that black women were better prepared for the subsequent maintenance of efficient production. They did not share the black man's view that field work was woman work. Colonial managers therefore used the brutality of the death threat in order to impose upon black men a work regime that ran counter to their gender identity and consciousness. Black men found the reversal of sex roles a major challenge to their masculine identity, and they responded with both outright violence and demands for entry into prestigious, non-agricultural occupations. By the mid-eighteenth century, the artisanal, supervisory labour aristocracy had become dominated by males; so, too, the visible organizational military vanguard of plantation-based anti-slavery rebellions.

As the frontier receded, the centring of black women within the slave complex occurred in two stages. First, by the mid-seventeenth century, slave owners legislated the principle of matrilineal reproduction of slave status. This provided that only the offspring of slave women were born into slavery. All children at birth took the same legal status as their mothers. Womanhood was thus legally constituted as a reproductive device that offered the slave system continuity and functionality. Slave owners agreed that the white race must not be reduced to chattel slavery, so the gender identity of white women could not be linked to enslavement and only the offspring of black and 'coloured' women could be born into slavery. On arrival in the West Indies, therefore, African women were placed strategically in the labour supply mechanism in order to restrict access to freedom. By distancing the white woman from the black man (a principal objective of race discourse) while exposing the black woman to all men, the patriarchy hoped to ensure that free-born children from the black race would always be a very small minority.

The second stage was the adoption of the natural reproduction of slaves as an important strategy for maintaining the supply of labour. Because women were a minority in the slave trade and many of them 'had already used up some of their potential fecundity by the time they had arrived,' slave populations in the Caribbean 'could only have experienced a negative growth rate'.[14] This fact was not well understood by slave owners, but over time they problematized the negative growth rates of blacks and produced an extensive discursive literature about it. As they debated demographic trends and patterns, concluding colony by colony that natural reproduction was cheaper and more consistent with 'progressive' managerial policies, owners bombarded the slave woman with new gender representations in an ideological frenzy.

Plantation slavery, therefore, was not just a system of material production and human reproduction. Work and social relations on the estates also contributed to the reproduction of significant social categories such as 'male' and 'female'. Work constituted the context within which the normative expectations attached to labour were gendered. The work regime thus had as much to do with the reproduction of the gender order as with the production of sugar and other agricultural commodities. Field work came to be viewed by black males as slave work rather than women's work; it could be assigned to any blacks but to no white women. In an ideological construct that eventually created an escape hatch for landless white males, field work and other forms of unskilled manual labour were deemed consistent with the 'essential nature' of blacks. These shifts of class, race and gender relations within the division of labour are indicative of West Indian planters' capacity for conceptualizing the nature of their social world and formulating hegemonic means of managing its paradoxical and contradictory tendencies.

Africans arriving in the West Indies were subjected to a process of physical acclimatization as well as regenderization generally referred to as 'seasoning'. During this initial phase of two to three years, they were at first protected from the physical rigours of plantation life. The objective of this policy was to allow slaves time to recover their physical and psychological strength, build up some immunity in the new disease environment, and learn the political economy of the new gender order. Their induction into the gender culture was at once an ideological, biological and labour apprenticeship.

Slave owners in the West Indies were familiar with the gender traditions of agriculture in West Africa. They understood that black women could be thrown into the deep end of the labour regime and be productive. Their belief that there were no productivity differentials between the sexes explains in large measure their refusal to shelter black women from the most arduous physical tasks. Mature women hoed the soil, dug drains, cut and bundled canes, planted new canes, carried baskets of manure to the fields, and performed other physically demanding tasks. Younger women did what was considered light work, such as weeding, grass picking, tending cattle and miscellaneous plantation tasks. Female children looked after stocks, carried water to the fields and performed other tasks.

The egalitarian labour regimes that the women experienced formed the context within which gender ideologies were constructed to promote the political economy of the colonial enterprise. The gender representation of black women was formalized in ways that offered coherence to the relations between sex, labour productivity and capital accumulation. The colonial gender discourse assaulted traditional concepts of womanhood in both Europe and Africa and sought to redefine notions of black feminine identity. The black woman was conceived as essentially 'non-feminine' in so far as primacy was placed upon her alleged physical strength, aggressive carriage and sturdiness. Pro-slavery writers presented her as devoid of the feminine tenderness and graciousness in which they wrapped the white woman. Although her capacity for strenuous work belied their explanations of the high rates of mortality and of crippling injuries that characterized enslavement, those were mentioned only in order to portray her as clumsy, brutish and ignorant of the scientific facts about bodily functions. She was represented as ideally suited to manual labour, which itself was represented as part of a wider civilizing social experience. Edward Long, an eighteenth-century pro-slavery ideologue in Jamaica, had no doubt that the black woman was a perfect brute, though one upon which the plantation's future rested. Her low fertility was for him one more feature that indicated her essentially non-feminine identity.[15]

Defeminization of the black woman, recast as the 'Amazon', allowed slave owners to justify her subjugation to a destructive social and material environment. In the slavery discourse she was said to be able to 'drop' children at will, work without recuperation, manipulate at ease the physical environment of the sugar estate and be more productive than men. These opinions articulated by white males were contradicted, however, by the evidence of commonplace miscegenation, and Long's text also reveals the threat of ideological subversion posed by white men's sexual attraction to black women. Their 'goatish embraces,' he wrote, invariably produced a 'tawny breed', who in turn tantalized like sirens all categories of gentle-men.[16] Long was thus aware of the socio-sexual reality of ethnic relations in Jamaica, and a gender reading of his work exposes the contradictory nature of the race discourse. The discursive mechanism that Long adopted as a protective cloak was the invention of a white feminine degeneracy that, if left unchecked, threatened the future of the white male colonizing project.

Long's pro-slavery text also reveals a fear of feminine subversion of hegemonic representations. The metaphor of the black woman's sexual embrace speaks to the black community's claim that its irrepressible humanity restored life to a morally exhausted conquistadorial élite, and miscegenation, of course, was a double-edged sword. It provided evidence both of the capacity of human sexuality to transcend crudely constructed ideological boundaries and of the fragility and irrelevance to personal lives of the race discourse.

The ideological defeminization of the black woman also contributed to a gender order that devalued black motherhood. Before the 1780s slave women in the advanced stages of pregnancy were given only a short respite from labour. When William Dickson arrived at Barbados in the early 1770s, he reported being

> astonished to see some women far gone in pregnancy, toiling in the field, and others whose naked infants lay exposed to the weather sprawling on a goat skin, or in a wooden tray. I have heard with indignation, drivers curse both them and their squalling brats, when they were suckling them.[17]

Hostility to pregnant women reflected planters' perceptions that it was cheaper to buy slaves than to let them reproduce naturally. That is not how it was explained in pro-slavery texts, however. Slave owners wrote instead about black women's disregard for motherhood and nurturing, and they offered this as further evidence of their brutishness and lack of femininity. Since it was 'natural', they argued, for women to desire motherhood, black women's low fertility, given their alleged sexual promiscuity, must be the result of arrested moral development rather than physical inability.

Subversive resistance to these gender representations by women invariably incurred punishments. Slave drivers had the authority to use the whip to enforce conformity to the social norms of the gender order. African-born women did not expect to be required to work during advanced pregnancy or in the three months after childbirth. Those who resisted the new regime were punished as part of the gender retraining. Richard Ligon described the mid-seventeenth-century plantation regime in Barbados:

> The woman is at work with her pickaninny at her back . . . If the overseer be discreet, she is suffered to rest herself a little more than ordinary, but if not, she is compelled to do as others do. Times they have of suckling their children in the fields, and refreshing themselves, and good reason, for they carry burdens on the back, and yet work too.[18]

Unfamiliarity with this labour culture contributed to the black population's low fertility and high infant mortality rates, which rendered it unable to naturally reproduce itself.

Eighteenth-century records placed the depletion rate of the population (the excess of its crude death rate over its crude birth rate) as high as 50 or 60 per cent, but modern historians using case study analysis place it much lower. Estate records for Jamaica in the third quarter of the eighteenth century suggest a depletion rate of about 20 per cent, while slave import and re-export records suggest 30 per cent between 1700 and 1750 and 25 per cent between 1750 and 1775. The depletion rate in Barbados in the first half of the eighteenth century seems to have been worse than in Jamaica; 49 per cent between 1701 and 1725 and 36 per cent from 1726 to 1750, though it fell to less than 12 per cent between 1775 and 1800. The demographic experiences of the Leewards approximated those of Barbados with depletion rates of 40 to 50 per cent up to the 1760s and less than 15 per cent in the last quarter of the century. By the time of the general registration of slaves between 1814 and 1818 and the collapse of slavery in the 1830s, depletion rates in Barbados and the Leewards were between 3 and 4 per cent.[19]

It was common for eighteenth-century visitors to the islands, unfamiliar with the gender order of plantation slavery, to express horror on observing the physical brutalization of females and the slave owners' disregard for black motherhood and maternity. Accustomed to a gendered culture in which women were perceived as needing social and moral protection from male tyranny, some individuals who remained pro-slavery during the debate on abolition were moved to support policies for radical reformation of slave women's conditions. To such observers, enslavement of women was the most vile, unjust and corrupting of civilized values. Not surprisingly, there-fore, abolitionists after the 1780s used evidence of corporal punishments inflicted on females, splitting up of black families and disregard for domesticity in making their principal moral charge against slavery. Their arguments forced West Indian planters to address as a separate issue slave women's social and domestic conditions. An important consequence of their political campaign was the owners' reformulation of gender representa-tions. For the first time in the Caribbean the notion of the black woman as a member of the 'gentler sex' – hence physically inferior to males – became the basis of policy initiatives in slave management.

Abolitionists also used the rate of natural decrease, or depletion rate, as proof of the unnatural character of the hegemonic gender order. They argued that the order was hostile to slave women's domestic lives and destroyed their natural tendency to be mothers.

Centring the slave woman as the principal victim of nutritional deficiency, K. F. Kiple considers high infant mortality the single most important factor in explaining the high depletion rate. Mothers were often helpless as their children suffered and died of lockjaw, yaws, worms and a bewildering array of unfamiliar infections and diseases. Most of these diseases, Kiple argues, were related to malnutrition which was an endemic consequence of consciously applied gendered policies.[20]

J. H. Bennett's account of the Codrington estates in Barbados during the eighteenth century highlights the personal aspects of women's daily social experience of high infant mortality. Assessing the effects of underfeeding and overworking pregnant and lactating mothers, he describes the horror experienced by enslaved women.[21] In the personal emotional world that existed behind the aggregate statistics of depletion rates, women watched their children die in quick succession and buried more than those who lived to become adults.

These experiences were spiritually and emotionally crippling for many, but they enabled most to find subversive ways to survive and to maintain and define their feminine self-identities. Enslaved black women protected and proclaimed their feminine identities in many different ways. They insisted on procuring fine clothing and decorative jewellery, provided love and care for their kith and kin, pursued market engagements through huckstering, participated in revolutionary struggles, and loved white men into a kind of oblivion by producing coloured children with them who took their names and, more importantly, their properties.

'Monk' Lewis, a Jamaican planter in the early nineteenth century, provided piercing insights into the gender identity, childrearing and motherhood of slave women in this social world. In accordance with the dominant slave owners' representation of black women in the age of 'amelioration', he described the women on his estate as 'kind-hearted creatures' who were 'particularly anxious to rear children'.[22] Despite the agony of high infant mortality, Lewis argued that childrearing, domesticity and family life exerted a steadying and maturing influence upon slave women. To him, slave mothers appeared more moral and less sexually promiscuous.[23]

New reproduction policies were adopted in the late eighteenth century to promote motherhood, domesticity and the care of children. In order to give coherence to this social and economic fine tuning of managerial imperatives, gender representations were destablized and reconstructed. There was widespread commitment then to pro-natal policies that were intended to encourage natural reproduction as a method of ensuring a labour supply in the long term. Hence a new 'woman policy' had to be conceived, formulated and implemented on the estates. Traditional managerial attitudes and actions towards slave women had to be reconsidered and reshaped in a manner conducive to higher fertility levels. This was the beginning of a broad-based programme of celebrating and promoting black motherhood that culminated in the representation of the black woman as a natural nurturer – everyone's nanny, granny or auntie.

It should be stated, however, that slave owners had no evidence that their females had consciously imposed restraints upon their fertility, or that hegemonic gender representation contributed to its suppression, even though some believed that to be the case. No one supposed that the slave woman, constructed as Jezebel, could possibly practise sexual abstinence (gynaecological resistance), but some believed that she possessed deep-rooted hostility towards childrearing in slavery, especially within the context of hostility to motherhood. Slave owners proposed to overcome female indifference or resistance to childrearing by systematically offering socio-material incentives and reshaping the ideological aspects of the gender order.

This fundamental managerial departure centred the woman as nurturer, so new gender ideas had to be formulated, tested and evaluated. As a consequence there was an upsurge in literature for the pro-slavery cause which directly addressed slave-breeding policies. Most contributors, many of them posing as experienced authorities on slave management, sought to encourage the new trend, conceiving it as new progressive organizational thought. Successful reproduction policies also promised to take some of the wind out of the sails of abolitionists who argued that the endemic ill-treatment of slave women sprang from conceptual sources deep within the gender order.

Table 10.2 Sex ratios of slave population in the British West Indies, *c.* 1817 and *c.* 1832[24]

Colony	Males per 100 females	
	1817	1832
Barbados	83.9	86.3
St Kitts	92.4	91.9
Jamaica	100.3	94.5
Nevis	95.3	98.1
St Vincent	102.1	95.2
Trinidad	123.9	112.6
Demerara/Essequibo	130.9	110.2

One influential work, a pamphlet published in London in 1786 entitled 'The Following Instructions Are Offered to the Consideration of Proprietors and Managers of Plantations', was written by prominent absentee Barbadian planters. The central thesis was printed in bold capital letters in the introduction:

'THE INCREASE IS THE ONLY TEST OF THE CARE WITH WHICH THEY ARE TREATED.'

The Barbadians had already achieved natural growth and were now offering for emulation by other, less fortunate planters the key secrets of their success. The critical step, of course, was the attainment of a female majority in the slave population. Barbados had already achieved that (see Table 10.2), and it attributed its success to the demographic restructuring. The pamphlet emphasized the need for planters to implement a set of pre-natal policies to assist pregnant women in delivering healthy babies and to establish post-natal facilities to assist lactating mothers in the lowering of the high level of infant mortality. Most important, it stressed the need to protect fertile women from the tyranny of overseers. In addition to recommending marginal reductions in the labour hours of pregnant and lactating field women and improved material care, the authors also promoted a representation of black women as members of the 'gentler sex' whose fragility required specific policy protection. In effect, they recommended a significant reconstruction of the gender order.

Tinkering with gender to remove as many irritants as possible from women's sexual and domestic oppression was considered necessary. Slave owners were urged to encourage young slaves to form Christian-style marriages, as monogamous relations were considered more conducive to high fertility than African polygyny. The nuclear family structure, as an institutional arrangement, was also considered useful for attaining the objective of high levels of reproduction. On many estates, then, Christian-style married slaves were found living in single households. Slave owners also institutionalized the use of financial incentives as stimuli to reproduction. Evidence from plantation account books show that by the 1790s financial payments were commonplace.

'Monk' Lewis of Jamaica was not satisfied with crude monetary and material rewards for the creation of life. Money was important, but for him it was insufficient and brutally inadequate when offered as an incentive to motherhood. He needed something more philosophical, befitting the nature of the new, moral, gender order. Slave women, he believed, were entitled to 'honour' and 'respect'. These were also needed to encourage fertile women, who were altogether too few on his estate. Lewis described his practices as follows:

> I then gave the mothers a dollar each, and told them, that for the future they might claim the same sum, in addition to their usual allowance of clothes and provisions, for every infant which should be brought to the overseer alive and well on the fourteenth day; and I also gave each mother a present of a scarlet girdle with a silver medal in the centre, telling her always to wear it on feasts and holidays, when it should entitle her to marks of peculiar respect and attention.[25]

This 'belly-woman' initiative was just the kind of counter-offensive West Indian slave owners needed in order to protect their regime from the moral assault of metropolitan anti-slavery campaigners. Offering money to slave women for the delivery of infants was depicted by abolitionists as more degrading than the purchase of the mothers in the first instance; it constituted proof of the cultural and moral degeneration of the gender order within the slave-owning community. The notion of 'an order of honour' was intended to rebut the abolitionists' description of 'reforming' slave owners as vulgar materialists who used sexual manipulation and exploitation to secure an adequate labour supply.

Abolitionists, therefore, also centred the slave woman with respect to their campaign strategies, propaganda and analytical critiques. The slave woman was thus placed at the centre of the debate between those who sought to protect and prolong slavery and those who sought to undermine and destroy it. The discourse was trans-Atlantic in nature. On the estates in the West Indies increases in the slave woman's fertility were hailed as conclusive proof of the 'good treatment' thesis. In Europe, the slave woman was depicted as the principal tragic victim of the worst system of masculine tyranny known to the modern world.

The debate over the slave woman was part of a wider gender discourse that sharpened opinion on both sides of the Atlantic and focused attention on slavery as a particular kind of gender power. The paternalist idea of the 'woman' as the gentler sex placed tremendous ideological ammunition in the hands of the anti-slavery movement. Campaigners sought to portray the evil of West Indian slave society as resulting from the biased sex structure of labour gangs and its adoption of natural reproduction in the wake of the abolition of the slave trade in 1807. While some hard-line pro-slavery advocates continued to defend corporal punishment of females on the grounds of 'the Amazonian cast of character' of the black woman, anti-slavery forces believed that they had finally discovered in gender the soft, vulnerable underbelly of the slavery structure.[26]

Slave owners now found themselves in a difficult and paradoxical position. While they claimed to possess an egalitarian ideology within which black women were not considered inferior or subordinate to black men, as demonstrated in their labour productivity, they had no intention of weakening dominant patriarchal systems to which the black men also subscribed and by which they were partially empowered and privileged. The subsequent conceptual imprisonment of the black woman within the restructured gender representation that promoted notions of difference and inferiority had the effect of supporting her claim to legal emancipation at the same time as it deepened her victimization within the gender order. By promoting gender egalitarianism under the whip, slave owners sought to defeminize her by implying a sameness with the male.

The abolitionist discourse also needed to cross a few turbulent rivers before it reached a comfortable resting place with respect to the objectification of the black woman. She was a woman, but in what did her femininity consist? In what ways, and to what extent, was she different from the white woman? Should she be regarded as a 'sister' by white women, or be subsumed under the categories of chattel and brute? Was she a victim of both white and black masculine tyranny, stemming from a malehood that saw all women as 'less than' and 'other'? The answers to these questions had policy implications for the movement, particularly with respect to issues such as the separation of children from mothers, attitudes toward family life, corporal punishment and the relations of sex, gender and work.

By the mid-1820s both male and female English abolitionists were satisfied that playing the 'woman' card was their best strategy in the struggle to win the hearts and minds of a seemingly indifferent public, which, according to John Bull, was 'almost sick of this black business'. Throughout England, middle-class white women formed anti-slavery organizations and campaigned against slavery by emphasizing the 'feminine' character-istics of the black woman, their 'sister' in the search for a new moral, Christian order.[27] In most cases white female abolitionists claimed a special understanding of the plight of black women, derived in part from their 'essential nature' as female. The author of *A Vindication of Female Anti-*

Slavery Associations argued that the movement was part of a general struggle against human misery, social oppression and moral injustice. Elizabeth Heyrick, a popular anti-slavery campaigner, stated in her pamphlet *Appeal to the Hearts and Conscience of British Women* (1828) that a woman was ideally suited to advance the cause because 'the peculiar texture of her mind, her strong feelings and quick sensibilities, especially qualify her, not only to sympathize with suffering, but also to plead for the oppressed'.[28]

Another strategy of the British female anti-slavery movement was to construct a gendered trinity composed of woman, child and family that slavery had denied to black people. Without the emotional, spiritual and institutional bonds to ensure the viability of this trinity, they argued, civilization was not possible in the West Indies; those responsible for their absence were guilty of contributing to the pool of human misery and backwardness. The West Indian slave plantation was depicted as a 'Hell' where men enslaved and beat women, alienated them from their children, placed a market price upon infants at birth, and denied them the rights to religion, education and moral guidance.

Gender lay at the core of the discourses on slavery and freedom in modernity. Extracted from West Africa by the slave trade and deposited in the Americas in considerably fewer numbers than men, women initially constituted a minority in frontier Caribbean societies. Minority demographic status gave way to numerical majority as socio-economic formations matured and were rationalized. Significant gender implications resulted from the fact that the entire system of slavery became increasingly female-focused as enslaved black women came to be seen as the conduit through which black infants acquired slave status. Successive gender representations of black women developed from the need to align changing sex compositions and demographic requirements with the political economy of efficient resource use. This was illustrated by the empirical evidence and conceptual articulations of the late eighteenth century when slave owners shifted their labour supply policy from 'buying' to 'breeding'. As the slave woman figured centrally in the new method of slave reproduction, new gender representations were used to rationalize owners' choice of it. Similarly, the anti-slavery movement in Europe privileged the gender discourse in order to emphasize slave women's relatively greater exploitation and brutalization. Abolitionists also used gender representations of black women to highlight the extreme moral and social oppressiveness and backwardness of societies based on slavery and the degeneracy of the élites that maintained and defended it.

The considerable turbulence in the evolution of gender concepts in the time of slavery requires that events and processes be placed in historical contexts with a view to obtaining critical forms of feminist knowledge about male domination. Feminist theorizing is best served by readings of history that illustrate how evolving communities actually thought about gender and how their thoughts were formed within changing social, economic and philosophical contexts. As a historical moment, slavery was characterized by considerable internal turmoil, but it enables us to map the contours of the complex interactions between gender and relations of race and class. An understanding of the 'enterprise of the Indies' as a project of modernity, therefore, requires the development of knowledge of gender as a socially constructed relation of domination. Liberation from gender's capacity to differentiate in order to dominate should be guided by an understanding of how and why we came over time to think about the things we think about (and do not think about).

Notes

1 See Hilary McD. Beckles, 'Sex and Gender in the Historiography of Caribbean Slavery', in Verene Shepherd *et al.* (eds.) *Engendering History: Caribbean Women in Historical Perspective* (Kingston, 1995), pp. 125–40; Bridget Brereton, 'Text, Testimony, and Gender: An Examination of Some Texts by Women on the English-Speaking Caribbean, from the 1770s to the 1920s', in *Engendering History*, pp. 63–94; and Rosalyn Terborg-Penn, 'Through an African Feminist Theoretical Lens: Viewing Caribbean Women's History Cross-culturally', in *Engendering History*, pp. 3–19.
2 Kamau Braithwaite, 'The Black Woman of the Caribbean during Slavery', Elsa Goveia Memorial Lecture, University of the West Indies, Cave Hill Campus, Barbados, 1984; Rhoda Reddock, 'Women and Slavery in the Caribbean: A Feminist Perspective', *Latin American Perspectives* 12, no. 1, pp. 63–80; Hilary McD. Beckles, *Natural Rebels: A Social History of Enslaved Black Women in Barbados* (New Brunswick, NJ, 1989); Marietta Morrissey, 'Women's Work, Family Formation and Reproduction among Caribbean Slaves', *Review* 9 (1986), pp. 339–67.
3 See for the wider relevance of this discussion Hilary McD. Beckles, 'Black Masculinity in Caribbean Slavery', Women and Development Unit, University of the West Indies, Barbados, *Occasional Paper* 2/96 (1996); Lindon Gordon, 'What's New in Women's History', in Teresa de Lauretis (ed.) *Feminist Studies/Critical Studies* (Bloomington, IN, 1986), pp. 20–3; Louise M. Newman, 'Critical Theory and the History of Women: What's at Stake in Deconstructing Women's History', *Journal of Women's History* 2, no. 3 (1991); Mary Poovey, 'Feminism and Deconstruction', *Feminist Studies* 14 (1988).
4 See Beckles, *Natural Rebels*; Arlette Gautier, 'Les esclaves femmes aux Antilles françaises, 1635–1848', *Réflexions historiques* 10, no. 3 (1983), pp. 409–35; B. W. Higman, 'Household Structure and Fertility on Jamaican Slave Plantations', *Population Studies* 27 (1973), pp. 527–50; Higman, *Slave Population and Economy in Jamaica, 1802–1834* (New York, 1976); H. S. Klein and S. L. Engerman, 'Fertility Differentials between Slaves in the United States and the British West Indies', *William and Mary Quarterly* 35 (1978), pp. 357–74; Michael Craton, 'Changing Patterns of

Slave Families in the British West Indies', *Journal of Interdisciplinary History* 10, no. 1 (1979), pp. 1–35.

5 The protracted violent war between Africans and Europeans on the Caribbean frontier in the sixteenth and seventeenth centuries has been well documented, but the contribution of changing gender identities and roles to social turbulence and instability has not been accounted for despite the considerable evidence found in slave owners' texts. See Hilary McD. Beckles, 'Caribbean Anti-Slavery: The Self-Liberation Ethos of Enslaved Blacks', *Journal of Caribbean History* 22, nos 1–2 (1988), pp. 1–19; Bernard Moitt, 'Women, Work and Resistance in the French Caribbean during Slavery, 1700–1848', in *Engendering History*, pp. 155–75; Barbara Bush, *Slave Women in Caribbean Society, 1650–1838* (Bloomington, IN, 1990); Marietta Morrissey, *Slave Women in the New World: Gender Stratification in the Caribbean* (Lawrence, KS, 1989).

6 See David Brion Davis, *The Problem of Slavery in Western Culture* (Ithaca, NY, 1966) and *Slavery and Human Progress* (New York, 1984); David Eltis and James Walvin (eds), *The Abolition of the Atlantic Slave Trade: Origins and Effects in Europe, Africa and the Americas* (Madison, WI, 1981); Thomas Hodgkin, 'Kingdoms of the Western Sudan', in Roland Oliver (ed.), *The Dawn of Africa History* (London, 1961); Jan Vansina, *Paths in the Rainforests* (London, 1990); Philip D. Curtin, 'Africa and the Wider Monetary World, 1250–1850', in John F. Richards (ed.), *Precious Metals in the Later Medieval and Early Modern Worlds* (Durham, NC, 1982), pp. 231–68; John Fage, 'The Effects of the Export Trade on African Populations', in R. P. Moss and R. J. Rathbone (eds), *The Population Factor in African Studies* (London, 1975), pp. 15–23; Joseph Inikori (ed.), *Forced Migration: The Impact of the Export Trade on African Societies* (London, 1981); Ray Kea, *Settlement, Trade and Politics in the Seventeenth Century Gold Coast* (Baltimore, MD, 1982); Claire Robertson and Martin A. Klein (eds), *Women and Slavery in Africa* (Madison, WI, 1983); Claude Meillassoux, 'Female Slavery', in *Women and Slavery*, pp. 49–66; Walter Rodney, 'African Slavery and Other Forms of Social Oppression on the Upper Guinea Coast in the Context of the Atlantic Slave Trade', *Journal of African History* 7, no. 3 (1966), pp. 431–43; Rodney, 'Gold and Slaves on the Gold Coast', *Transactions of the Historical Society of Ghana* 10 (1969), pp. 13–28.

7 Claire C. Robertson and Martin A. Klein, 'Women's Importance in African Slave Systems', in *Women and Slavery*, pp. 4–5.

8 *Ibid.*; see also Martin Klein, 'Women in Slavery in the Western Sudan', in *Women and Slavery*, pp. 67–92.

9 See Robertson and Klein, 'Women's Importance', p. 9.

10 See Robertson and Klein, 'Women's Importance', p. 18; see also J. D. Fage, 'Slave and Society in Western Africa, *c.* 1455–1700', *Journal of African History* 21 (1980), pp. 289–310; M. Klein, 'The Study of Slavery in Africa: A Review Article', *Journal of African History* 19 (1978), pp. 599–609; I. Kopytoff, 'Indigenous African Slavery: Commentary One', *Historical Reflections* 6 (1979), pp. 62–77; I. Kopytoff and S. Miers, 'African "Slavery" as an Institution of Marginality', in S. Miers and I. Kopytoff (eds), *Slavery in Africa* (Madison, WI, 1977).

11 Meillassoux, 'Female Slavery', p. 49; Robertson and Klein, 'Women's Importance', pp. 10–11.

12 Herbert S. Klein, 'African Women in the Atlantic Slave Trade', in *Women and Slavery*, pp. 29–32.

13 B. W. Higman, *Slave Populations of the British Caribbean, 1807–1834* (Baltimore, MD, 1984), p. 116.

14 *Ibid.*, p. 37.

15 Edward Long, *The History of Jamaica*, 3 vols (London, 1774), pp. 274–6, 327–8, 330–1.

16 *Ibid.*, p. 328.

17 William Dickson, *Letters on Slavery* (1789; Westport, CT, 1970), p. 12.

18 Richard Ligon, *A True and Exact History of the Island of Barbados* (London, 1657), p. 48.
19 See J. R. Ward, *British West Indian Slavery, 1750–1834: The Process of Amelioration* (Oxford, 1988), pp. 121–2.
20 See K. F. Kiple, *The Caribbean Slave: A Biological History* (Cambridge, 1981); K. F. Kiple and V. H. Kiple, 'Slave Child Mortality: Some Nutritional Answers to a Perennial Puzzle', *Journal of Social History* 10 (1979), pp. 284–309; Kiple and Kiple, 'Deficiency Diseases in the Caribbean', *Journal of Interdisciplinary History* 11, no. 2 (1980), pp. 197–205.
21 J. H. Bennett, *Bondsmen and Bishops: Slavery and Apprenticeship on the Codrington Plantations of Barbados, 1710–1838* (Berkeley, 1958), p. 55.
22 M. G. Lewis, *Journal of a West Indian Proprietor, 1815–17* (1834; London, 1929), p. 87.
23 *Ibid.*
24 *Ihid.*, p. 33 (table 2.6).
25 Lewis, *Journal of a West Indian Proprietor*, pp. 108–9.
26 *Report on the Debate in Council on a Dispatch from Lord Bathurst to Governor Warde of Barbados* (London, 1828), pp. 21–3.
27 See Clare Midgley, *Women against Slavery: The British Campaigns, 1780–1870* (London, 1992), pp. 93–117; Louis Billington and Rosamund Billington, '"A Burning Zeal for Righteousness": Women in the British Anti-Slavery Movement, 1820–1900', in Jane Rendall (ed.), *Equal or Different: Women's Politics, 1800–1914* (Basingstoke, UK, 1985), pp. 82–111; bell hooks, 'Sisterhood: Political Solidarity between Women', *Feminist Review* 23 (1986), pp. 125–38.
28 *A Vindication of Female Anti-slavery Associations* (London, n. d.), pp. 3–4; Elizabeth Heyrick, *Appeal to the Hearts and Conscience of British Women* (Leicester, UK, 1828), p. 3 (also cited in Midgley, *Women against Slavery*, p. 94).

= 11 =

Those Who Remained Behind: Women Slaves in Nineteenth-century Yorubaland[1]

Francine Shields

The commercial interface between European and African slave traders on the coast of West Africa linked the Middle Passage and slavery in the Americas with the African domestic slave trade and with the institution of slavery in Africa.[2] Indeed, many slaves remained in West Africa as part of domestic systems of slavery that continued until the early twentieth century. Hence, the experiences of individual slaves from the time of their capture to their embarkation from West Africa are integral parts of the history of the African diaspora.

It is possible to trace the names and establish the ages, ethnic origins and experiences of some slaves through various primary sources,[3] including missionary journals and the correspondence and reports of colonial officers and agents. They begin to answer some of the questions raised in 'revisionist' interpretations of slavery and relate slaves' experiences to local and wider historical contexts. This paper explores some of these questions with respect to women and domestic slavery in the Yoruba area of south-western Nigeria in the nineteenth century.[4]

The gender division of labour meant a considerable demand for female slaves in nineteenth-century Yorubaland. This paper examines the life histories of some of the female slaves in the context of the commercial expansion of the palm oil and kernel trade. It draws upon journals in the archives of the Anglican 'Yoruba Missions'[5] written by missionaries who resided in various Yoruba towns in the second half of the nineteenth century,[6] and on documents in British Foreign Office and Colonial Office archives written by various British officials and Sierra Leonean and Yoruba agents. Although the British officials were based at Lagos, their reports cover interior visits and include information supplied by Yoruba sources.[7] Statements in these sources made by or, more commonly, on behalf of female slaves provide information on their backgrounds and experiences, which can be related to the local and wider historical events that influenced their experiences of domestic slavery. These events produced some similarities in many women's experiences, but individual personalities and other factors created a diversity of experiences for them.

Militarism and warfare dominated the history of Yorubaland in the nineteenth century. The Yoruba wars included the Ilorin mutiny of 1817, the destruction of Owu in the early 1820s, and the collapse of Old Oyo in the 1830s.[8] The rest of the century saw extensive political restructuring. The frequent wars displaced people from each defeated town, and eventually the Oyo themselves had to disperse south and resettle in pre-existing or new towns such as Ibadan, in the centre of Yorubaland (established c. 1829), Abeokuta, in the south-west (c. 1830), and New Oyo, about eighty miles south of the old town (c. 1837). Abeokuta suffered an almost continuous threat of attack from her powerful western neighbour, the Kingdom of Dahomey, until the 1870s. Abeokuta was further embroiled in conflict with the British, Ibadan and Ijebu at various times from 1865 onwards. Ibadan, the most militaristic state, was almost constantly at war; major battles occurred in 1840, with the defeat of Ilorin at Osogbo; between 1861 and 1863, against Ijaye; and from the late 1870s to 1893, against the Ekitiparapo coalition, in what has been termed the Sixteen Years War.[9]

The social implications of militarism, recurrent warfare and the consequent insecurity, which fostered lawlessness, were complex. Warfare had a considerable effect on occupational aspirations, social status and gender roles.[10] One consequence was an increase in the slave population, which altered the sexual, generational and ethnic division of labour in many towns.

Captives made up a large proportion of slaves entering the domestic market, and prevalent fears of being killed or captured during battles or by marauding troops and kidnappers on farms and on trade routes are well supported by numerous reports contained in primary sources.[11] For example, in 1862, H. S. Freeman reported that the people of the Egba villages 'dare not cultivate far from their homes lest they should be kidnapped'.[12] As Governor Glover noted, the Abeokuta people complained that they were in danger of being abducted from their farms. Indeed, in 1864, they alleged that no fewer than thirty people had been taken in the space of a month by Ofin marauders; five were known to have been killed.[13] Men, women and children were harassed or abducted from their farmlands in all parts of Yorubaland in the following years.[14]

Women were particularly vulnerable to these dangers. Trade routes were generally unsafe, and when women traders ventured out, they were usually accompanied by armed guards. They often travelled in large caravans for security.[15] None the less, many women and children were captured and enslaved. For example, in 1889, Mary Dota stated that she, two other women and a man had been captured by an Epe man named Galadima while they were on a trading trip from Lokoja. Galadima took six valuable homespun cloths that Mary intended to sell and four pairs of handmade slippers belonging to one of the other women. He then attempted to sell the captives at Aiyesan.[16]

People tried to find safer haven in the various Yoruba towns, but some towns were better protected than others. In those that were defensively weak and often attacked, women, children and the elderly were regularly forced to neglect their households and occupations and seek a precarious refuge in the outlying forests and farmlands, despite the dangers there. In Ota, people stayed away for up to five months each year. Women and children constituted the majority of those uprooted. White lamented in 1865 that constant upheaval and rumours of war had left the townspeople of Ota confused, anxious and superstitious.[17]

War captives were often exchanged for war goods. Ibadan in particular maintained a considerable trade in slaves with Ijebu, which supplied guns and ammunition.[18] According to White, when Ibadan defeated Ijaye in 1862,

> a good many of the Ijaye women were exiled from their homes and dispersed about different places, Abbeokuta, Lagos, and this place [Ota], seeking some means of subsistence. Today all of a sudden some 20 of them rushed into our premises begging for protection.[19]

They said that the Egba were capturing women in the streets of Ota to sell at Okeodan for ammunition.

Slaves who had been absorbed into households were vulnerable to resale in exchange for ammunition or food in time of crisis. According to

Olubi's observation, a high proportion of sick, aged and defenceless Ilesa women and children were captured by Ibadan forces when they defeated Ilesa in 1870.[20] On one occasion, when Ibadan was short of supplies, the town's wealthy women had to contribute some of their slaves to be exchanged for powder.[21] In 1886 Samuel Johnson reported that many of the chiefs were compelled to part with their slave wives to procure arms and meet war expenses.[22] Individuals convicted of crimes were sometimes exchanged for war goods.[23]

Even in the war camps, imminent attack sometimes made it necessary for vulnerable groups to evacuate to avoid capture or death.[24] Women and children most often fell victim to marauding troops and kidnappers in the treacherous zones around the camps. In 1896 a Hausa woman named Asiki recounted that when she, another woman, Ajara, and their two children had tried to reach a camp near Ikirun for refuge, they were captured by two Ilorin soldiers. Asiki and her child were taken to Ilorin, where they were presented to the Balogun Alanomu, who gave the soldier cowries as a reward. Asiki was then sold at the slave market to a man from Oloro named Idowu, who required her to pluck long reeds to weave mats.[25] Asiki's account demonstrates that people were still being enslaved as late as the 1890s, after most of the towns involved in the Sixteen Years War had disbanded their war camps and agreed to peace.[26]

In their efforts to eradicate the export slave trade in the mid-nineteenth century, the British promoted exports of palm oil and kernels, which were in demand in industrial Europe to produce machine lubricants, soap, candles and, later, margarine.[27] The Baptist missionary William Clarke was among many who observed the growth of the palm oil trade in Yorubaland. He commented that the industry,

> in the palm districts employs a large number of labourers and presents more the appearance of a manufactory than any other department of labour. I have seen establishments of this kind where perhaps fifty persons or more were engaged in labour.[28]

Palm oil production was also accessible to producers operating on a smaller scale.[29]

The production, processing and trade of palm products both for local consumption and to provision slave ships was long-established as women's work.[30] Indeed, in the years of economic transition after the abolition of the British slave trade in 1807, gender ideology was so strong that it contributed to a reluctance on the part of male rulers and slave traders to adapt to the requirements of palm oil production and trade, which depended upon female labour. In 1855 a group of Egba chiefs declared that the end of the export trade in slaves had left them short of labour: 'Those that have 300 slaves, now [are] left 50; and they that have 200, left 40; and that of 100, left 20; that of 50, left 5. So they remember that it would have been better if they have been trading in slaves as they used to do.' When the Egba war chief Sodeke asked what they should do now – 'the white man told them to trade palm oil; so they ask how is that: is not a woman to sell oil, how can a man sell oil like a woman?'[31] Methods of palm and kernel oil extraction were both time-consuming and labour-intensive, and much of the labour was considered women's work. The men were not retaining enough slaves within their households to engage in palm oil production on a scale that would earn enough to match the profits they had previously made by selling slaves for export.

Robert Campbell gave this detailed account of palm oil processing in 1860, describing both the techniques and the division of labour:

> The nuts are gathered by men. From one to four or five women separate them from the integuments. They are then passed on to other women, who boil them in large earthen pots. Another set crush off the fibre in mortars. This done they are placed in large clay vats filled with water, and two or three women tread out the semi-liquid oil, which comes to the surface as disengaged from the fibre, where it is collected and again boiled to get rid of the water which mechanically adheres to it.[32]

Machinery to save time and labour in the large-scale production of oil became available in the 1880s, but until the end of the century, most women still used the hands-on techniques that had been employed since the beginning of the century, indicating that small-scale production was common.[33] The extra labour needed for the palm industry, together with the expansion of other female crafts and trades, paradoxically stimulated the rapid growth of a domestic trade in slaves. Women made up a large proportion of these domestic slaves because of the demands of 'legitimate' trade.[34]

The sexual division of labour[35] in the palm produce industry, whether carried out on a small or large scale, increased demand for female skills.[36] The labour of women could be harnessed in two main ways: through the family, primarily via polygyny, and through slavery. The options of polygyny and slavery were by no means mutually exclusive, for many slave women were added to households as slave wives or concubines from the mid-century onwards.[37] Possession of slave wives, concubines and female slaves was not only an outward sign of wealth, but also an investment in their productive and reproductive output.[38] Polygyny became far more widespread in the latter half of the century,[39] reflecting the rising demand for female labour in the palm produce trade and other female industries and the availability of female slaves.

The acquisition of female labour was advantageous for senior wives.[40] Although men sought female slaves and slave wives, senior wives largely controlled their labour and indeed the labour of free-born co-wives.[41] Often women themselves encouraged their husbands to take another wife or concubine to free time for themselves and lighten their domestic workload.[42] If a slave woman was taken as a concubine, the man had sexual relations with her, but she was not formally taken as an additional wife.[43]

The case of a female slave who escaped to Lagos in 1865 is particularly illustrative of these points. Henry Robbin, a prominent cotton producer and trader connected with the Church Missionary Society in Abeokuta, bought a woman named Awa who had been supplied from Ibadan and was probably a war captive. Awa stated that she and nine other slave women had been kept by Robbin as concubines. Her duties included both transporting Robbin's tobacco supplies and assisting his principal wife in trade; she 'constantly employed [her] to carry and count cowries'. On one occasion, Robbin's senior wife sent Awa and seven other concubines to the Aro gate to collect the bulky money. Like many other female captives, Awa and her companions laboured in expanding business ventures.[44]

Free-born wives maintained exclusive rights to their own income and property during this period. As Bowen explained, the husband had 'no claim on her property . . . [and] the woman is the sole owner of her property and her earnings. She is not obliged to work for her husband . . .'[45] However, the domestic slaves and concubines who provided the extra labour needed by developing industries had no such rights to income; ultimately, distribution of their earnings was controlled by their owners or overseers. Consequently, male owners were able to circumvent established marital rights and gain access to the income and goods generated by slave women, whether taken as wives or concubines; they shared the benefits with their senior wives.

From the 1860s, more slave men and children entered the palm produce industry. This development reflected the consequences of increasing warfare, the need for more labour as the industry expanded, and the diversion of male and child slaves into the domestic slave market as the Atlantic slave trade dried up. By the late 1860s, the entry of slave men and children into the production, transport and trade of palm oil radically altered the sexual division of labour in the industry, long dominated by women. In particular, male slaves of Hausa origin became prominent in both the transport and trade of palm produce in the south of Yorubaland.[46]

The life expectancy of children in Yoruba towns was generally very low, but children's labour was becoming increasingly valuable with the rise in demand for food and vegetable products for the domestic and export trade, respectively, and the impetus this gave to related occupations.[47] Apart from the *iwofa* or pawnage system, which was a common way to recruit child labour, slavery provided another considerable source of child labour.[48] The demand was met to some extent through the widespread sale of slave children supplied mainly by the Egba and, in particular, the Ibadan army, which frequently captured children while raiding enemy towns, as both Revd Olubi and Revd Allen noted in 1870, during the Ibadan–Ilesa war.[49] By 1855 there was already a keen demand for child slaves in Lagos, where they were used as domestics.[50] Even in interior towns, the demand for children outstripped that for adults, as Campbell noted later that year.[51]

Transport demands of the domestic and export products provided extra stimulus for the exploitation of children's labour.[52] The introduction of the Registration of Alien Children Ordinance by the British authorities in 1878 caused panic among traders in both Lagos and the surrounding areas where slavery was outlawed and the ordinance was to be applied. No fewer than thirty-nine prominent female traders pointed out to the consulate that the 'produce of the country . . . is generally brought into the settlement by the domestic slaves and children of slaves of the natives of the countries around the settlement'.[53] The women feared that their slaves and slave children would be encouraged to desert at Lagos. (The Yoruba situation evidently differed from that of the Krobo of southern Ghana[54] and of the Ngwa of eastern Nigeria,[55] where slaves were not the main source of labour for palm oil production.) By 1867, some of the Brazilian population of Lagos were complaining that prohibitions limiting their ownership of slaves meant 'that they could not compete in productions on their farms with the natives of the interior', who were not affected by the restrictions.[56]

Contemporary accounts and later sources emphasize the relatively benign nature of domestic slavery in nineteenth-century Yorubaland.[57] In 1857 the Sierra Leonian repatriate John Davis stated that 'the privileges of a freeman and a slave are nearly equal'.[58] The Yoruba sociologist N. A. Fadipe later asserted that domestic slavery was 'mild' in nature, that the slave found little difficulty in securing redemption, and that there was no obvious social stigma attached to slave status.[59] The biographical data discussed here suggest otherwise.

James Johnson, a firm campaigner against domestic slavery, wrote in 1877, 'instances of individual cruelty and barbarity to slaves are not wanting'.[60] Johnson had an interest in discrediting the slave trade, but his assertion is supported by evidence in accounts related by slaves themselves. Physical abuse and isolation were prevalent features of domestic slavery. Violence was a reality of slavery, and although to say that violence occurred may be stating the obvious, it must be recognized that physical abuse of female slaves in particular was bound up with a well-established and socially accepted use of violence against women in the household to instil obedience and to reaffirm male (and sometimes also female) authority.[61] The violent treatment of female domestic slaves was linked to wider and more institutionalized methods of control directed specifically, although not always exclusively, at women.

One of the most pernicious abuses by the male master was the sexual exploitation of female slaves. Exploitation of free-born women was not socially or officially accepted. Fadipe states that in theory 'a female slave was at the entire disposal of her master and, if he decided to establish sexual relations with her, he made her his wife and thereby automatically gave her her freedom'.[62] Samuel Johnson asserted that in Ibadan 'any slave woman taken as a wife becomes *ipso facto* a free woman'.[63] However, female slaves were not always accorded full marital rights, freedom or better treatment when their owners established a sexual relationship with them.[64]

One account, given in 1886 by two female slaves, provides painful details of women's experiences of domestic slavery. The two slaves, named Ramatu and Asatu, belonged to the Balogun of Ikorodu. They were both Nupe and described each other as 'good friends'. They had had children with the Balogun and were married to him, though without a full marriage ceremony, which clearly suggests that they were concubines. The Balogun had employed them to trade palm oil and kernels on his behalf. They testified that they had been cruelly treated by both the Balogun and his family. Ramatu stated that when her child died,

> 5 days afterwards I was put in irons – a ring was put round my neck and
> a chain was attached thereto and fastened to the ceiling so as to prevent

me from lying down. I could only stand on my feet. I was put in irons in the evening and kept there until the evening of the next day.[65]

Asatu said that after her child died, the Balogun 'treated me worse than ever. Several times I was put in chains and tied to a post.'[66] Although they were concubines, both women stated that they felt they had always been treated as slaves: clearly, the women themselves perceived a difference between their status and rights and those of the Balogun and his family.

In 1865 Awa stated that she and several other slaves had been added to Henry Robbin's household as his concubines, which suggests that he had established sexual relations with them. Awa testified to the harsh measures used by Robbin on his female slaves: shackling, denial of food and water and flogging with a horse whip. Awa described how Robbin had re-sold other slave women and their children; in one case, two women were exchanged for two rolls of tobacco. After about a year with Robbin, Awa was sold by a senior woman in his household to two women at the slave market in Okeodan. She was then sold to a man at Porto Novo who intended to sell her at Lagos, but she escaped.[67]

Awa passed through many hands in a short time. Her experience of slavery is representative of the discontinuous and insecure lives of slaves. Her account also traces the geographical route of her experience of enslavement, starting in the east and moving progressively south-west. Indeed, other accounts that allow slave routes to be traced often show the movement of people toward commercial centres such as coastal ports that were still engaged in the illicit export of slaves from the Yoruba area or to markets where slaves loaded with valuable trade items were sold along with the goods that they carried. Like the captives exchanged for war goods, slaves were used as porters and units of exchange for other products. This was a common feature of both the Atlantic and domestic slave systems and a practice which was reinforced during this period of increasing commercialization.[68] Even as late as 1891, when foreign money was widely available, Alvan Millson considered that 'cowries and slaves were the two main forms of currency, slaves being particularly preferred for larger transactions over longer distances'.[69]

The experiences of Ramatu, Asatu, Awa and her companions are not consistent with Fadipe's glossy account of the rights of female slaves. None of the women in these cases were formally married or accorded full marital rights, none were freed and none were well treated even when their owners decided to have sexual relations with them. Sexual relationships offered some slave women the possibility of securing better conditions both for themselves and for the children born from the relationship, but such options were not available to male slaves. In theory, such children were automatically free and assimilated. However, conditions may not have been as favourable in practice, at least not in every town. Indeed, the majority of fugitive slave women took their children with them when they ran away from their owners. According to Henry Townsend, the children of slave women at Abeokuta were not free and a stigma was attached to slave status and slave ancestry.[70] Thomas Champness, a Methodist missionary also based at Abeokuta, stated in 1861 that a slave woman and her children remained the property of their owner even if she married or had children with another man. Indeed, Champness had intervened in several cases where owners had taken their 'property' back.[71]

An established mode of disciplining slaves was to threaten them with sale to coastal slave merchants. However, as the Atlantic slave trade diminished, slave owners could no longer rely on this threat to gain obedience or compliance, as Consul Campbell noted.[72] Ijebu troops told Olubi in 1867 that whereas formerly they had sold disobedient slaves to the Portuguese, now, 'because of the English presence, their slaves, wives and children are intensely disobedient'.[73] This statement further implies what much other evidence strongly indicates: a widespread deterioration in gender relations over the period.

Slaves were still reprimanded, and slaves were re-sold even within Yorubaland itself. Female slaves were sometimes re-sold or given as gifts to notable individuals for use as victims of human sacrifice on important occasions. For example, as late as 1894, three old slave women belonging to notable men and women in the Makun area made their escape, claiming sanctuary with the British: Oshamfumi (of Ijebu origin), Ibeyemi (of Ikole origin) and Ekundayo (of Ife origin) stated that they had escaped from owners who were going to sell them to Chief Ewusi of Sagamu in the Ijebu area for sacrifice at his enthronement ceremony.[74] The possibility of being sacrificed was a very real one for all domestic slaves.[75] The use of female slaves for sacrifice was particularly prominent in Ondo. In 1878, one young woman was bought as a child by an Ondo chief for the specific purpose of being sacrificed at his funeral years ahead. The girl was brought up with the privileges of a senior wife but was administered anti-fertility drugs to prevent conception so that she would not leave any children behind. Apparently this was common practice among wealthy chiefs in Ondo.[76]

Most slave women could not appeal to indigenous authorities for protection, and physical distance or estrangement from their own families meant that family support was not an option either. The missions became their refuge; indeed, female slaves were disproportionately represented among the mission attendants in many towns.[77] Likewise, after the formal establishment of the Lagos colony in 1861, increasing numbers of slaves abandoned their 'homes' in the interior in search of liberation and protection at Lagos.[78] A fair number of slave wives, concubines, other female slaves and even free-born women took their perceived 'disobedience' to its conclusion and fled to Lagos. In addition, women continued to escape to other towns, seeking protection or better conditions from other men, as they had done before the colony was established.[79] Female slave owners lost slaves through flight.[80]

Masters called fugitive female slaves 'wives', often for the benefit of British ears, to bolster claims of legal and moral rights. In many cases, the women perceived themselves as concubines or slaves, with fewer rights than wives had. Often, Sierra Leonean repatriates put up the redemption money for female slaves and employed them as 'domestic servants' in their households. This ambiguous term suggested that the women were freely employed when in fact they were indebted to and, whether by choice or not, dependent upon their patrons for paying their manumission costs and taking them into their households.[81]

The flight of so many domestic slaves caused a crisis in the interior, which highlights the crucial role that women and children played in the economy in general and the palm industry in particular and the fact that many producers and traders were ultimately dependent on them for labour. In 1872 the Alake and the trade chiefs of Abeokuta complained to the consul:

> Our slaves . . . our wives, our children, are all running away to Lagos, and for which we dare institute no enquiry . . . our slaves here are used in the same way as children of our own body begotten, they are to help us in working our farms to obtain the produce needed in the European market, this is the only investment we had here, by taking them from us [you are] reducing people of importance to abject beggary in a day.[82]

They now fully appreciated the vital role of female and child labour, both slave and free-born, in the palm oil and kernel industry. The crisis was ongoing in 1887, when Soranke, the Jaguna of Igbein, expressed similar fears:

there are those who are assisting us in working to get enough palm oil, palm kernels for trading, and when they who will assist us in working will be running away so furiously every day . . . it will cause trading to be lessened.[83]

The reluctance to part with female slaves, especially if they had been taken as wives and concubines, is evident in the following statement, issued by the Ikorodu authorities following the escape of Ramatu and Asatu, the two female slaves who belonged to the Balogun:

slaves running to Lagos we understand, but as the two women in question were the Balogun's wives the Governor should be able to send them back. That forty-eight men slaves of the Balogun had been away to Lagos, but he never asked for them.[84]

In this period an increasing number of owners allowed their slaves to work part-time for their own benefit in the hope that this would foster self-sufficiency and loyalty. Slave women in particular saved their earnings from trade at the palm oil markets. These developments, however, did not foster loyalty. As the British consul, Benjamin Campbell, noted, 'many of them by care and frugality soon amass sufficient cowries to pay a heavy sum for the redemption of themselves and their children'.[85] The rates of manumission requested by the owners of female slaves were 'at an exorbitant rate compared with the price formerly paid [before 1860]', and owners often proved more reluctant to part with female slaves with daughters than male slaves.

The rise in redemption costs may have resulted from slave owners' reluctance to lose female labour as female-skill-based industries expanded. It was difficult for women to liberate themselves, as an Oyo woman named Ohlomo found out; in 1860 her master, Bada, reluctantly freed her for 100 heads of cowries.[86] Fadipe's assertion that redemption was fairly accessible to all slaves is misleading. Even if a slave secured his or her freedom, it could never be guaranteed. As Acting Consul McCoskry sadly noted in 1861, speaking of numerous cases involving freed slaves, 'I find many who have been here have fallen into bad hands, and have again been sold into slavery'.[87] Manumission operated like many of the other aspects of the domestic system of slavery, and significant distinctions in status, rights, and treatment were largely based on gender.[88]

Notes

1 An earlier draft of this paper was presented at the UNESCO/SSHRCC Summer Institute, 'Identifying Enslaved Africans: The "Nigerian" Hinterland and the African Diaspora', York University, Toronto, 1997. I would like to thank the participants for their useful comments on the draft, especially Edna Bay, LaRay Denzer, Robin Law and Paul Lovejoy. I also greatly appreciate the financial assistance to attend the Institute, which was provided by the Department of History at the University of Stirling, and the hospitality of Elena and Paul Lake and Peggy Cade.

2 Paul Lovejoy, 'The African Diaspora: Revisionist Interpretations of Ethnicity, Culture and Religion under Slavery', *Studies in the World History of Slavery, Abolition and Emancipation* 2, no. 1 (1997).

3 See Paul Lovejoy, 'Biography as Source Material: Towards a Biographical Archive of Enslaved Africans', in R. Law (ed.), *Source Material for Studying the Slave Trade and the African Diaspora* (papers from a conference at the Centre of Commonwealth Studies, University of Stirling, UK, April 1996), Occasional Paper 5 (1997).

4 For a fuller discussion of women and domestic slavery in Yorubaland at this time, see Francine Shields, 'Palm Oil and Power: Women in an Era of Economic and Social Transition in 19th-Century Yorubaland (South-West Nigeria)' (PhD thesis, University of Stirling, UK, 1997).

5 The Anglican 'Yoruba Missions' were initiated in the middle of the nineteenth century, when the British government established a colony at Lagos. The journals were maintained on a daily, quarterly or yearly basis, and are both quantitatively and qualitatively rich. Over half the missionaries were identified as Yoruba or claimed Yoruba origin. On the growth and development of the missions, see E. A. Ayandele, *The Missionary Impact on Modern Nigeria, 1842–1914: A Political and Social Analysis* (London, 1966) and J. F. A. Ajayi, *Christian Missions in Nigeria, 1841–1891* (London, 1981). For historical details on the colony of Lagos, see Robert Smith, 'The Lagos Consulate: An Outline, 1851–1861', *Journal of African History* 15, no. 3 (1974).

6 Earlier material on the Yoruba area can be found in the Sierra Leone series in the Church Missionary Society Archives at the University of Birmingham (hereafter cited as CMS), classified under CA1. Yoruba mission journals prior to 1880 are classified under CA2 0 and ordered alphabetically, by author. Those after 1880 are classified under G3 A2 and ordered consecutively, by year. I would like to thank John Peel for his invaluable advice on the Yoruba mission archives, and the staff of the Heslop Rooms at the University of Birmingham Library for their assistance in retrieving the documents.

7 These are held at the Public Record Office (hereafter cited as PRO), Kew, England. Selected documents on the slave trade are reproduced from the originals by the Irish Universities Press as Parliamentary Papers (hereafter cited as PP). I would like to thank the staff of the PRO for their help while consulting these documents.

8 See J. A. Atanda, 'The Fall of the Old Oyo Empire: A Reconsideration of Its Cause', *Journal of the Historical Society of Nigeria* 5, no. 4 (1971); Robert Smith, *Kingdoms of the Yoruba* (London, 1976), p. 155; R. Law, 'The Owu War in Yoruba History', *Journal of the Historical Society of Nigeria* 7, no. 1 (1973).

9 J. F. Ade Ajayi and R. Smith, *Yoruba Warfare in the Nineteenth Century* (Cambridge, 1964).

10 CMS, CA2 049/104, Hinderer, 4 October 1851; CMS, CA2 049/116, Hinderer, Half Yearly Report to April 1859; CMS, CA2 056/50, J. Johnson, February–April 1877; CMS, CA2 069/12, Meakin, 24 April 1859; Samuel Johnson, *The History of the Yorubas: From the Earliest Times to the Beginning of the British Protectorate* (London, 1921), pp. 365, 374–5, 438.

11 See Sydney Emezue, 'Warfare and Slaving in Nineteenth-Century Igboland', paper presented at the UNESCO/SSHRCC Summer Institute, 'Identifying Enslaved Africans: The "Nigerian" Hinterland and the African Diaspora', Toronto, 1997.

12 PRO, CO147/3, Freeman to Newcastle, 1863.

13 PRO, CO147/4, no. 74, (Slave Trade, no. 14) encl., Gov. Glover to Henry Robbin, August 1863. Also CMS, CA2 070/51, Moore, 25 February 1864.

14 For example, PRO, CO147/8, no. 35, encl. 6, Glover, 1865; PRO, CO147/27, no. 23, Berkley to R. N. Keale (Governor in Chief), Visit to the Eastern District, 1873; PRO, CO147/42, no. 224, encl., T. Tickel to Griffith, Visit to Weme, Western District, 1880; PRO, CO147/43, no. 300, Griffith to Ussher, Seizure in Ijebuland, 1880; PRO, CO147/48, no. 40, encl. 8, Statement of the King Ore, Head of the Ekitiparapo, January 1882; PRO, CO147/64, no. 192, encl., Moloney to Knutsford, Correspondence with Ilorin, Ibadan and Ekitiparapo, 1888; PRO, CO147/65, no. 256, encl., Moloney to Knutsford, 1888. Anna Hinderer noted that the farms around Ibadan were not safe in 1860, at the start of the Ijaye war; see Hinderer, *Seventeen Years in the Yoruba Country* (London, 1872), p. 228.

15 CMS, CA2 049/104, Hinderer, 3 October 1851. See also William Clarke, *Travels and Explorations in Yorubaland (1854–1858)*, ed. J. A. Atanda (Ibadan Nigeria), pp. 22, 65, 73; PP, vol. 63, no. 2, encl. 10, S. Johnson to Moloney, 21 May 1886 (part of the Ibadan army had been reserved at home to escort trade caravans going to and from Orun once a month); Samuel Johnson, *History*, p. 338. See T. Falola, 'The Yoruba Caravan System of the Nineteenth Century', *International Journal of African Historical Studies* 24, no. 1 (1991).

16 PRO, CO147/69, no. 55, Moloney to Knutsford and encl. 1, 'Statement of Mary Dota', 1889.

17 CMS, CA2 087/67, White, 5 March 1865; for previous occasions, see CMS, CA2 087/52, White, 1, 2, 3 October 1856, and CA2 087/65, White, 25 March 1863.

18 CMS, CA2 049/103, Hinderer, 7 June 1851; CA2 049/107, 26 August 1853; CA2 049/110, 4 November 1854; CMS, CA2 056/50, J. Johnson, February–April 1877; PP, vol. 47, no. 3, encl. 2, Extract from 'Iwe-Irohin', 24 March 1860; PP, vol. 63, no. 8, encl. 1, Report by Samuel Rowe, 1887, 412.

19 CMS, CA2 087/63, White, Ota, 9 January 1862.

20 CMS, CA2 075/24, Olubi, 8 June 1870. See also J. Iliffe, 'Poverty in Nineteenth-century Yorubaland', *Journal of African History* 25, no. 1 (1984), and Iliffe, *The African Poor: A History* (Cambridge, 1987). Anna Hinderer noted the case of an Efon woman and her daughter who were displaced, kidnapped and separated in the 1854 Ibadan–Efon war; see Hinderer, *Seventeen Years*, p. 143.

21 PRO, CO147/46, no. 124, 'The War between Ibadan and Neighbouring Tribes', encl. 3, extract of letter from Mr Scott (CMS Ibadan) to Mr Hethersett (Aremo, Ibadan) August 1881.

22 PP, vol. 63, no. 26, encl. 10, S. Johnson to Moloney, May 1886.

23 CMS, CA2 075/24, 24 December 1869.

24 PRO, CO147/8, no. 32, Glover to Cardwell, 14 March 1865. In one unfortunate case in 1886, Chief Mosaderin sadly confided in Henry Higgins that two of his wives had been shot dead by Ibadan troops in the middle of his war camp. PP, vol. 63, no. 8, encl., part 2 of a report by Higgins and Smith, 20 June 1887, 62.

25 PRO, CO879/45/509, no. 39, encl. 1, Acting Governor Rohrweger to Mr Chamberlain, 1896.

26 Ilorin refused to sign peace agreements negotiated by the British and remained hostile. British agents established a camp at Odo Otin, four miles north of Ikirun; this is probably where Asiki was heading when the Ilorin soldiers captured her. See Smith, *Kingdoms*, p. 149.

27 The main items of exchange imported to West Africa were textiles, spirits, salt, iron, guns, gunpowder and tobacco. On the commercial transition in Lagos and the immediate hinterland, see A. G. Hopkins, 'Economic Imperialism in West Africa: Lagos 1880–92', *Economic History Review* 21 (1968), and Hopkins, *An Economic History of West Africa* (London, 1973); R. Law (ed.), '"Legitimate" Trade and Gender Relations in Yorubaland and Dahomey', in Law, *From Slave Trade to 'Legitimate' Commerce* (Cambridge, 1995); R. Law, 'The Historiography of the Commercial Transition in 19th Century West Africa', in Toyin Falola (ed.), *African Historiography: Essays in Honour of Jacob Ade Ajayi* (Harlow, UK, 1993).

28 Clarke, *Travels*, p. 274. See also Robert Campbell, *A Pilgrimage to My Motherland: Journey among the Egbas and Yorubas of Central Africa* (London, 1861), p. 51, and R. H. Stone, *In Afric's Forest and Jungle, or Six Years among the Yorubans* (Edinburgh, 1900), p. 24.

29 CMS, CA2 029/18, Cole, 25 January 1875; CMS, CA2 056/52, J. Johnson, Ilaro to Awaye, August–November 1878; PRO, CO879/15, no. 192, 1879.

30 CMS, CA2 049/104, Hinderer, 4 October 1851; T. J. Bowen, *Adventures and Missionary Labours in Several Countries in the Interior of Africa* (London, 1968), p. 308; Clarke, *Travels*, p. 245; Campbell, *Pilgrimage*, pp. 48, 51; Samuel Johnson, *History*, p. 124. Susan Martin notes a similar long-standing sexual division of labour among the Ngwa in 'Slaves, Igbo Women and Palm Oil in the Nineteenth Century', in Law, *From Slave Trade to 'Legitimate' Commerce*; Martin, *Palm Oil and Protest: An Economic History of the Ngwa Region of South Eastern Nigeria 1800–1980* (Cambridge, 1988); Martin, 'Gender and Innovation: Farming, Cooking and Palm Processing in the Ngwa Region, South Eastern Nigeria 1900–1930', *Journal of African History* 25, no. 4 (1984).

31 PRO, FO84/976, no. 22, Campbell to Clarendon, 2 October 1855 (reproduced in PP, Africa Consular, vol. 42, class B, no. 17 and enclosures).

32 Campbell, *Pilgrimage*, pp. 51–2. For similar production methods in West Africa and Yoruba area, see Captain J. Adams, *Remarks on the Country Extending from Cape Palmas to the River Congo* (1834; London, 1966), pp. 171–2; Clarke, *Travels*, p. 274; Stone, *In Afric's Forest*, p. 24; PRO, FO881/5622.X, Precis of Information on the Colony of Lagos and the Neighbouring Tribes, compiled by R. E. Darwin, February 1888, p. 22.

33 By 1880 E. G. Gunnell's 'Palm Nut and Kernel Machinery' was advertised in the *Lagos Times*. A sifter, cracker, separator and palm-pulp press were introduced, apparently to meet 'constant demand from Native Merchants and Traders for such a machine'. PRO, CO147/48, no. 50, encl. 5, *Lagos Times*, 24 August 1881; PRO, CO147/57, *Lagos Times*, 24 October 1883.

34 As LaRay Denzer's paper ('Indigenous Slavery and Yoruba Historiography', presented at the UNESCO/SSHRCC Summer Institute, 'Identifying Enslaved Africans: The "Nigerian" Hinterland and the African Diaspora, Toronto, 1997) highlights, domestic slavery in Yorubaland has remained a neglected area of research; consequently, very few studies are available on the topic, but see E. Adeniyi Oroge, 'The Institution of Domestic Slavery in Yorubaland, with Particular Reference to the Nineteenth Century' (PhD thesis, University of Birmingham, UK, 1971); Toyin Falola, 'Missionaries and Domestic Slavery in Yorubaland in the Nineteenth Century', *Journal of Religion in Africa* 14 (1986); Ann O'Hear, *Power Relations in Nigeria: Ilorin Slaves and Their Successors* (Rochester, NY, 1997). On women and slavery in general in a number of African societies, see C. Robertson and M. A. Klein (eds), *Women and Slavery in Africa* (Madison, WI, 1983); Kristin Mann, 'Owners, Slaves and the Struggle for Labour in the Commercial Transition at Lagos', in Robin Law (ed.), *From Slave Trade to 'Legitimate' Commerce*; B. I. Obichere, 'Women and Slavery in the Kingdom of Dahomey', *Revue française d'histoire d'outre-mer* 65 (1978); Marcia Wright, 'Women

in Peril: A Commentary on the Life Stories of Captives in Nineteenth-Century East-Central Africa', *African Social Research* 20 (December 1975).

35 For historical studies of the sexual and generational division of labour in nineteenth-century Yorubaland, see Shields, 'Palm Oil and Power'; R. Law, '"Legitimate" Trade and Gender Relations in Yorubaland and Dahomey', in Robin Law (ed.), *From Slave Trade to 'Legitimate' Commerce*. Many studies deal with twentieth-century or present-day developments and incorporate a small section on the pre-colonial situation. See S. Afonja, 'Changing Modes of Production and the Sexual Division of Labour among the Yoruba', *Signs* 7, no. 2 (1981), pp. 299–313; J. I. Guyer, 'Food, Cocoa, and the Division of Labour by Sex in Two West African Societies', *Comparative Studies in Society and History* 22, no. 3 (1980), pp. 355–73; N. Sudarkasa (formerly Gloria Marshall), 'The Division of Labour by Sex in Yoruba Society', chap. 2 in Sudarkasa, *Where Women Work: A Study of Yoruba Women in The Market Place and in the Home* (Ann Arbor, MI, 1973); C. Johnson, 'Class and Gender: A Consideration of Yoruba Women during the Colonial Period', chap. 13 in C. Robertson and I. Berger (eds), *Women and Class in Africa* (New York, 1986). For studies on Nigeria and Africa in general see S. Afonja, 'Historical Evolution in the Sexual Division of Labour in Nigeria' (paper presented at a meeting on 'Theoretical Frameworks and Methodological Approaches to Studies on the Role of Women in History', 1984); R. A. LeVine, 'Sex Roles and Economic Change in Africa', in J. Middleton (ed.), *Black Africa: Its Peoples and Their Cultures Today* (London, 1970).

36 See S. Martin, 'Slaves, Igbo Women and Palm Oil in the Nineteenth Century', in R. Law (ed.), *From Slave Trade to 'Legitimate' Commerce*; K. Mann, 'Owners, Slaves' (forthcoming); Sandra Greene, *Gender, Ethnicity and Social Change on the Upper Slave Coast: A History of the Anlo-Ewe* (London and Portsmouth, NH, 1996); Louis Wilson, 'The Bloodless Conquest in South-Eastern Ghana: The Huza and Territorial Expansion of the Krobo in the 19th Century', *International Journal of African Historical Studies* 23, no. 2 (1990); Wilson, *The Krobo People of Ghana to 1892: A Political and Social History* (Athens, OH, 1991), especially chap. 5; Onaiwu Ogbomo, 'Esan Woman Traders and Pre-Colonial Economic Power', in B. House-Midamba and F. K. Ekechi (eds), *African Market Women and Economic Power* (Greenwood, CT, 1995).

37 For interesting studies of aspects of polygamy in nineteenth-century Yorubaland see Anthony Copley, 'The Debate on Widow Re-Marriage and Polygamy: Aspects of Moral Change in Nineteenth-Century Bengal and Yorubaland', *Journal of Imperial and Commonwealth History* 7, no. 2 (1979); J. B. Webster, 'Attitudes and Policies of the Yoruba African Churches towards Polygamy', in C. Baeta (ed.), *Christianity in Tropical Africa* (London, 1968).

38 PRO, CO147/4, no. 96, encl. 2, Chiefs, Traders and People of Lagos to Gov. Glover, 1863; Wesleyan Methodist Missionary Society, Revd W. Hoad, Oyo, 18 March 1896.

39 Francine Shields, '"Is Not a Woman to Sell Oil, How Can a Man Sell Oil Like a Woman?" Women, Labour and the Commercial Transition in 19th Century Yorubaland' (paper presented at the African Studies Association of the UK biennial conference, Bristol, September 1996).

40 Richard Burton, *Abeokuta and the Cameroons Mountains* (London, 1863), vol. 1, p. 208.

41 Stone, *In Afric's Forest*, pp. 98–9. See also H. Carr, O. Johnson, C. A. Sapara-Williams, E. H. Oke, A. Edun and W. Lawson (ed. A. G. Hopkins), 'A Report on the Laws and Customs of the Yoruba, 1910', *Journal of the Historical Society of Nigeria* 5, no. 1 (1969), p. 80; N. A. Fadipe, *The Sociology of the Yoruba*, (Ibadan, Nigeria, 1939), pp. 80, 115.

42 PRO, CO879/15, no. 178, 'Information Respecting the Settlement of Lagos', by Lieut. Gov. Lees, 1879, 21.

43 For a study of this issue in northern Nigeria see P. Lovejoy, 'Concubinage and the Status of Women Slaves in Early Colonial Northern Nigeria', *Journal of African History* 29 (1988).

44 CMS, CA2 080/39, Robbin, Abeokuta, CA2 011/32, Deposition of Awa, 12 November 1865.

45 T. J. Bowen, *Adventures and Missionary Labours in Several Countries in the Interior of Africa* (London, 1968), pp. 304–5, 343. See also Burton, *Abeokuta*, vol. 1, p. 81; Campbell, *Pilgrimage*, p. 60; CMS, CA2 087/76, White, 23 May 1870.

46 On production, see PRO, CO147/51, no. 250, Acting Administrator Simpson, 1881. On transport, CMS, CA2 056/50, J. Johnson, 21 March 1877. On transport and trade, PRO, CO147/4, no. 68, Deposition of Amodu, Lagos, 1863; CO147/6, no. 7, Freeman to Newcastle, February 1864; CO147/40, no. 3, encl., Statement of Jemetoh and Whasu, 1880; CO147/40, no. 65, Kojo to Tickel, 1880; CO147/40, no. 66, encl., Statement of Bada, 1880; CO147/72, no. 309, Denton to Knutsford, October 1889.

47 Evidence indicating low birth rates and poor life expectancy among children in nineteenth-century Yorubaland can be found in R. Hallet (ed.), *The Niger Journal of Richard and John Lander* (London, 1965), pp. 70, 72; Bowen, *Adventures and Missionary Labours*, p. 305; Burton, *Abeokuta*, vol. 1, p. 207; CMS, CA2 085/1, Revd Townsend to Captain Trotter, letter dated 31 January 1849.

48 CMS, CA2 056/50, J. Johnson, February–April 1877, Journey from Lagos to Ibadan. For individual studies of pawnship in African societies, including Yorubaland, see T. Falola and P. E. Lovejoy, eds, *Pawnship in Africa: Debt Bondage in Historical Perspective* (Boulder, CO, 1994). For a detailed study on nineteenth-century Yorubaland, see E. A. Oroge, 'Iwofa: An Historical Survey of the Yoruba Institution of Indenture', *African Economic History* 14 (1985), pp. 75–106.

49 CMS, CA2 069/13, Meakin, Oyo, 31 October 1859; CMS, Allen, CA2 019/9, 8 June 1870; Olubi, CA2 075/25, 8 June 1870 and earlier, in the 'Report of the Ijaye Relief Committee', CMS, CA2 011/25, 1 October 1861.

50 PP, vol. 42, no. 16, Campbell to Clarendon, 1 October 1855.

51 PRO, FO84/976, vol. 19, no. 35, Campbell to Earl of Clarendon, 7 December 1855.

52 For transport of goods in this period, see F. A. Ogunremi, 'Human Porterage in Nigeria in the Nineteenth Century: A Pillar in the Indigenous Economy', *Journal of the Historical Society of Nigeria* 8, no. 1 (1975).

53 PRO, CO147/35, no. 18, encl., Dumaresq to Freely, 1878.

54 Wilson, 'Bloodless Conquest', pp. 292–7, notes a similar use of children's labour among the Krobo of southern Ghana during the rise of the palm oil and kernel trade. But he concludes that the children were largely drawn from within the family or community and were not generally slaves, domestic slaves not being the main source of labour for palm oil production among the Krobo. See also Wilson, *Krobo People*, pp. 95–6.

55 Martin, 'Slaves, Igbo Women', concludes that slave labour was not used to any great degree in the Ngwa palm oil industry; rather, as among the Krobo, there was more use of family and community members. Although Ngwa men, like Yoruba men, acquired more wives, most of the women were free-born and not predominantly drawn from the slave population. The Yoruba situation also differs from that among the Aro of eastern Nigeria, documented by G. Ugo Nwokeji, '"Did We Bring Land with Us from Aro?": The Contradictions of Mmuba among the Aro of Nigeria, c. 1750–1890', paper presented at the UNESCO/SSHRCC Summer Institute, 'Identifying Enslaved Africans: The "Nigerian" Hinterland and the African Diaspora', Toronto, 1997.

56 PRO, CO147/13, no. 12, Blackall to the Duke of Buckingham, Visit to Lagos, 1867.

57 PP, vol. 6, Report of the Select Committee on the African Slave Trade, Evidence of Revd Henry Townsend, May 1849. Townsend stated that in Abeokuta domestic slaves were generally treated 'with the greatest kindness'.

58 PP, vol. 44, no. 14, encl. 1, Mr Davis to Campbell, 18 May 1857.

59 Fadipe, *Sociology*, pp. 180–9.

60 CMS, CA2 056/50, James Johnson, Interior Inspection Tour, February–April 1877. See especially Falola, 'Missionaries and Domestic Slavery'.

61 See Shields, 'Palm Oil and Power', chap. 5.

62 Fadipe, *Sociology*, p. 182.

63 Samuel Johnson, *History*, p. 325.

64 Kristin Mann, 'Women's Rights in Law and Practice: Marriage and Dispute Settlement in Colonial Lagos', in M. J. Hay and M. Wright (eds), *African Women and the Law: Historical Perspectives* (Boston, 1982).

65 PRO, CO147/57, no. 288, encl. 1, Evans to Granville, September 1886.

66 *Ibid.*

67 PP, vol. 50, class B, no. 1, Glover to Russell, 6 December 1865, encl., 'Deposition of Awa, A Slave Woman of Mr. Henry Robbin at Abeokuta'.

68 For example, in 1852 an enslaved Ondo woman was exchanged by her master to settle a trade account: CMS, CA2 078/19, Phillips Junior, 11 August 1877. Also see PP, vol. 60, no. 34, encl. 2, Statement of Wheto of Badagry, 7 January 1889, in which Wheto states, 'Sometimes they [slaves] are sold for goods and cash, gin, rum, tobacco, and sometimes exchanged for Egba slaves or Jebu [sic] slaves'.

69 The language in Millson's explanation highlights the extent to which both the Atlantic and domestic slave trades de-humanized and commoditized the slaves: 'A slave, be it remembered, combines the security of a bank note with the carrying power of a pack horse.' PRO, CO147/85, no. 168, Carter to Knutsford, encl., 'Yoruba', by Alvan Millson of the Royal Geographical Society, 1891, 4.

70 The person was generally considered of a 'lower caste'. PP, vol. 6, H. Townsend.

71 In one case, a slave woman called Mrs Green, belonging to a man named Jeremiah, was granted permission by her master to marry; she did so and had children. Some time later Jeremiah took the slave woman and her children back, as they were still his property. Wesleyan Methodist Mission Society (WMMS) Notices, vol. xvi, letter from T. Champness, 25 November 1861 and WMMS archives, letter no. 42, Champness, dated 4 September 1862.

72 PP, vol. 45, no. 11, Campbell to Clarendon, 28 March 1858.

73 CMS, CA2 075, Olubi, 25 August 1867.

74 PRO, CO879/41/475, no. 3, encl. 2, Carter to Ripon, 1894.

75 For some of the many examples, see PRO, CO147/61, no. 345, Moloney to Knutsford, encl. 2, 'Human sacrifices at Itebu', 1887; CO147/61, no. 351, Moloney to Holland, encl. 6, Phillips to Moloney, Ondo, 1887; CO147/42, no. 246 and encl., Griffith to Ussher, Report on a Visit to Eastern District, 1880. Griffith reported of Ondo's slaves that 'whenever they had cause to fear that the Lisa [chief] would sacrifice they would arm themselves'. When the Lisa died, leaving orders that more than forty-five slaves were to be sacrificed, his slaves abandoned the household, armed themselves and refused to return until the Ondo authorities struck a bargain with them, which, ironically, permitted them to substitute for sacrifice slaves they had bought.

76 CMS, CA2 078/21, Phillips, 20 November 1878.

77 WMMS, no. 18, Bickersteth, Ijaye, letter dated Abeokuta, 6 May 1861; CMS, CA2 011/117, N. Ogbonaiye, Itebu, 5 October 1879; WMMS, no. 30, J. Thomas, Abeokuta, 27 November 1882; PRO, CO147/71, no. 261, encl. 1, Denton to Knutsford, 1889. In this last document a group of missionaries stated that the proportion of females to males in the Christian community of Lagos at the time was 3:1. The total female population of Lagos was calculated to be less than the male.

78 See E. A. Oroge, 'The Fugitive Slave Question in Anglo-Egba Relations 1861–1886', *Journal of the Historical Society of Nigeria* 8, no. 1 (1975); Kristin Mann, 'The

Emancipation of Female Slaves in Colonial Lagos' (unpublished paper, 1991), and Mann, 'Owners, Slaves' (forthcoming).

79 For example, CMS, CA2 075/32, Olubi, 6 October 1875; CA2 075/30, Olubi, 17 March 1874; CA2 011/70, 10 February 1874. In 1887 the Ife authorities demanded the return of a woman who had run away from her husband to Oke-Igbo; the Oke-Igbo authorities refused, saying that many of their own women and slaves had run away to Ife. See PRO, CO147/61, no. 353, encl. 2, Derin, Oni elect of Ife to Moloney, 1887.

80 For example PRO, CO147/1, Freeman to Newcastle, 4 June 1862.

81 Compare PP, vol. 44, no. 14, Campbell to Clarendon, 2 July 1857, with encl. 4, Mr Williams to Campbell, 18 June 1857. See also Nwokeji, '"Did We Bring Land?"'

82 PRO, CO147/21, no. 49, encl. in Pope Hennesy to Kimberley, 1872, 'Letter from Alake, Ogboni, Baloguns and Parakoyi of Abeokuta to Governor Pope Hennesy'. By the end of the century, Carter reported that at Abeokuta, desertion of women, children, and slaves was still the major preoccupation of the chiefs: PRO, CO879/45/509, no. 16, Carter to Chamberlain, 1896.

83 PRO, CO879/27/345, no. 16a, encl. 2, 1887, 'Soranke, the Jaguna of Igbein, to Moloney'. Many more letters with similar complaints were submitted to the consulate over the period: see PRO, CO147/6, no. 49, encl. in Glover to Cardwell, 23 July 1864, 'Ogundipe to Glover'; CO147/3, no. 41, encl., Captain William-Rice Mulliner to Duke of Newcastle, 1863; CO147/59, no. 127, encl., Mr Kester to Acting Administrator Evans, 'Visit to Ijebu-Ode', 1887; CO147/38, no. 135, encl. 2, Ussher to Sir Hicks-Beach Bart, 'Letter from Awujale of Ijebu-Ode', 1879. See also CMS, CA2 029/15, Cole, 15 February 1874.

84 PRO, CO147/57, no. 288, encl. 2, 'News from Ikorodu Market', 1886.

85 PP, vol. 45, class B, no. 11, Campbell to Clarendon, 28 March 1858.

86 PP, vol. 46, no. 11, Brand to Russell, 31 December 1859. See also PP, vol. 46, no. 12, Brand to Russell, 18 January 1860.

87 PP, vol. 47, no. 19, McCoskry to Russell, 3 September 1861.

88 See also Nwokeji, '"Did We Bring Land?"' which highlights distinct differences between the rights and treatment of male and female slaves among the Aro.

═ 12 ═

'She Voluntarily Hath Come': A Gambian Woman Trader in Colonial Georgia in the Eighteenth Century[1]

Lillian Ashcraft-Eason

In mid-May 1772 Fenda Lawrence left the slave-trading entrepôt of Kau-Ur in the kingdom of Saalum to relocate in colonial Georgia, eventually settling in Savannah. Taking leave of her native land on the Gambia river, she boarded the *New Brittannia*, a slaving vessel, in the company of 220 Africans who were being transported into bondage to grow rice and other products in the coastal lowlands of Georgia and South Carolina.[2] By contrast with the captives on board, Fenda Lawrence was a black, free woman of material substance and in fact a slave trader herself. Because of her status as a free passenger and the former spouse of an Englishman, she was set apart from both the African captives and the crew, so her presence was sure to invite curiosity aboard the ship. It was rare for any African merchant to cross the Atlantic. Lawrence's gender makes her passage even more exceptional.

Slave trading was the established business at Kau-Ur, a small settlement upriver from James Island, the headquarters of British trade on the Gambia. The Senegambia region had been a source of slaves for both the trans-Atlantic and trans-Saharan trades, and there was a strong local demand for slaves as well. In the eighteenth century, Saalum was ruled by a military élite that preyed on the peasantry and was involved in the slave trade.[3] Moreover, the town of Kau-Ur was connected with the Muslim commercial network in the interior of the western Sudan. Muslim merchants, who

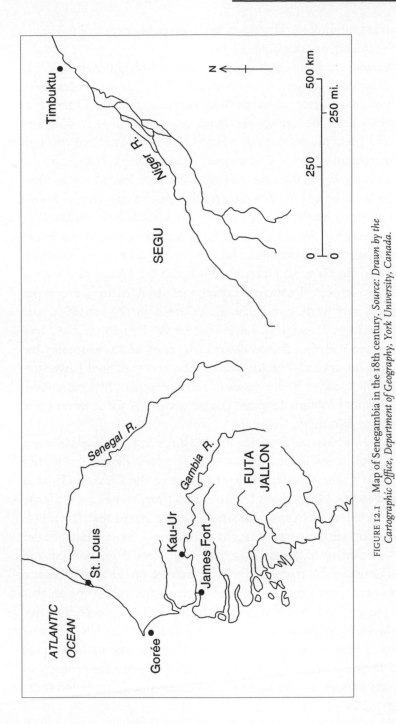

FIGURE 12.1   Map of Senegambia in the 18th century. *Source: Drawn by the Cartographic Office, Department of Geography, York University, Canada.*

were known as Mandinka, Jakhanke or Juula, probably supplied the slaves on board Fenda Lawrence's ship.[4]

As at other ports along the Senegambia coast, including Gorée, Rufisque and St-Louis, women traders were common.[5] These prominent women (*signares*) dominated local trade in provisions, fish and food, but they also played a major role in the import–export trade in gum, slaves, textiles and other commodities. Many of these women had been attached through marriage or concubinage to a European trader, often French in the eighteenth century, but as the case of Fenda Lawrence demonstrates some women also became involved with British merchants. Hence Fenda Lawrence's presence on the coast of Senegambia would have evoked little interest, but in colonial America, the response would have been otherwise.

After thirty-six days of sailing, the *New Brittannia* docked in Charleston harbour. The *South Carolina Gazette* announced the arrival of the ship, and an advertisement featuring raffia-skirted, African stereotypes announced that 220 'healthy and likely slaves' from the ship's holds would be put up for sale on Tuesday, 30 June. There was no mention that a free Gambian woman had also arrived aboard this ship, and presumably the 220 slaves did not include the five slaves who accompanied Lawrence. After placing the captives in the hands of slave merchant Miles Brewton, the *New Brittannia*'s captain, Stephen Deane, accompanied Lawrence and her entourage to Savannah, Georgia.[6]

Two documents have survived that establish Fenda Lawrence's identity. Upon her arrival in Savannah, Captain Deane gave a deposition on her behalf to Noble Jones (Senior Assistant Justice in the General Court of Georgia) and James Habersham (Acting Governor) issued a certificate granting her residency.[7] In his deposition, Deane stated that Lawrence, whom he had known for seven or eight years, was a considerable trader in 'Kau-Ur'. According to Deane, Lawrence was 'a free Black Woman and heretofore a Considerable trader in the River Gambia on the Coast of Africa [who] hath voluntarily come to be and Remain for sometime in this province'.[8] He said she had brought with her 'sundry goods' and five domestic slaves, 'a Woman named Camilla and her Child Nancy, one Woman named Morria and her Child Tony, also one Boy named James Lawrence'.[9] Deane testified that 'the goods and slaves are the property of the said Fenda Lawrence, She having been concerned in trade for some years past'.[10]

Captain Deane attempted to lessen the risks of Lawrence's immigration. He was sufficiently interested in her to provide safe passage to Charleston

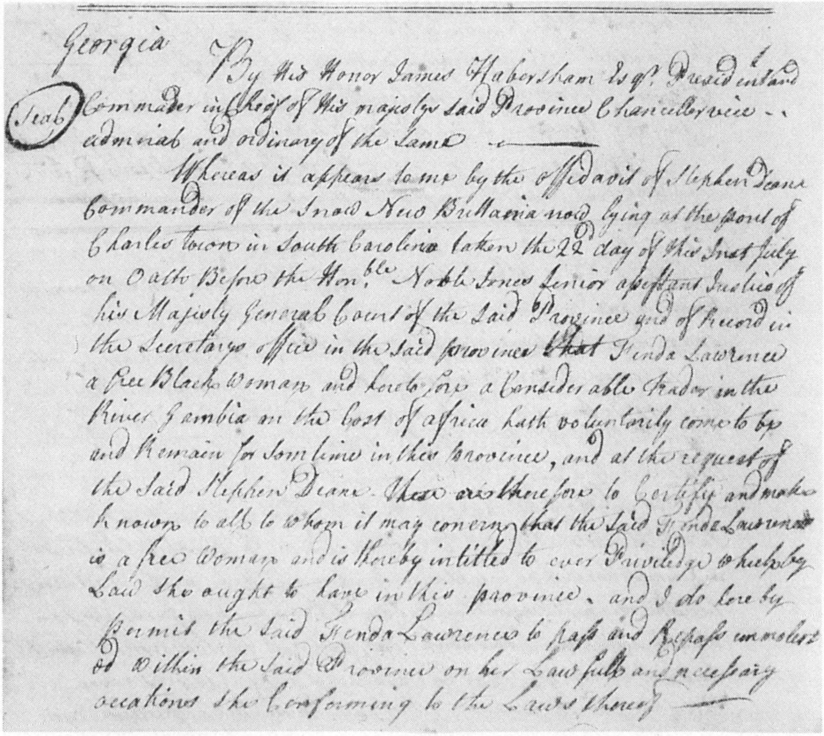

FIGURE 12.2   Affidavit of Captain Stephen Deane, commander of the ship *New Brittannia*, concerning Fenda Lawrence, a former resident of 'a place called Cower on the River Gambia in Africa', 2 July 1772. *Source:* Georgia (Colony). Bonds, Bills of Sale, Deeds of Gift, Powers of Attorney, 1772–1774 (pages 13–4). *Courtesy of Georgia Department of Archives and History.*

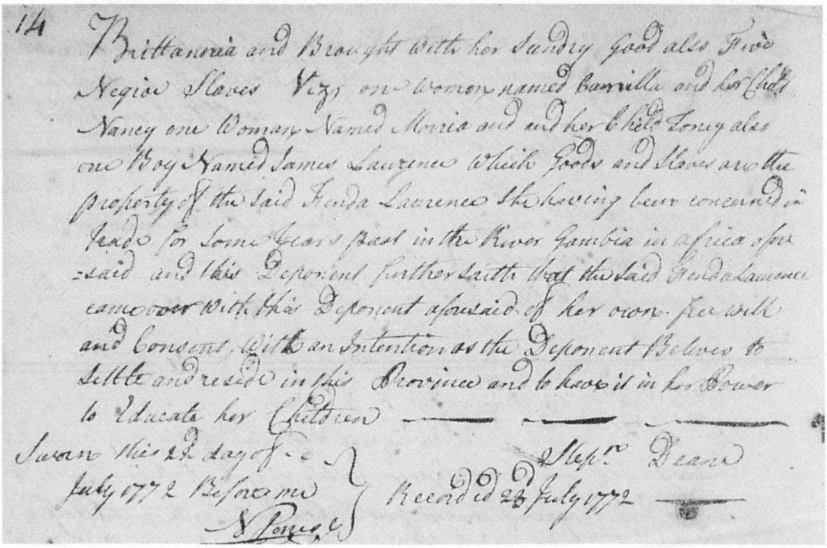

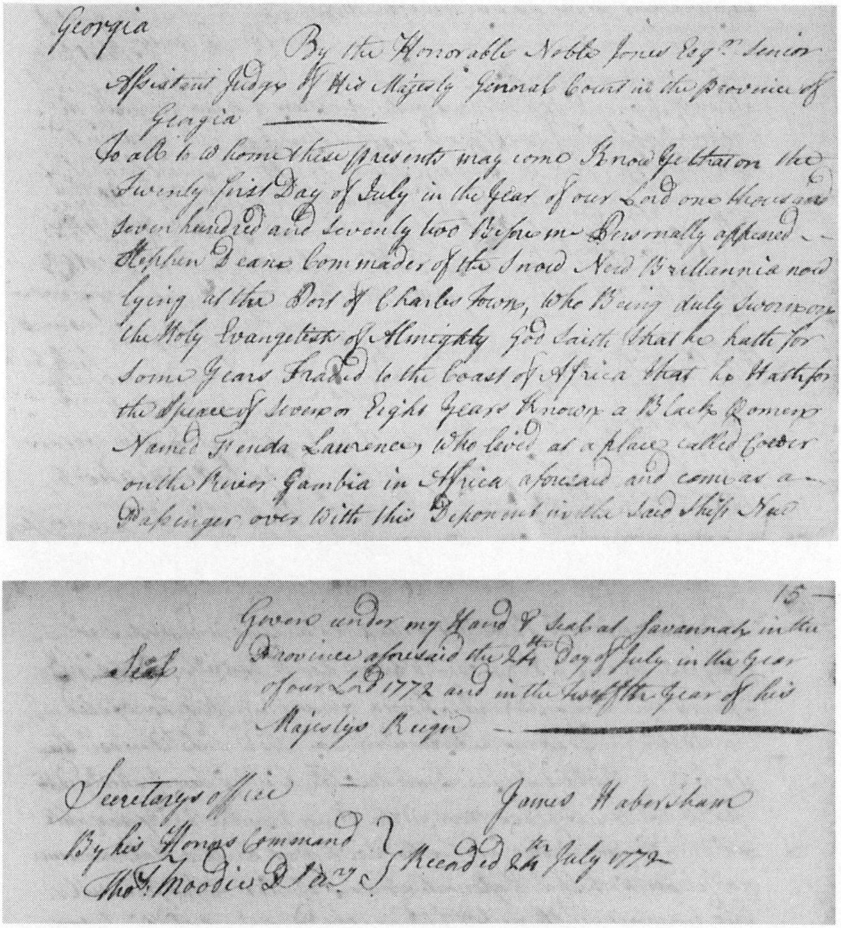

Georgia
By the Honorable Noble Jones Esqr. Senior Assistant Judge of His Majestys General Court in the province of Georgia ——
To all to whome these presents may come Know Yee that on the Twenty first Day of July in the Year of our Lord one thousand seven hundred and seventy two Before me Personally appeared — Stephen Deane Commander of the Snow New Brittannia now lying at the Port of Charles Town, who Being duly sworn on the Holy Evangelists of Almighty God saith that he hath for some Years Traded to the Coast of Africa that he Hath for the Space of seven or Eight Years Known a Black Women Named Fenda Lawrence who lived at a place called Cotoer on the River Gambia in Africa aforesaid and came as a — Passinger over with this Deponent in the said Ship New

15 —
Given under my Hand & Seal at Savannah in the Province aforesaid the 24th Day of July in the Year of our Lord 1772 and in the twelfth Year of his Majestys Reign ——
Seal
Secretarys office — James Habersham
By his Honors Command
Thos. Moodie D. Secy } Recorded 24th July 1772

FIGURE 12.3 Acknowledgement by James Habersham, president of the Governor's Council and acting governor of the Colony of Georgia ('His Honor James Habersham Esq President and Commander in Chief of His majestys said Province Chanceller vice-admiral and ordinary of the Same'), certifying that Fenda Lawrence is a free Black woman 'intitled to every Priviledge which by Law she aught to have in this province', 24 July 1772. *Source:* Georgia (Colony). Bonds, Bills of Sale, Deeds of Gift, Powers of Attorney, 1772–1774 (pages 14–15). *Courtesy of Georgia Department of Archives and History.*

and then to Savannah, to promote her cause before Georgian authorities, and to secure for her residency and safe passage within Georgia. Her status as a trader of some means establishes that Lawrence must have been well known along the Gambia, both to local people and apparently to Europeans. None the less Deane must have been aware that no matter what she owned or achieved, this woman of ebony hue never would receive respect equal to that of a white woman of means. The contemporary colonial mind-set cast any woman arriving from Africa aboard a slave ship in a negative light. Lawrence needed official papers to protect her free status. Therefore, Deane emphasized Lawrence's status as a free person with purpose and personal means: 'The said Fenda Lawrence came over with this Deponent aforesaid of her own free will and Consent.' Deane stated that it was her 'Intention . . . to Settle and reside in this Province and to have it in her Power to Educate her Children'.[11] Because she was a free woman, Deane requested that Lawrence be 'intitled to every Priviledge which by Law she aught to have in this province'.[12]

On 28 July, in response to Deane's deposition, Habersham issued Lawrence a certificate acknowledging her freedom, permitting her to settle in Georgia, and extending to her protection. With the full weight of his authority, Habersham declared: 'I do hereby permit the said Fenda Lawrence to pass and Repass unmolested within the said Province on her Lawfull and necessary occasions she Conforming to the Laws thereof.'[13]

What in her cultural background prepared this woman to venture to North America? Fenda Lawrence had spent her formative years in a region where trade and commerce were influenced by both the British and the French. She had apparently met her husband, Lawrence, in Gambia. At the time of her departure in 1772, there had been a long association between the kingdom of Saalum, at the mouth of the Gambia, and Britain. As early as the 1620s, English traders began trafficking in slaves along the Gambia river, which gave English merchants access to the trade of the western Sudan.[14] British influence increased after 1663, when a company was chartered for the specific purpose of trading in slaves.[15] In 1672, the Royal African Company was chartered; it dominated the Gambia trade until this company was in turn superseded in 1750 by the Company of Merchants Trading into Africa. After 1765, the Company of Merchants shifted its trade to more lucrative areas of West Africa, and it may be that this withdrawal southwards of British merchants left Fenda Lawrence behind.

At the time, the Senegambia region was truly multicultural. There were diverse languages and ethnic groups throughout the region (Mandinka, Wolof, Serer, Fulbe and smaller numbers of other people), and the several small kingdoms near the coast, including Saalum, were ethnically mixed.[16] Hence the presence of a mixed European and African population, which has sometimes been referred to as 'Atlantic creole', was another feature of this ethnic and cultural diversity. Individuals like Lawrence became mediators of the multiple cultures that came into contact, and they depended on international trade for self-maintenance and profits.[17]

Merchants in Saalum were under the authority of a local official, the *alcati*, a term derived from the Arabic al-qadi, or judge, but in the Senegambia a term often used to designate a village head. Every person intending to conduct slave trading in Kau-Ur had to have her or his business sanctioned by the *alcati*.[18] The male-dominant ruling élite controlled the economy, and as one of the most lucrative aspects of trade, the commerce in slaves was regulated strictly. To be 'a Considerable trader', as Deane described Lawrence, a woman had to be successful, regardless of her caste status. She was able to enter this male-dominated world through the patronage she had secured and then by using it to her advantage.[19] Because her trading business occurred on a 'considerable' level, Lawrence would have had numerous encounters with the *alcati* as the king's representative and the highest local authority responsible for regulating trade, dealing with foreigners, collecting taxes, networking with area chiefs and dispensing justice.

We can be reasonably sure that Fenda Lawrence was exposed to some of the concepts embedded in the songs and poetry of the military élite of Saalum, yet she married outside traditional circles. Tradition emphasized destiny, faithfulness to one's ancestors and loyalty to one's caste, and women were expected to perpetuate traditional values that tended to underpin the patriarchy.[20] Labour was sexually divided, allowing women a modicum of independence and control over their lives and resources, but generally subordinating women to the male-dominated economy.[21]

Unlike Lawrence, most African women never achieved recognition in commerce. Those who ventured into the processes of buying and selling other humans were generally confined to servicing the trade because of negligible amounts of capital, and hence they operated on the fringes of trans-Atlantic commerce. Women usually worked in local marketplaces, where they traded in foodstuffs and small wares suited to local needs.[22]

As Fenda Lawrence's story reveals, women were sometimes able to take advantage of economic opportunities not only on a local level but occasionally also in distant markets.[23] In order to build a lucrative business in the slave trade and manœuvre around patriarchal obstacles, a large outlay of capital was necessary. Ambitious women, or their daughters, established relationships with European men, and even married them, to consolidate business partnerships and thereby gain access to trade. A few notable women were daughters of biracial marriages, but Lawrence was probably widowed for she certainly was separated from her spouse. The first name of the man from whom she took her English name is not known, but apparently he had left the business and his possessions as her dowry. Deane's statement that Lawrence 'heretofore was a Considerable trader' suggests that her business may have suffered after her husband's death or departure.[24]

By the time Lawrence became a successful slave trader in the 1760s, there had been several generations of women slavers in the Senegambia. As the trade reports and personal journals of Europeans record, it was not unusual for women to sell captives along the riverways.[25] In this respect, there was nothing unique about Lawrence's vocation. At Rufisque, for example, an early Portuguese trading centre north of the Gambia, women traders were involved in the slave trade as early as 1634, when Senhora Philippa was a major trader. In 1669, an unnamed woman with Portuguese connections is also reported as a principal merchant. The most famous of these women merchants was the formidable Bibiana Vaz, a Euro-African who maintained an extensive trading empire between the Gambia and Sierra Leone rivers in the 1670s and 1680s. In 1684, the widow Senhora Catti, a Wolof woman who had married a Portuguese trader, was the commercial agent for the *damel* (ruler) of Kaajor. According to Wolof inheritance customs, Catti retained ownership of her husband's business and, under protection of or with authorization from the damel, continued to pursue a flourishing trade.[26] Women continued to be prominent in the coastal trade. By 1749, for example, women owned nine of the thirteen commercial properties on Gorée Island.[27]

Like the women who preceded her, Fenda Lawrence benefited from her relationship with a European male. She combined her African background with European thought and practice to espouse an Atlantic cultural ethos. She lived in a British trading post that was a marketplace of multicultural ideas, images and information, and a port of call for seafaring adventurers. These and other dynamics had the potential for cultivating a mind-set conducive to emigration. Lawrence did not fit the mould of a conventional Gambian woman, who cultivated rice, traded in local marketplaces and strove to safeguard cultural traditions and ancestral legacies. She had a non-traditional marriage that was also a business partnership. Although her lifestyle was not unprecedented, it was rare. She enjoyed mobility as a trader beyond that of more traditionally employed women.

Considering that she had opportunities for achievement within the context of her indigenous society, what factors impelled Fenda Lawrence to emigrate? The push from Kau-Ur may have been the patriarchal enforcement of cultural traditions, social practices and political manœuvrings that conflicted with her personal and business interests. Among the most probable issues with which she contended were those related to her marriage, her apparent status as a widow, concerns to protect her inheritance or dowry and her business dealings with Captain Stephen Deane.

The patriarchal, paternalistic and communal tendencies within the kingdom of Saalum could have interfered with Lawrence's business in Kau-Ur if the *alcati* and local chiefs questioned her dower rights or for other reasons withdrew their support. It is conceivable that this was her fate, for women who married outsiders often were denied such privileges as usufruct land rights and access to labour, including domestic slaves. Prevailing traditions regarding inheritance rights for widows of clan members were oppressive. The inheritance of a deceased male went to the eldest brother or other appropriate male in the family, not to the widow or her children. The senior male administered the inheritance on behalf of the larger family and kin network. Whether a woman with Lawrence's stature who had married a European merchant would retain the right to control her inheritance in a trading post presided over by the *alcati* and a local chief is unclear. The fact that her stated intent was 'to have it in her Power to Educate her Children' seems to indicate that she was protecting her estate and may suggest that her rights were being challenged.[28] Lawrence may also have been motivated to leave the Gambia partly because of a decline in trade.

Captain Stephen Deane who looked after her interests had been trading to the Gambia for several years, and he may have traded with Fenda Lawrence and perhaps her husband in one or more of his slaving voyages. Deane's first recorded expedition to the Gambia occurred in 1768, when he purchased 170 slaves for the *Brittannia* and took them to Savannah.[29] Between 1768 and 1771, he carried at least 500 slaves from West Africa to Georgia, a fifth of the 2500 captives arriving in the Georgia colony between 1766 and 1771.[30] In 1771, however, he only acquired 90 slaves, which he took to Charleston.[31] Business seems to have rebounded in 1772, the year of Lawrence's emigration, when Deane transported 220 captives to Charleston. This was his largest shipment to date.

After assisting Lawrence resettle in Georgia, Deane sailed for London on 23 July, met the owner of the *New Brittannia*, and then left for West Africa on November 5. His business on the Gambia river proceeded at a fast pace. He took less than 90 days to load and stock the ship for his return to Charleston; while it normally took approximately 130 days for loading ships on the African coast in the 1770s, ships tended to stay in port nearly 173 days on voyages to the Senegambian region.[32] However his plans to leave for Charleston with a cargo of 236 captives at the end of February were aborted.[33] Some slaves who belonged to the trading company armed the restive captives on the *New Brittannia* with carpenters' tools so that they could rip open the deck to steal gunpowder and guns.[34] The plot was foiled, however, but when the crew were about to overpower the insurgents, the slaves lit the gunpowder, causing the ship to blow up. All the 236 captive Africans, 96 free Africans who were still on board, and almost all the European crew were killed. Only Deane and one other man escaped, 'by their having providentially got into the boat . . . a few minutes before, to take up some slaves who had thrown themselves over board'.[35] Deane did not arrive in Charleston until the third week of May, but he managed to acquire another ship, the sloop *Swift*, and to transport to Charleston in record time 65 captives, presumably some of those who had jumped off the *New Brittannia* before it exploded.[36]

It is not clear if Deane continued to ship Africans into slavery after this disaster. A Savannah obituary announced his death in 1783, ten years after the explosion on the *New Brittannia*.[37] It seems likely, therefore, that he settled in the Savannah area, as Fenda Lawrence had earlier. Whatever the influence of the abortive rising on ship, it may be that Deane and Lawrence were pulling out of the Gambia trade or were forced by circumstances to do so.[38]

Having pondered reasons for her push out of Kau-Ur, we have to ask what pulled Fenda Lawrence to Georgia? To address this issue, we are compelled to consider the connections between Lawrence, Deane and Habersham that made it possible for Lawrence to obtain residency in Georgia. When Lawrence arrived in Savannah in 1772, Deane introduced her to slave merchants and government officials. His familiarity with them was the result of a well-established trade connection between the Gambia and the two southern colonies of Georgia and South Carolina. Deane was captain of one of the ships that had helped to forge the connection.

James Habersham, who signed Lawrence's certificate, was not only a government official but also a slave trader. Indeed he was an agent for the *Brittannia* and helped sell its slaves in Savannah.[39] It seems that Deane had been dealing with Habersham for some time and they were familiar enough that Deane was willing to broach the subject of residency for Fenda.

Deane apparently felt that he was taking no risk in recommending Lawrence to Habersham in the latter's capacity as caretaker of a colony with large numbers of enslaved Africans. In giving the deposition, Deane implied that Lawrence, like him, was in the business of slave trading. 'A Considerable trader' in Kau-Ur was almost certainly a slave trader. No European slaver would use this description for an African woman who only sold rice or traded in other products in the local market, for at that time men simply would not have been able to envision such 'woman's work' as 'considerable'.

Lawrence and Deane conceivably could have been induced to relocate to Georgia because of the threat of an embargo by the colonists on British vessels. The tensions leading up to the American war for independence may have discouraged further trade with Africa. At the time of Lawrence's arrival, the number of shipments from Senegambia had declined relative to those from other West African ports to the south.[40] Fear that the trade would decline further as the colonists began to defy Britain's Navigation Acts would have influenced the decisions of those who invested in the slave trade. Virginia was threatening to end its trans-Atlantic slave trade totally, figuring on a domestic trade market within the colonies to maintain Virginian prosperity. Sentiments attacking the trans-Atlantic slave trade escalated concomitantly with slumping slave exports from Senegambia. These factors may have motivated both Lawrence and Deane to relocate to Georgia.

A successful African woman trader would have been resourceful enough to abandon a Gambian-based trade venture at a time of apparent vulnerability in the South Carolina–Georgia markets. In Georgia, it was possible to invest in the cultivation of rice, which in fact was a common occupation for women along the Gambia.[41] Georgia had been a colony for only forty years when Lawrence arrived in 1772, and a slave code had only been enacted in 1750, when the colonists were successful in repealing the prohibition against the use of slaves. Thereafter, the Board of Trade permitted the introduction of slaves. In 1770, two years before Lawrence's arrival, the Georgia Committee of Correspondence wrote to Benjamin Franklin, the colony's agent in London, complaining about the Board of Trade's decision that 'Slaves should be made real Estate and go with the Lands they . . . [are] employed upon'.[42] Habersham and other members of the Committee claimed that this restriction on the sale of slaves would cause hardship. They pleaded that 'in a young and extensive Country like this, where Property must necessarily be frequently Aliened and new

Settlements daily made, many cogent Reasons might be urged against such a Measure'.[43] Habersham was fully committed to the expansion of slavery in Georgia, but as his encouragement of the immigration of a free, black woman with slaves demonstrated, he was not necessarily committed to the racialized slavery that was being consolidated in the colony.

When Lawrence arrived in 1772, there were approximately 15,000 people of African ancestry in Georgia, along with 18,000 British and other Europeans. Two-thirds of all enslaved Africans lived within twenty miles of the coast.[44] In 1771, there were 821 enslaved blacks in Savannah, while the free black population was probably less than one hundred.[45] The number of free blacks was low throughout the colonial era; manumission could only be obtained by presenting individual cases to the legislature, and fewer than fifty enslaved people were manumitted between 1751 and 1776.[46] Wherever she went in Georgia, therefore, this free woman of colour would have found herself an unusual figure among the vast majority of Africans, some of whom had clearly been shipped from ports in Senegambia.

Black folk, enslaved or free, who aspired to improve their lot clamoured to be in the coastal town of Savannah, which offered opportunities for trade and work at small wages. None the less, the town was not safe for blacks, as Olaudah Equiano, the Igbo youth who had been kidnapped in c. 1756 and sold into trans-Atlantic slavery, found out in the 1760s, a few years before the arrival of Fenda Lawrence. White patrols and ruffians frequently interfered with blacks and subjected them to physical and verbal abuse. It was difficult for black people to maintain their dignity in Savannah or any other place in Georgia in this era. Equiano visited Savannah several times in the 1760s as a slave and came to know a number of people there. When he returned in 1767 as a free man, he ran into trouble for violating the curfew. He had visited an enslaved friend in the men's quarters but had remained beyond the curfew imposed on all black people, as decreed in the slave code of 1750 and its subsequent revisions.[47] As a result, Equiano barely escaped a whipping, but he had already suffered physical abuse and threats on previous occasions and received more on the day after the threatened whipping. Because of these incidents, Equiano was always glad to leave Savannah and indeed Charleston, too, where there were similar dangers of abuse at the hands of white racists.[48]

As a stranger, Lawrence was exposed to the dangers of such assaults on black people. Whereas the hostility toward Equiano may have stemmed in part from his occupation as a sailor, Lawrence was unusual because she owned property. But as a slave owner, Lawrence was certain to seem less threatening than Equiano to the interests of white folk. Black vendors and other workers, among whom she (or her domestic slaves) was sure to compete for trade or other business, must have been her most ardent foes, as evidence regarding friction between free and enslaved blacks and between black and white competitors indicates.[49]

Lawrence would have encountered numerous people who were enslaved, and also would have met a few indentured Africans and their offspring in Savannah. They were to be found in the marketplace, various business establishments and private homes of both black and white residents.[50] She would see that black women enjoyed a 'pre-eminent position' as vendors, an economic role that was common among women in West Africa as well.[51] These slave women wore badges that served as passes authorizing them to conduct trade. In the same way, Habersham's certificate provided Lawrence with her mark of freedom and gave her permission to be in Georgia.[52]

The African women in Georgia must have been curious about Lawrence, and some of them would have recognized her feat of relocating to the colonies voluntarily as something to marvel at and even to be annoyed about. However, the deference that people extended to their superiors in Senegambia was likely to have been so ingrained that women in servitude would have hidden any deeper anger. They were likely to show a person of Lawrence's accomplishments respect and tolerance until, perhaps, a later, more appropriate time.[53] Despite any overt and covert hostility, they surely provided tips incidental to the local code of marketplace dealings and otherwise provided a degree of familiarity that would have eased Lawrence's adjustment to her new home.

Africans who had been brought to the colonies as adults might have speculated that Lawrence was a slave trader or was otherwise involved in the trans-Atlantic slave trade. Since there was an identifiable number of slaves from Senegambia, information about her may have spread among them. It is likely that some people she met knew Kau-Ur, considering Deane's shipments alone. They would have assessed her role in the slave trade according to their individual experiences. A number of the dispersed captives had encountered women slave traders and other women provisioning the trade in slaves prior to their departure from the African continent. Equiano, for example, had been kidnapped by a woman and two men who climbed over the compound walls and snatched him, his sister and two other relatives, selling them at a slave market where a 'wealthy' woman purchased him, apparently to absorb any harm that might befall the woman's son. Equiano also met other women associated with the trade.[54]

Lawrence probably knew something about the low country of Georgia from Deane before her arrival. Deane and his crew certainly would have had much from their travels to Charleston and Savannah with which to dazzle their associates in Africa. Mariners had a knack for sharing tales about wondrous scenes they saw at every port. They had talked, no doubt, about African women trading in the marketplaces of Savannah and Charleston. Fenda was a business woman, as Deane's testimony makes clear, not just the wife of a trader. Her achievements caught the eye of British traders.

Deane's reference to Lawrence's dowry was an allusion to one of the most important legal rights of colonial white women, the right to inherit a third of her deceased husband's real estate and a third of his personal property. Even where husbands left no wills, the courts designated that this dower right be extended to women. Although the real estate became the property of his heirs after the widow's death, the personal property a woman acquired was hers to dispose of as she saw fit. The dower right was a rare provincial concession at a time when women were believed to be irrational, dependent on the strength of male family members, and of limited physical and mental capacities.[55] These dower rights primarily benefited free, white women of means in the colonies and were extended to women of darker hue as a matter of individual favour.

It may be because she expected to have free rein over her dower that she had brought from the Gambia and intended to use it to educate her children that Lawrence settled in the Savannah area. Evangelical schools for teaching the catechism and the rudiments of reading, writing and ciphering to enslaved Africans and Native Indians were established as far south as South Carolina and Georgia, particularly in the Savannah–Augusta area. Clerics sent out to the colonies by the Society for the Propagation of the Gospel of the Church of England continued these educational sessions in Augusta and nearby locations until the decade of the American Revolutionary War.[56] Lawrence's intention, then, may well have been to take advantage of these or other opportunities, such as hiring tutors, to educate James Lawrence, Tony and Nancy, the children known to have been in her household at the time of her arrival.

We may never know the full measure of Lawrence's success or what negative and positive encounters she experienced in Georgia as a result of racism and the patriarchy that persisted there. We do know she traversed for at least a time the diverse cultures of two continents – the 'Atlantic creole' trading community of Senegambia and British America. She may have lived uncomfortably among enslaved and dispersed Africans as one who was complicit in the slave trade, carrying the moral baggage of a former slave merchant. Prevailing white supremacist notions might have pre-empted Lawrence's plans to acquire a formal education for her children and to control her dowry. In the end, Fenda Lawrence may not have perceived significant differences in the basic bureaucratic and oppressive natures of the African indigenous and the British colonial societies.

Lawrence's initial acquaintances and potential guardians against racial attacks – Habersham, Noble and Deane – died within the decade, in October 1775, November 1775 and December 1783.[57] That no records, other than the deposition and the certificate, of Fenda Lawrence's life or death in Georgia have been located in the archives suggests either that her basic civil status was that of *persona non grata* or that she had only a short stay there.[58]

The image of Lawrence that emerges from the archival records is one of a business woman from a town that was widely known for its role in the trans-Atlantic slave trade. With a fate presumably tied to Captain Stephen Deane, she seems to have turned her back on the trans-Atlantic slave commerce in 1772, and he seems to have followed suit in 1773. As a woman of means, a resourceful person of eighteenth-century vintage, and a former indigene of a slave-trading/owning society, this woman would continue to use but apparently also to elevate her own domestic slaves. This free African woman's immigration into the colony with goods and slaves was unprecedented.

As one prospering from the agonies of the captive and the enslaved, she is not likely to have addressed, in depth or at length, either the moral issues related to commodifying human beings or the long-term social and political implications of that commodification for the future of the African continent and its dispersed people.[59] When she was a trans-Atlantic slave trader, Lawrence followed in the tradition of several generations of Senegambian women slave merchants. Her experiences in a British-influenced area of Africa and her work as a slave merchant helped prepare her to negotiate the 'Atlantic culture' on both sides of the Atlantic Ocean.

Present-day preoccupations with race would have been foreign to Lawrence. She had little consciousness of racial solidarity. Emigrating from a well-ordered society, she must have found the basic social and political organization as well as the patriarchy, class structure and slavery of the colony familiar, but probably not its racism.

Lawrence endured the discomforts, which the most hardened sailors despised, of passage on a slave ship in order to advance her interests or escape problems at home. Yet she had a sensitivity that caused her to retain in the new setting the familiar and caring faces of women and children as her domestic slaves, which constituted her extended family, from Kau-Ur. Her migration out of Africa as an individual woman was rare, but probably not unprecedented, in the late eighteenth century. Moreover, a few women continued to cross the Atlantic as part of this ongoing tradition of 'Atlantic creole'. About twenty years later, Elizabeth Holman, a woman from the Sierra Leone region, accompanied her British husband, John (a slave merchant), and their five children and slaves on a slave ship to settle in South Carolina and establish a rice plantation.[60]

Lawrence's story points to the independence, accomplishments, strengths, weaknesses and vulnerabilities of some African women during an irrational, proto-capitalistic era. It broadens our knowledge of the diverse experiences of enslaved Africans prior to their landing in the colonies and of the societies from which they were snatched. It reminds us that the history of Africans in British North America is about many different individuals and not some stereotypical African woman. On a wider scale, it implies troubling questions about the participation of women in the good and evil processes of history. African–American history texts neglect the role of African women in the slave trade. Understandably, the descendants of the victims dispersed by the slave trade find it difficult to identify an African ancestress with the immorality and avarice synonymous with trafficking in humans.

Notes

1 This essay was written with the support of the Institute for the Study of Culture and Society, Bowling Green State University. I am particularly grateful to Martin A. Klein, Rowland Abiodun, Donald Wright and Paul E. Lovejoy for suggestions on research and interpretation.
2 For the number of captives on board, see the *South Carolina Gazette*, 18 June 1772. That Lawrence was aboard the ship is recorded in a deposition from the ship's captain, Stephen Deane; see *Deed Book*, 1772–1775, pp. 13–14, Georgia Department of Archives and History, Atlanta.
3 Boubacar Barry, *Senegambia and the Atlantic Slave Trade* (Cambridge, 1998).
4 Philip D. Curtin, *Economic Change in Precolonial Africa: Senegambia in the Era of the Slave Trade* (Madison, WI, 1975); and Lamin O. Sanneh, *The Jakhanke: The History of an Islamic Clerical People of the Senegambia* (London, 1979); Paul E. Lovejoy, 'The

Muslim Factor in the Trans-Atlantic Slave Trade', in Lovejoy (ed.), *Slavery on the Frontiers of Islam: The Central Sudan and the African Diaspora* (Princeton, NJ, 2000). Martin Klein makes the point about Mandinka middlemen in Martin A. Klein, *Islam and Imperialism in Senegal: Sine-Saloum, 1847–1914* (Stanford, CA, 1968), p. 4. Also see J. Suret-Canale, 'The Western Atlantic Coast, 1600–1800', in J. F. A. Ajayi and Michael Crowder (eds), *History of West Africa* (New York, 1972), 1:387–8.

5 James Searing, *West African Slavery and Atlantic Commerce: The Senegal River Valley, 1700–1860* (Cambridge, 1993), pp. 77, 93–108.

6 *South Carolina Gazette*, 25 June 1772.

7 *Ibid.*

8 *Ibid.*, pp. 14–15.

9 *Deed Book*, 1772–1775, pp. 13–14. For a description of domestic slavery in the region, see Martin A. Klein, *Slavery and Colonial Rule in French West Africa* (Cambridge, 1998); and Klein, *Islam and Imperialism in Senegal*, pp. 10–11. As Klein has noted, 'there was a distinction between trade and domestic slaves; the former were captives who generally were sold before they formed ties with the owner's family, while domestic slaves were members of an extended family and dependants of the head of that family.' Based on discussions with Klein and Donald Wright, I assume that James Lawrence was an enslaved child precocious enough to have earned the affection that prompted his mistress to give him her surname, but he could have been her son.

10 *Deed Book*, 1772–1775, pp. 13–14.

11 *Ibid.*

12 *Deed Book*, 1772–1775, p. 15.

13 *Ibid.* The latter phrase in this statement is reminiscent of sentiments expressed in a 1765 slave-code draft encouraging free Blacks to settle in the colony; see Betty Wood, *Slavery in Colonial Georgia, 1730–1775* (Athens, GA, 1984), pp. 125–9.

14 It was officially acquired with permission of Queen Elizabeth I in 1588. This summary is based on Curtin, *Senegambia in the Era of the Slave Trade*, 1:29–36; Suret-Canale, 'The Western Atlantic Coast, 1600–1800', 1:387–8. James A. Rawley, *Transatlantic Slave Trade: A History* (New York, 1981), p. 151, notes that slave trading was not mentioned.

15 Rawley, *Transatlantic Slave Trade*, pp. 152–3.

16 See Boubacar Barry, *Senegambia and the Atlantic Slave Trade* (Cambridge, 1998), especially parts 1 and 2 on ethnicity and cultural unity, and page 88 on the 'cosmopolitan mix' in Saalum; Donald R. Wright, *The World and a Very Small Place in Africa* (London, 1997), passim, on ethnic diversity and similarity within the Senegambian region; Klein, *Islam and Imperialism in Senegal*, p. 4.

17 For the recent debate on creolization within the context of the trans-Atlantic slave trade, consult Philip D. Morgan, 'The Cultural Implications of the Atlantic Slave Trade: African Regional Origins, American Destinations and New World Developments', *Slavery and Abolition* 18, no. 1 (1997); Bernard Bailyn, 'The Idea of Atlantic History', *Itinerario* 20, no. 1 (1996); Ira Berlin, 'From Creole to African: Atlantic Creoles and the Origins of African-American Society in Mainland North America', *William and Mary Quarterly* 53, no. 2 (1996); and Paul Lovejoy, 'Identifying Enslaved Africans in the African Diaspora', in this volume.

18 B. Barry, 'Senegambia from the Sixteenth to the Eighteenth Century', in B. A. Ogot (ed.), *Africa from the Sixteenth to the Eighteenth Century: General History of Africa*, vol. 5 (Berkeley, 1992), p. 283. For a description of the responsibilities and authority of the *alcati* at Kau-Ur in 1730–5, see the account of Francis Moore, *Travels into the Inland Parts of Africa* (London, 1738), pp. 127–8, as cited in Klein, *Islam and Imperialism in Senegal*, pp. 25–6.

19 John K. Thornton, *Africa and Africans in the Making of the Atlantic World, 1400–1680* (Cambridge, 1992), p. 69, discusses bureaucratic aspects of African commerce and patronage.

20 Barry, 'Senegambia', p. 284.

21 George E. Brooks, Jr., 'The Signares of St-Louis and Gorée: Women Entrepreneurs in Eighteenth-Century Senegal', in Nancy J. Hafkin and Edna G. Bay (eds), *Women in Africa: Studies in Social and Economic Change* (Stanford, CA, 1976), p. 20; Suret-Canale, 'The Western Atlantic Coast, 1600–1800', pp. 15–16; and Niara Sudarkasa, 'Status of Women in Indigenous African Societies', in Hafkin and Bay (eds), *Women in Africa*, pp. 25–6.

22 L. Bernhard Venema, *The Wolof of Saalum: Social Structure and Rural Development in Senegal* (Wageningen, Netherlands, 1978), pp. 26, 287, 298.

23 Hafkin and Bay (eds), *Women in Africa*, p. 6.

24 *Deed Book*, 1772–1775, p. 15.

25 Brooks, 'Signares of St-Louis and Gorée', pp. 19–24.

26 *Ibid.*; Bruce L. Mouser, 'Women Slavers of Guinea-Conakry', in Claire C. Robertson and Martin A. Klein (eds), *Women and Slavery in Africa* (Madison, WI, 1983), pp. 321–5.

27 Brooks, 'Signares of St-Louis and Gorée', pp. 23, 30, 38–9.

28 Venema, *Wolof of Saalum*, p. 15.

29 Figures from the W. E. B. DuBois Institute Transatlantic Slave Voyage Data Set which indicate that Deane brought in more captives than is reported in Elizabeth Donnan, *Documents Illustrative of the History of the Slave Trade to America*, 4 vols (New York, 1969), 4:413.

30 *Ibid.*, 4:624–25; Betty Wood, *Women's Work, Men's Work: The Informal Slave Economies of Low Country Georgia* (Athens, GA, 1995). The connection between Georgia and South Carolina is documented in the *Gazettes* of South Carolina and Georgia. Both routinely posted the activity of ships in the Charleston and Savannah ports. E.g. the *South Carolina Gazette* reported the arrival of the *New Brittannia* on 18 June 1772, the date of Lawrence's entry.

31 These figures are taken from the W. E. B. DuBois Institute Transatlantic Slave Voyage Data Set; see David Eltis, Stephen D. Behrendt, David Richardson and Herbert S. Klein (eds), *The Transatlantic Slave Trade, 1527–1867: A Database* (Cambridge, 1999).

32 S. D. Behrendt, David Eltis and David Richardson, 'The Bights in Comparative Perspective: The Economics of Long-Term Trends in Population Displacement from West and West-Central Africa to the Americas before 1850' (paper presented at the UNESCO/SSHRCC Summer Institute, 'Identifying Enslaved Africans: The "Nigerian" Hinterland and the African Diaspora', York University, Toronto, 1997). Their analysis of the Du Bois data set of slaving voyages acknowledges that there were 'large variations in times spent at the coast by region, with ships tending to stay for rather shorter periods of time at ports in the Bights compared to those that traded further west'.

33 Donnan (ed.), *Documents*, 4:453, n. 4; *Gentleman's Magazine* (October 1773), p. 523.

34 Donnan, *Documents*, 4:453.

35 *Ibid.*; *Gentleman's Magazine* (October 1773), p. 512.

36 I wish to thank David Eltis and David Richardson for information on the *Swift* that is contained in the W. E. B. DuBois Institute Transatlantic Slave Voyage Data Set.

37 *Georgia Gazette*, 4 December 1783; *Early Deaths in Savannah, Ga., 1763–1803: Obituaries and Legal Notices* (Savannah: Georgia Historical Society), Georgia Department of Archives and History, Atlanta, Drawer 17, p. 153.

38 *Ibid.* Despite a regional slump in the market, which was down to 157,000 in the 1770s, from 206,000 in the 1760s, Deane had managed to gather a sizeable number of captives in both 1772 and 1773.

39 Donnan, *Documents*, 4:624–6.
40 The decline in the slave trade has been attributed to the Futaanke *jihad* in the interior which cut off slave caravans headed west. See Philip D. Curtin, 'Abolition of the Slave Trade from Senegambia', in David Eltis and James Walvin (eds), *Abolition of the Atlantic Slave Trade: Origins and Effects in Europe, Africa, and the Americas* (Madison, WI, 1981), p. 94.
41 Curtin, *Senegambia in the Era of the Slave Trade*, 1:175, 274, 296.
42 See 'Letters from the Georgia Committee of Correspondence to Benjamin Franklin' in *Georgia Historical Quarterly* 36 (1952), pp. 279–80. The letters were delivered to Franklin by Captain Stephen Deane.
43 *Ibid.*, p. 280.
44 Betty Wood, 'Some Aspects of Female Resistance to Chattel Slavery in Low Country Georgia, 1763–1815', in Paul Finkelman (ed.), *Women and the Family in a Slave Society* (New York, 1989), p. 425.
45 Philip D. Morgan, 'Black Life in Eighteenth-Century Charleston', *Perspectives in American History*, n. s., 1 (1984), p. 188.
46 Wood, *Women's Work, Men's Work*, pp. 7, 131; Wood, *Slavery in Colonial Georgia*, pp. 115, 123, 128–9.
47 Olaudah Equiano, *The Interesting Narrative of the Life of Olaudah Equiano*, ed. Robert J. Allison (Boston, 1995), pp. 108–14, 133–6.
48 *Ibid.*
49 Wood, *Slavery in Colonial Georgia*, p. 128.
50 Wood, *Women's Work, Men's Work*, pp. 83–4.
51 There are several first-hand accounts and secondary works on women traders and the marketplace in Africa; a useful one is Niara Sudarkasa, *Where Women Work: A Study of Yoruba Women in the Market Place and in the Home* (Ann Arbor, MI, 1973); see also Brooks, 'Signares of St-Louis and Gorée'; Bernard I. Belasco, *The Entrepreneur as Culture Hero: Preadaptations in Nigerian Economic Development* (New York, 1980); Wood, *Women's Work, Men's Work*, chap. 5, discusses African women traders within the context of the Georgia low country and slavery.
52 Wood, *Women's Work, Men's Work*, pp. 80–7.
53 Here I am referring to both the deference generally extended to one's seniors and rulers as well as to the annual day or days set aside in some societies for mocking and criticizing rulers and other superiors for misdeeds, etc. through songs and recitations.
54 Equiano, *Interesting Narrative*, pp. 47–52.
55 Nancy Woloch (ed.), *Early American Women: A Documentary History, 1600–1900* (Belmont, CA, 1992), pp. 119–20; Woloch, *Women and the American Experience* (New York, 1996), pp. 38–41.
56 See also Lillian Ashcraft-Eason, 'Black Women and Religion in the Colonial Period', in Rosemary Radford Ruether and Rosemary Skinner Keller (eds), *Women and Religion in America: The Colonial and Revolutionary Periods* (New York, 1983), pp. 238–40, 248.
57 *Georgia Gazette*, 4 December 1783; *Early Deaths in Savannah*, Drawer 17, p. 153.
58 The following sources were examined for further evidence: Superior Court Records for Deeds; Savannah newspapers, 1763–99 and 1800–5; Indices to Georgia Wills, 1733–1860; *General Index to Wills, Estates, Administrations, Etc.* in Chatham County Courthouse, Savannah, GA; the Index to badges (passes for marketplace vending); church memberships for Baptist, Episcopal and Methodist churches; *Register of Deaths in Savannah*, vols 3–6; records from the Mayor's Court of Common Pleas; petitions; *Register of Free Persons of Color*, 1780–1865; *Index to Marriages*, book 2, 1806–1950; court dockets; the *Tax Digest*; and *Fiats for Grants Book*. I found no mention of

Lawrence or her domestic servants and their offspring. I have yet to locate Stephen Deane's will.

59 For the ideological aspects of African involvement in the slave trade, see the contributions in Paul E. Lovejoy (ed.), *Ideology of Slavery in Africa* (Beverly Hills, 1981), and Patrick Manning, *Slavery and African Life: Occidental, Oriental, and African Slave Trade* (Cambridge and New York, 1990).

60 Donnan, *Documents* 4:453; L. Koger, *Black Slaveowners: Free Black Slave Masters in South Carolina, 1790–1860* (Jefferson, NC, 1985), pp. 39, 104, 110–19.

Bibliography

Archives and Collections

Anlo Traditional Council Archives, Anloga, Ghana.
Archivo General de Indias, Seville, Spain.
Arquivo Nacional, Rio de Janeiro, Brazil.
Chatham County Courthouse, Savannah, GA.
Church Missionary Society Archives, University of Birmingham Library, UK.
Diocese of St Augustine Catholic Center, Jacksonville, FL, Catholic Parish Records.
Georgia Department of Archives and History, Atlanta.
National Archives of Ghana, Accra.
Public Record Office, Kew, UK.
University of Florida, Gainesville, P. K. Yonge Library of Florida History, John B. Stetson Collection.
University of Ghana, Legon, Balme Library.

Newspapers and Magazines

O Carbonário, 1886.
A Federação, Porto Alegre, 1935.
Gentleman's Magazine, 1773.
Georgia Gazette, 1783.
Granma International, Havana, 1992.
Granma Weekly Review, Havana, 1987.
Lagos Times, 1881, 1883.
South Carolina Gazette, 1772.

Theses, Dissertations, Scholarly Papers, and other Unpublished Works

Afonja, S., 'Historical Evolution in the Sexual Division of Labour in Nigeria', paper presented at meeting on 'Theoretical Frameworks and Methodological Approaches to Studies on the Role of Women in History' (1984).
Behrendt, S. D., Eltis, David and Richardson, David, 'The Bights in Comparative Perspective: The Economics of Long-Term Trends in Population Displacement from West-Central Africa to the Americas before 1850', paper presented at UNESCO/SSHRCC Summer Institute, 'Identifying Enslaved Africans: The "Nigerian" Hinterland and the African Diaspora', York University, Toronto (1997).
Braithwaite, Kamau, 'The Black Woman of the Caribbean during Slavery', Elsa Goveia Memorial Lecture, University of the West Indies, Cave Hill, Barbados (1984).
Chambers, Douglas B., 'Eboe, Kongo, Mandingo: African Ethnic Groups and the Development of Regional Slave Societies in Mainland North America, 1700–1800', working paper no. 96–14, International Seminar on 'The History of the Atlantic World, 1500–1800', Harvard University (1996).

———'"He Gwine Sing He Country": Africans, Afro-Virginians, and the Development of Slave Culture in Virginia, 1690–1810', PhD thesis, University of Virginia (1996).

Denzer, LaRay, 'Indigenous Slavery and Yoruba Historiography', paper presented at UNESCO/SSHRCC Summer Institute, 'Identifying Enslaved Africans: The "Nigerian" Hinterland and the African Diaspora', York University, Toronto (1997).

Emezue, Sydney, 'Warfare and Slaving in Nineteenth-Century Igboland', paper presented at UNESCO/SSHRCC Summer Institute, 'Identifying Enslaved Africans: The "Nigerian" Hinterland and the African Diaspora', York University, Toronto (1997).

Faria, Sheila de Castro, 'A colônia em movimento: Fortuna e família no cotidiano colonial', PhD thesis, Universidade Federal Fluminense, Brazil (1994).

Fiawoo, Dzigbodi Kodzo, 'The Influence of Contemporary Social Changes on the Magico-Religious Concepts and Organization of the Southern Ewe-Speaking Peoples of Ghana', PhD thesis, University of Edinburgh (1959).

Gaba, Kue Agbota, 'The History of Anecho, Ancient and Modern', Balme Library, University of Ghana, Legon, manuscript (c. 1942).

Greene, Sandra E., 'The Anlo-Ewe: Their Economy, Society, and External Relations in the Eighteenth Century', PhD thesis, Northwestern University (1981).

Kea, Ray A., 'Trade, State Formation, and Warfare on the Gold Coast, 1600–1826', PhD thesis, University of London (1974).

Lovejoy, Paul E., 'The Muslim Factor in the Trans-Atlantic Slave Trade', paper presented at conference on 'West Africa and the Americas: Repercussions of the Slave Trade', University of the West Indies, Mona, Jamaica (1997).

Lovejoy, Paul E. and Law, Robin, 'Deconstructing the African Diaspora: The Slave Trade of the "Nigerian" Hinterland', paper presented at conference on 'The African Diaspora and the "Nigerian" Hinterland', York University, Toronto (1996).

Lovejoy, Paul E., Law, Robin and Soumonni, Elisée, 'The Development of an African Diaspora: The Slave Trade of the "Nigerian" Hinterland, 1650–1900', UNESCO Slave Route Project, Cabinda, Angola, working paper (1996).

Mann, Kristin, 'The Emancipation of Female Slaves in Colonial Lagos', unpublished paper (1991).

Miller, Ivor, 'Cuban Abakuá History and Contemporary Practice: The Testimony of Andres Flores, Elder', paper presented at conference on 'West Africa and the Americas: Repercussions of the Slave Trade', University of the West Indies, Mona, Jamaica (1997).

Montoute, Annita, 'The Search for Kele: A Dying Religion', Caribbean Studies essay, Department of History, University of the West Indies, Jamaica (1996).

Moore, Robin, 'Nationalizing Blackness: Afrocubanismo and Artistic Revolution in Havana, 1920–1940', PhD thesis, University of Texas at Austin (1995).

Nwokeji, G. Ugo, '"Did We Bring Land with Us from Aro?": The Contradictions of Mmuba among the Aro of Nigeria, c. 1750–1890', paper presented at the UNESCO/SSHRCC Summer Institute, 'Identifying Enslaved Africans: The "Nigerian" Hinterland and the African Diaspora', York University, Toronto (1997).

O'Hear, Ann, 'Ilorin as a Slaving and Slave-Trading State', paper presented at UNESCO/SSHRCC Summer Institute, 'Identifying Enslaved Africans: The "Nigerian" Hinterland and the African Diaspora', York University, Toronto (1997).

Oroge, E. Adeniyi, 'The Institution of Domestic Slavery in Yorubaland, with Particular Reference to the Nineteenth Century', PhD thesis, University of Birmingham, UK (1971).

Peixoto, Antonio da Costa (ed.), *Obra Nova de Lingua Geral de Mina* (manuscrito da Biblioteca Publica de Evora e da Biblioteca Nacional de Lisboa, Publicado e apresentado por Luis Silveira e acompanhado de comentario filologico de Edmundo Correia Lopes (1741; Lisbon, 1945).

Pintado, Ana Celia Perera, 'La regla ocha: Sus valores religiosos en la sociedad cubana contemporánea', Departamento de Estudios Socioreligosos, Havana, mimeographed (1996).

Shields, Francine, '"Is Not a Woman to Sell Oil, How can a Man Sell Oil like a Woman?" Women, Labour and the Commercial Transition in 19th Century Yorubaland', paper presented at the African Studies Association of the UK biennial conference, Bristol (1996).
––––––– 'Palm Oil and Power: Women in an Era of Economic and Social Transition in 19th-Century Yorubaland (South-Western Nigeria)', PhD thesis, University of Stirling, UK (1997).
Sorensen, Caroline, 'Badagry 1784–1863: The Political and Commercial History of a Pre-Colonial Lagoonside Community in South West Nigeria', PhD thesis, University of Stirling, UK (1995).
Togby, Richard Tetteh, 'The Origin and Organization of the Yewe Cult', BA essay, Department for the Study of Religions, University of Ghana (1977).
Tosu, L. P., 'A Short Account of the Awada-da Stool of Anlo', Anlo Traditional Council Archives, manuscript, n.d.
Wilks, Ivor, 'Akwamu, 1650–1750: A Study of the Rise and Fall of a West African Empire', MA diss., University of Wales (1958).

Published Works

Abrahams, Roger and Szwed, John (comps), *After Africa: Extracts from British Travel Accounts* (New Haven, CT, 1983).
Adams, John, *Remarks on the Country Extending from Cape Palmas to the River Congo* (1823; London, 1966).
––––––– *Sketches Taken during Ten Voyages to Africa, between the Years 1786 and 1800* (1823; New York, 1970).
Adediran, 'Biodun, 'Yoruba Ethnic Groups or a Yoruba Ethnic Group? A Review of the Problem of Ethnic Identification', *Africa: Revista do centro do estudos africanos de USP* 7 (1984).
Aduamah, E. K., *Ewe Traditions* 3, no. 13, Institute of African Studies, University of Ghana, Legon (n. d.).
Afigbo, Adiele, *Ropes of Sand: Studies in Igbo History and Culture* (Ibadan, Nigeria, 1981).
Afonja, S., 'Changing Modes of Production and the Sexual Division of Labour

among the Yoruba', *Signs* 7, no. 2 (1981).
Ajayi, J. F. Ade, *Christian Missions in Nigeria, 1841–1891* (London, 1981).
––––––– 'Samuel Ajayi Crowther of Oyo', in Philip D. Curtin (ed.), *Africa Remembered: Narratives by West Africans from the Era of the Slave Trade* (Madison, WI, 1967).
Ajayi, J. F. Ade and R. Smith, *Yoruba Warfare in the Nineteenth Century* (Cambridge, 1964).
Akindele, A. and Aguessy, C., *Contribution à l'étude de l'histoire de l'ancien royaume de Porto-Novo* (Dakar, 1968).
Akinjogbin, I. A., *Dahomey and Its Neighbours, 1708–1818* (Cambridge, 1967).
Akintoye, S. A., *Revolution and Power Politics in Yorubaland, 1840–1893: Ibadan Expansion and the Rise of Ekiti Parapo* (London, 1971).
Allen, William, *A Narrative of the Expedition Sent by Her Majesty's Government to the River Niger in 1841* (London, 1848).
Alleyne, Mervyn C., 'Continuity versus Creativity in Afro-American Language and Culture', in Salikoko S. Mufwene (ed.), *Africanisms in Afro-American Language Varieties* (Athens, GA, 1991).
Allsopp, Richard (comp.), *Dictionary of Caribbean English Usage* (Oxford, 1996).
Alutu, John O., *Nnewi History*, 2nd edn (1963; Enugu, Nigeria, 1985).
Anaikor, Chike C., 'The Omabe Cult and Masking Tradition', in *The Nsukka Environment* (1978; reprint, Enegu, 1985).
Anderson, Michael, *Aproximaciones a la historia de la familia occidental 1500–1914* (Madrid, 1988).
Angarica, Nicolás, *Manual de Orihaté: Religión lucumí* (n. d, n. p.).
Arrom, José Juan and Arévalo, Manuel A. García, *Cimarrón* (Santo Domingo, Dominican Republic, 1986).
Asante, Molefi Kete, *The Afrocentric Idea* (Philadelphia, 1987).
––––––– 'Afrocentricity', in William Andres, Frances Smith Foster and Trudier Harris (eds), *The Oxford Companion to American Literature* (Oxford, 1997).
Ashcraft-Eason, Lillian, 'Black Women and Religion in the Colonial Period', in Rosemary Radford Ruether and Rosemary Skinner Keller (eds), *Women and Religion in America: The Colonial*

and Revolutionary Periods (New York, 1983).

Atanda, J. A. 'The Fall of the Old Oyo Empire: A Reconsideration of Its Cause', *Journal of the Historical Society of Nigeria* 5, no. 4 (1971).

Ayandele, E. A., *The Missionary Impact on Modern Nigeria, 1842–1914: A Political and Social Analysis* (London, 1966).

Baikie, William B., *Narrative of an Exploring Voyage up the Rivers Kwora and Binue* (1856; London, 1966).

Bailyn, Bernard, 'The Idea of Atlantic History', *Itinerario* 20, no. 1 (1996).

Barber, Karin, 'How Man Makes God in West Africa: Yoruba Attitudes towards the Orisa', *Africa* 51, no. 3 (1981).

—— 'Discursive Strategies in the Texts of Ifá and in the "Holy Book of Odù" of the African Church of Òrúnmìlà', in P. F. de Moraes Farias and Karin Barber (eds), *Self-Assertion and Brokerage* (Birmingham, UK, 1990).

—— 'Oriki, Women and the Proliferation and Merging of Orisa', *Africa* 60, no. 3 (1990).

Barbot, Jean, *A Description of the Coast of North and South Guinea* (London, 1732).

Barnes, Sandra T. (ed.), *Africa's Ogun: Old World and New* (Bloomington, IN, 1989).

Barnet, Miguel, *Memórias de um cimarrón* (São Paulo, 1986).

—— 'La hora de Yemayá', *Gaceta de Cuba* 34, no. 2 (1996).

Barry, Boubacar, *La Sénégambie du XVᵉ au XIXᵉ siècle: Traite négrière, Islam, conquête coloniale* (Paris, 1988).

—— 'Senegambia from the Sixteenth to the Eighteenth Century', in B. A. Ogot (ed.), *Africa from the Sixteenth to the Eighteenth Century: General History of Africa*, vol. 5 (Berkeley, CA, 1992).

—— *Senegambia and the Atlantic Slave Trade* (Cambridge, 1998).

Bascom, William, *Sixteen Cowries: Yoruba Divination from Africa to the New World* (Bloomington, IN, 1980).

Bassanezzi, Maria S. C. B., 'Considerações sobre os estudos do celibato e da idade de casar no passado brasileiro', in *Anais do IX encontro de estudos populacionais*, 3 vols (Caxambú, Brazil, 1994).

Bastide, Roger, *As religiões africanas no Brasil*, 2 vols (São Paulo, 1971).

Beckles, Hilary McD., 'Caribbean Anti-Slavery: The Self-Liberation Ethos of Enslaved Blacks', *Journal of Caribbean History* 22, nos 1–2 (1988).

—— *Natural Rebels: A Social History of Enslaved Black Women in Barbados* (New Brunswick, NJ, 1989).

—— 'Sex and Gender in the Historiography of Caribbean Slavery', in Verene Shepherd et al. (eds), *Engendering History: Caribbean Women in Historical Perspective* (Kingston, Jamaica, 1995).

—— 'Black Masculinity in Caribbean Slavery', occasional paper 2/96, Women and Development Unit, University of the West Indies, Barbados (1996).

Belasco, Bernard I., *The Entrepreneur as Culture Hero: Preadaptations in Nigerian Economic Development* (New York, 1980).

Bennett, J. H., *Bondsmen and Bishops: Slavery and Apprenticeship on the Codrington Plantations of Barbados, 1710–1838* (Berkeley, 1958).

Berlin, Ira, 'From Creole to African: Atlantic Creoles and the Origins of African-American Society in Mainland North America', *William and Mary Quarterly* 53, no. 2 (1996).

Billington, Louis and Billington, Rosamund, '"A Burning Zeal for Righteousness": Women in the British Anti-Slavery Movement, 1820–1900', in Jane Rendall (ed.), *Equal or Different: Women's Politics, 1800–1914* (Basingstoke, UK, 1985).

Blanco, Carlos Larazzábal, *Los negros y la esclavitud en Santo Domingo* (Santo Domingo, Dominican Republic, 1967).

Bolland, Nigel, 'Creolisation and Creole Societies', in Alistair Hennessy, ed. *Intellectuals in the Twentieth-Century Caribbean* (Basingstoke, UK, 1992).

Bosman, William, *A New and Accurate Description of the Coast of Guinea*, originally published in English in 1705 (London, 1967).

Bowen, T. J., *Adventures and Missionary Labours in Several Countries in the Interior of Africa* (London, 1968).

Brandon, George, *Santería from Africa to the New World: The Dead Sell Memories* (Bloomington, IN, 1993).

Braithwaite, Kamau Edward, *The Development of Creole Society in Jamaica, 1770–1820* (Oxford, 1971).

────── *Contradictory Omens: Cultural Diversity and Integration in the Caribbean* (Mona, Jamaica, 1974).

Brereton, Bridget, 'Text, Testimony, and Gender: An Examination of Some Texts by Women on the English-Speaking Caribbean, from the 1770s to the 1920s', in Verene Shepherd et al. (eds), *Engendering History: Caribbean Women in Historical Perspective* (Kingston, Jamaica, 1995).

Brooks, George E., Jr., 'The Signares of St-Louis and Gorée: Women Entrepreneurs in Eighteenth-Century Senegal', in Nancy J. Hafkin and Edna G. Bay (eds), *Women in Africa: Studies in Social and Economic Change* (Stanford, CA, 1976).

────── *Landlords and Strangers: Ecology, Society, and Trade in Western Africa, 1000–1630* (Boulder, CO, 1993).

Brown, Carolyn A., 'Testing the Boundaries of Marginality: Twentieth-Century Slavery and Emancipation Struggles in Nkanu, Northern Igboland, 1920–29', *Journal of African History* 37, no. 1 (1996).

Buckley, Anthony, *Yoruba Medicine* (Oxford, 1985).

Burton, Richard, *Abeokuta and the Cameroons Mountains* (London, 1863).

Bush, Barbara, *Slave Women in Caribbean Society, 1650–1838* (Bloomington, IN, 1990).

Cabrera, Lydia, *El Monte* (Havana, 1954).

────── *La sociedad secreta Abakuá* (Havana, 1954).

────── *Yemayá y Ochún* (Madrid, Spain, 1974; Miami, FL, 1980).

────── *Reglas de congo: palo monte y mayombe* (Miami, FL, 1979).

Campbell, Robert, *A Pilgrimage to My Motherland: Journey among the Egbas and Yorubas of Central Africa* (London, 1861).

Capo, Hounkpati, *A Comparative Phonology of Gbe* (Berlin, 1981).

Carneiro, Edison, *Os quilombos dos Palmares* (São Paulo, 1988).

Carr, H. et al. (ed. A. G. Hopkins), 'A Report on the Laws and Customs of the Yoruba, 1910', *Journal of the Historical Society of Nigeria* 5, no. 1 (1969).

Chambers, Douglas B., '"He Is an African but Speaks Plain": Historical Creolization in Eighteenth-Century Virginia', in Alusine Jalloh and Stephen E. Maizlish (eds), *The African Diaspora* (College Station, TX, 1996).

────── '"My Own Nation": Igbo Exiles in the Diaspora', *Slavery and Abolition* 18, no. 1 (1997).

────── 'Source Material for Studying Igbo in the Diaspora: Problems and Possibilities', in Robin Law (ed.), *Source Material for Studying the Slave Trade and the African Diaspora* (Stirling, UK, 1997).

Chandler, Allan D. and Knight, Lucien L. (eds), *Journal of William Stephens* (Atlanta, GA, 1904–16).

Chapeaux, Pedro Deschamps, *El negro en la economía habanera del siglo XIX* (Havana, 1971).

────── *Los cimarrones urbanos* (Havana, 1983).

Chukukere, Gloria, 'Analysis of Cultural Reflection in Igbo Proverbs', in R. N. Umeasiegbu (ed.), *The Study of Igbo Culture: Essays in Honour of F. C. Ogbalu* (Enugu, Nigeria, 1988).

Clarke, William, *Travels and Explorations in Yorubaland (1854–1858)*, ed. J. A. Atanda (Ibadan, Nigeria, 1972).

Cole, Herbert M. and Anakior, Chike C., *Igbo Arts: Community and Cosmos* (Los Angeles, 1984).

Copley, Anthony, 'The Debate on Widow Re-marriage and Polygamy: Aspects of Moral Change in Nineteenth-Century Bengal and Yorubaland', *Journal of Imperial and Commonwealth History* 7, no. 2 (1979).

Costa, Iraci del Nero, *Vila Rica: População (1729–1826)* (São Paulo, 1979).

Courlander, Harold, *The Drum and the Hoe: Life and Lore of the Haitian People* (Berkeley and Los Angeles, 1960).

────── *Haiti Singing* (Chapel Hill, NC, 1939).

Coursey, D. G., *Yams: An Account of the Nature, Origins, Cultivation and Utilisation of the Useful Members of the Dioscoreaceae* (London, 1967).

Craton, Michael, 'Changing Patterns of Slave Families in the British West Indies', *Journal of Interdisciplinary History* 10, no. 1 (1979).

Crow, Hugh, *Memoirs of the Late Captain Hugh Crow, of Liverpool* (1830; London, 1970).

Curtin, Philip D., *Two Jamaicas, 1830–1865: The Role of Ideas in a Tropical Colony* (Cambridge, 1955).

────── *The Atlantic Slave Trade: A Census* (Madison, WI, 1969).

—— *Economic Change in Precolonial Africa: Senegambia in the Era of the Slave Trade* (Madison, WI, 1975).

—— 'Abolition of the Slave Trade from Senegambia', in David Eltis and James Walvin (eds), *Abolition of the Atlantic Slave Trade: Origins and Effects in Europe, Africa, and the Americas* (Madison, WI, 1981).

—— 'Africa and the Wider Monetary World, 1250–1850', in John F. Richards (ed.), *Precious Metals in the Later Medieval and Early Modern Worlds* (Durham, NC, 1982).

—— *Cross Cultural Trade in World History* (New York, 1984).

—— *The Rise and Fall of the Plantation Complex: Essays in Atlantic History* (New York, 1990).

Cutter, Charles, *The Legal Culture of Northern New Spain, 1700–1810* (Albuquerque, NM, 1994).

Dalzel, Archibald, *History of Dahomey* (1793; London, 1967).

Dapper, O., *Naukeurige Beschrijivinge der Afrikaensche Gewesten* (Amsterdam, 1668).

Davidson, David M., 'Negro Slave Control and Resistance in Colonial Mexico, 1519–1650', *Hispanic American Historical Review* 66 (1966).

Davis, David Brion, *The Problem of Slavery in Western Culture* (Ithaca, NY, 1966).

—— *Slavery and Human Progress* (New York, 1984).

Deagan, Kathleen A. and Landers, Jane, 'Excavating Fort Mose: A Free Black Town in Spanish Florida', in Theresa A. Singleton (ed.), *I, Too, Am America: Archaeological Studies in African American Life* (Charlottesville, VA, 1999).

Deagan, Kathleen and MacMahon, Darcie, *Fort Mose: Colonial America's Black Fortress of Freedom* (Gainesville, FL, 1995).

DeCorse, Christopher, 'Culture Contact, Continuity, and Change on the Gold Coast, A.D. 1400–1900', *African Archaeological Review* 10 (1992).

—— 'The Danes on the Gold Coast: Culture Change and the European Presence', *African Archaeological Review* 11 (1993).

Deive, Carlos Esteban, *Los guerrilleros negros: Esclavos fugitivos y cimarrones en Santo Domingo* (Santo Domingo, Dominican Republic, 1989).

Deren, Maya, *Divine Horsemen: Voodoo Gods of Haiti* (New York, 1970).

Dickson, William, *Letters on Slavery* (1789; Westport, CT, 1970).

Dike, Kenneth O. and Ekejiuba, Felicia, *The Aro of South-Eastern Nigeria, 1650–1980: A Study of Socio-Economic Formation and Transformation in Nigeria* (Ibadan, Nigeria, 1990).

Donnan, Elizabeth, *Documents Illustrative of the History of the Slave Trade to America*, 4 vols (New York, 1969).

Drewal, Henry John, Pemberton III, John and Abiodun, Rowland, *Yoruba: Nine Centuries of African Art and Thought* (New York, 1989).

Edwards, Bryan, *The History, Civil and Commercial, of the British Colonies in the West Indies*, vol. 2 (London, 1793).

Egnal, Marc, *New World Economies: The Growth of the Thirteen Colonies and Early Canada* (Oxford, 1998).

Egudu, Romanus N. (trans. and comp.), *The Calabash of Wisdom and Other Igbo Stories* (New York, 1973).

Ejituwu, Nkparom C. and Kpone-Tonwe, Songpie, 'Atlantic Trade', in E. J. Alagoa and Tekena N. Tamuno (eds), *Land and People of Nigeria: Rivers State* (Port Harcourt, Nigeria, 1989).

Ellis, A. B., *The Yoruba-Speaking Peoples of the Slave Coast of West Africa* (1894; New York, 1970).

Eltis, David, *Economic Growth and the Ending of the Transatlantic Slave Trade* (New York, 1987).

—— 'Precolonial Western Africa and the Atlantic Economy', in Barbara L. Solow (ed.), *Slavery and the Rise of the Atlantic System* (Cambridge, 1991).

Eltis, David, Behrendt, Stephen D., Richardson, David and Klein, Herbert S. (eds), *The Transatlantic Slave Trade, 1527–1867: A Database* (Cambridge, 1999).

Eltis, David and Richardson, David, 'The "Numbers Game" and Routes to Slavery', *Slavery and Abolition* 18, no. 1 (1997).

Eltis, David and Walvin, James (eds), *The Abolition of the Atlantic Slave Trade: Origins and Effects in Europe, Africa and the Americas* (Madison, WI, 1981).

Emerson, Matthew C., 'African Inspiration in a New World Art and Artifact: Decorated Pipes from the Chesapeake', in Theresa A. Singleton (ed.), *I, Too, Am America: Archaeological Studies in*

African American Life (Charlottesville, VA, 1999).

Equiano, Olaudah, *The Life of Olaudah Equiano, or Gustavus Vassa, the African*, ed. Paul Edwards (London, 1988).

—— *The Interesting Narrative of the Life of Olaudah Equiano, Written by Himself*, ed. Robert J. Allison (Boston, 1995).

Fadipe, N. A., *The Sociology of the Yoruba* (Ibadan, Nigeria, 1939).

Fage, John, 'The Effects of the Export Trade on African Populations', in R. P. Moss and R. J. Rathbone (eds), *The Population Factor in African Studies* (London, 1975).

—— 'Slave and Society in Western Africa, c. 1455–1700', *Journal of African History* 21 (1980).

Falola, Toyin, 'Missionaries and Domestic Slavery in Yorubaland in the Nineteenth Century', *Journal of Religion in Africa* 14 (1986).

—— 'The Yoruba Caravan System of the Nineteenth Century', *International Journal of African Historical Studies* 24, no. 1 (1991).

Falola, Toyin and Lovejoy, Paul E. (eds), *Pawnship in Africa: Debt Bondage in Historical Perspective* (Boulder, CO, 1994).

Ferguson, Leland G., 'Looking for the "Afro" in Colono-Indian Pottery', in Robert L. Schuyler (ed.), *Archaeological Perspectives on Ethnicity in America* (New York, 1979).

—— *Uncommon Ground: Archaeology and Early African America, 1650–1800* (Washington, DC, 1992).

—— '"The Cross Is a Magic Sign": Marks on Eighteenth-Century Bowls from South Carolina', in Theresa A. Singleton (ed.), *I, Too, Am America: Studies in African American Archaeology* (Charlottesville, VA, 1999).

Fernández, Damián, 'Revolution and Religion in Cuba', in L. S. Gustafson and M. C. Moen (eds), *The Religious Challenge to the State* (Philadelphia, 1992).

Ferretti, Sérgio, *Querebetam de Zonadounu: Um estudo de antropologia da religião da Casa das Minas*, tese de mestrado apresentada a Universidade Federal do Rio Grande do Norte, Natal, Brazil, 1983.

Filho, Mello Moraes, *Festas e tradições populares do Brasil* (Rio de Janeiro, 1901).

Finnegan, Ruth, *Oral Literature in Africa* (Oxford, UK, 1970).

Fogel, Robert W., *Without Consent or Contract: The Rise and Fall of American Slavery* (New York, 1989).

Forde, Darryl and Jones, G. I., *The Ibo and Ibibio-Speaking Peoples of South-Eastern Nigeria* (London, 1950).

Franco, José Luciano, *La conspiración de Aponte* (Havana, 1963).

Freyre, Gilberto, *Casa-grande e senzala* (Rio de Janeiro, 1989).

Furé, Rogelio Martínez, *Diálogos imaginarios* (Havana, 1979).

Garcia, Rodolfo, 'Vocabulario Nago', in *Estudos Brasileiros*, trabalhos apresentados ao lo Congresso Afro-Brasileiro reunido em Recife em 1934, apresentação de Jose Antonio Gonsalves de Mello (1935; Recife, 1988).

Gautier, Arlette, 'Les esclaves femmes aux Antilles françaises, 1635–1848', *Réflexions historiques* 10, no. 3 (1983).

Genealogical Committee of the Georgia Historical Society (comp), *Early Deaths in Savanna, GA, 1763–1803: Obituaries and Legal Notices* (Savannah, 1993).

Genovese, Eugene D., *A terra prometida (o mundo que os escravos criarum)* (Rio de Janeiro, 1988); originally published in English, *The World the Slaves Made* (New York, 1972).

Georgia Writers' Project, Savannah Unit, *Drums and Shadows: Survival Studies among the Georgia Coastal Negroes* (Athens, GA, 1986).

Gilroy, Paul, *The Black Atlantic: Modernity and Double Consciousness* (Cambridge, 1993).

Góes, José R., *O cativeiro imperfeito* (Vitória, Brazil, 1993).

Gordon, Lindon, 'What's New in Women's History', in Teresa de Lauretis (ed.), *Feminist Studies/Critical Studies* (Bloomington, IN, 1986).

Green, M. M., *Ibo Village Affairs* (1947; New York, 1964).

Greene, Sandra E., 'From Whence They Came: A Note on the Influence of West African Ethnic and Gender Relations on the Organizational Character of the 1733 St. John Slave Rebellion', in George Tyson and Arnold Highfield (eds), *The Danish West Indian Slave Trade: Virgin Islands Perspectives* (Virgin Islands, 1994).

—— *Gender, Ethnicity and Social Change on the Upper Slave Coast: A History of the*

Anlo-Ewe (London and Portsmouth, NH, 1996).

Guanche, Jesús, 'Santería cubana e identidad cultural', *Revolución y cultura* (March 1996).

Gutman, Herbert G., *The Black Family in Slavery and Freedom, 1750–1925* (New York, 1976).

Guyer, J. I., 'Food, Cocoa, and the Division of Labour by Sex in Two West African Societies', *Comparative Studies in Society and History* 22, no. 3 (1980).

Hair, P. E. H., 'An Ethnolinguistic Inventory of the Lower Guinea Coast before 1700: Part II', *African Language Review* 8 (1969).

—— *Africa Encountered: European Contacts and Evidence 1450–1700* (Brookfield, VT, 1997).

Hair, P. E. H., Jones, Adam and Law, Robin (eds), *Barbot on Guinea: The Writings of Jean Barbot on West Africa, 1678–1712* (London, 1992).

Hall, Gwendolyn Midlo, *Africans in Colonial Louisiana: The Development of Afro-Creole Culture in the Eighteenth Century* (Baton Rouge, LA, 1992).

Hallet, R. (ed.), *The Niger Journal of Richard and John Lander* (London, 1965).

Hancock, David, *Citizens of the World: London Merchants and the Integration of the British Atlantic Community, 1735–1785* (Cambridge, 1995).

Hanger, Kimberly S., *Bounded Lives, Bounded Places: Free Black Society in Colonial New Orleans, 1769–1803* (Durham, NC, 1997).

Haraway, Donna, 'Situated Knowledges: The Science Question in Feminism and the Privilege of Partial Perspective', *Feminist Studies* 14, no. 3 (1988).

Harris, Joseph, 'Introduction', in *Global Dimensions of the African Diaspora*, 2nd edn (Washington, DC, 1993).

Herskovits, Melville, *Life in a Haitian Valley* (New York, 1937).

—— *The Myth of the Negro Past* (Boston, 1941).

—— *Dahomey: An Ancient West African Kingdom* (Evanston, IL, 1967).

Heyrick, Elizabeth, *Appeal to the Hearts and Conscience of British Women* (Leicester, UK, 1828).

Higman, B. W., 'Household Structure and Fertility on Jamaican Slave Plantations', *Population Studies* 27 (1973).

—— *Slave Population and Economy in Jamaica, 1802–1834* (New York, 1976).

—— *Slave Populations of the British Caribbean, 1807–1834* (Baltimore, MD, 1984).

Hill, Donald (producer) *Peter Was a Fisherman: The 1939 Trinidad Field Recordings of Melville and Frances Herskovits*, Rounder Records Corp., CD 1114, vol. 1, song 25 (Cambridge, MA, 1998).

Hinderer, Anna, *Seventeen Years in the Yoruba Country* (London, 1872).

Hodgkin, Thomas, 'Kingdoms of the Western Sudan', in Roland Oliver (ed.), *The Dawn of African History* (London, 1961).

Holms, John A., *Pidgins and Creoles: Theory and Structure*, 2 vols (Cambridge, 1988–89).

hooks, bell, 'Sisterhood: Political Solidarity between Women', *Feminist Review* 23 (1986).

Hopkins, A. G. , 'Economic Imperialism in West Africa: Lagos 1880–92', *Economic History Review* 21 (1968).

—— *An Economic History of West Africa* (London, 1973).

Hornberger, C., 'Etwas aus der Geschichter der Anloer', *Quartal-Blatt der Norddeutschen Missionsgesellschaft* 82 (1877).

Igé, John and Yai, Olabiyi, 'The Yoruba-Speaking People of Dahomey and Togo', *Yoruba: Journal of the Yoruba Studies Association of Nigeria* 1, no. 1 (1973).

Iliffe, J., 'Poverty in Nineteenth-century Yorubaland', *Journal of African History* 25, no. 1 (1984).

—— *The African Poor: A History* (Cambridge, 1987).

Inikori, Joseph (ed.), *Forced Migration: The Impact of the Export Trade on African Societies* (London, 1981).

Isichei, Elizabeth, *A History of the Igbo People* (London, 1976).

—— *Igbo Worlds: An Anthology of Oral Histories and Historical Descriptions* (Phildelphia, 1978).

—— *A History of Nigeria* (London, 1983).

Jackson, Richard, *Journal of a Voyage to Bonny River*, ed. Roland Jackson (1825–6; Letchworth, UK, 1934).

Jalloh, Alusine, 'Introduction', in Alusine Jalloh and Stephen E. Maizlish (eds), *The African Diaspora* (College Station, TX, 1996).

Johnson, C., 'Class and Gender: A Consideration of Yoruba Women

during the Colonial Period', in
C. Robertson and I. Berger (eds),
Women and Class in Africa (New York,
1986).

Johnson, Samuel, *The History of the Yorubas: From the Earliest Times to the Beginning of the British Protectorate* (London, 1921).

Jones, G. I., *The Trading States of the Oil Rivers: A Study of Political Development in Eastern Nigeria* (London, 1963).

——— 'Olaudah Equiano of the Niger Ibo', in Philip D. Curtin (ed.), *Africa Remembered: Narratives of West Africans from the Era of the Slave Trade* (Madison, WI, 1968).

——— *The Art of Eastern Nigeria* (Cambridge, 1984).

——— *Ibo Art* (Aylesbury, UK, 1989).

Kea, Ray A., 'Akwamu-Anlo Relations, c. 1750–1813', *Transactions of the Historical Society of Ghana* 10 (1969).

——— *Settlement, Trade and Politics in the Seventeenth Century Gold Coast* (Baltimore, MD, 1982).

Kellogg, Susan, *Law and the Transformation of Aztec Culture, 1500–1700* (Norman, OK, 1995).

Kent, R. K., 'Palmares; An African State in Brazil', *Journal of African History* 6 (1965).

Kiple, Kenneth F., *The Caribbean Slave: A Biological History* (Cambridge, 1981).

Kiple, Kenneth F. and Kiple, Virginia H., 'Slave Child Mortality: Some Nutritional Answers to a Perennial Puzzle', *Journal of Social History* 10 (1979).

——— 'Deficiency Diseases in the Caribbean', *Journal of Interdisciplinary History* 11, no. 2 (1980).

Klein, Herbert S., *The Middle Passage* (Princeton, NJ, 1978).

——— 'African Women in the Atlantic Slave Trade', in Claire Robertson and Martin Klein (eds), *Women and Slavery in Africa* (Madison, WI, 1983).

Klein, Herbert S. and Engerman, Stanley. L., 'Fertility Differentials between Slaves in the United States and the British West Indies', *William and Mary Quarterly* 35 (1978).

——— 'A demografia dos escravos americanos', in Maria L. Marcílio (ed.), *População e sociedade* (Petrópolis, Brazil, 1984).

Klein, Martin A., *Islam and Imperialism in Senegal: Sine-Saloum, 1847–1914* (Stanford, CA, 1968).

——— 'The Study of Slavery in Africa: A Review Article', *Journal of African History* 19 (1978).

——— 'Women in Slavery in the Western Sudan', in Claire Robertson and Martin Klein (eds), *Women and Slavery in Africa* (Madison, WI, 1983).

——— *Slavery and Colonial Rule in French West Africa* (Cambridge, 1998).

Koelle, Sigismund W., *Polyglotta Africana* (1854; Graz, Austria, 1963).

Koger, Larry, *Black Slaveowners: Free Black Slave Masters in South Carolina, 1790–1860* (Jefferson, NC, 1985).

Konetzke, Richard (ed.), *Colección de documentos para la historia de la formación social de Hispanoamérica.* (1953, Madrid).

Kopytoff, I., 'Commentary One', *Historical Reflections* 6 (1979).

Kopytoff, I. and Miers, S., 'African "Slavery" as an Institution of Marginality', in S. Miers and I. Kopytoff (eds), *Slavery in Africa: Historical and Anthropological Perspectives* (Madison, WI, 1977).

Kremser, Manfred, 'The African Heritage in the "Kele" tradition of the "Djine" in St. Lucia', in Manfred Kremser and Karl R. Wernhart (eds), *Research in Ethnography and Ethnohistory of St. Lucia: A Preliminary Report* (Horn-Wien, Vienna, 1986).

Labouret, Henri and Rivet, Paul, *Le Royaume d'Arda et son evangelisation au XVIIᵉ siècle* (Paris, 1929).

Lachatañeré, Rómulo, *El sistema religioso de los Afrocubanos* (Havana, 1992).

Landers, Jane G., 'Gracia Real de Santa Teresa de Mose: A Free Black Town in Spanish Colonial Florida', *American Historical Review* 95 (1990).

——— *Across the Southern Border: Black Society in Spanish Florida* (Urbana, IL, 1999).

Law, Robin, 'The Owu War in Yoruba History', *Journal of the Historical Society of Nigeria* 7, no. 1 (1973).

——— *The Oyo Empire, c. 1600–1836* (Oxford, 1977).

——— 'Trade and Politics behind the Slave Coast: The Lagoon Traffic and the Rise of Lagos, 1500–1800', *Journal of African History* 24 (1983).

——— 'Between the Sea and the Lagoons: The Interaction of Maritime and Inland Navigation on the Pre-Colonial Slave

Coast', *Cahiers d'études africaines* 29 (1989).

────── '"My Head Belongs to the King": On the Political and Ritual Significance of Decapitation in Pre-Colonial Dahomey', *Journal of African History* 30 (1989).

────── *The Slave Coast of West Africa, 1550–1750* (Oxford, 1991).

────── 'The Historiography of the Commercial Transition in 19th Century West Africa', in Toyin Falola (ed.), *African Historiography: Essays in Honour of Jacob Ade Ajayi* (Harlow, UK, 1993).

────── 'A Lagoonside Port on the Eighteenth-Century Slave Coast: The Early History of Badagry', *Canadian Journal of African Studies* 28, no. 1 (1994).

────── '"Legitimate" Trade and Gender Relations in Yorubaland and Dahomey', in Robin Law (ed.), *From Slave Trade to 'Legitimate' Commerce* (Cambridge, 1995).

────── 'Ethnicity and the Slave Trade: "Lucumí" and "Nago" as Ethonyms in West Africa', *History in Africa* 24 (1997).

Law, Robin and Lovejoy, Paul E., 'The Changing Dimensions of African History: Reappropriating the African Diaspora', in Kenneth King et al. (eds), *Interdisciplinary Perspectives* (Edinburgh, UK, 1997).

Law, Robin and Mann, Kristin, 'West Africa in the Atlantic Community: The Case of the Slave Coast', *William and Mary Quarterly* 56, no. 1 (1999).

Leith Ross, Sylvia, *African Women: A Study of the Ibo of Nigeria* (1939; London, 1965).

Leonard, A. G., *The Lower Niger and Its Tribes* (London, 1906).

'Letters from the Georgia Committee of Correspondence to Benjamin Franklin', *Georgia Historical Quarterly* 36 (1952).

'Letters of Montiano, Siege of St. Augustine', *Collections of the Georgia Historical Society* (Savannah, GA, 1909).

LeVine, R. A., 'Sex Roles and Economic Change in Africa', in J. Middleton (ed.), *Black Africa: Its Peoples and Their Cultures Today* (London, 1970).

Levi-Strauss, Claude, *The Savage Mind* (Chicago, 1966), originally published as *La Pensée sauvage* (Paris, 1962).

Lewis, Earl, 'To Turn as on a Pivot: Writing African Americans into a History of

Overlapping Diasporas', *American Historical Review* 100, no. 3 (1995).

Lewis, M. G., *Journal of a West Indian Proprietor, 1815–17*, ed. Mona Wilson (1834; London, 1929).

Ligon, Richard, *A True and Exact History of the Island of Barbados* (London, 1657).

Long, Edward, *The History of Jamaica*, 3 vols (London, 1774).

Lopes, Edmundo Correia, 'Os trabalhos de Costa Peixoto e a Lingua Evoe no Brasil', in Antonio da Costa Peixoto, *Obra Nova de Lingua Geral de Mina* [1741], manuscrito da Biblioteca Publica de Evora e da Biblioteca Nacional de Lisboa, publicado e apresentado por Luis Silveira e acompanhado de comentario filologico de Edmundo Correia Lopes (Lisbon, 1945).

López, José Luis Córtes, *Los origines de la esclavitud negra en España* (Madrid, 1986).

Lovejoy, Paul E., *Caravans of Kola: The Hausa Kola Trade, 1700–1900* (Zaria and Ibadan, Nigeria, 1980).

────── *Transformations in Slavery: A History of Slavery in Africa* (Cambridge, 1983).

────── *Salt of the Desert Sun: Salt Production and Trade in the Central Sudan* (Cambridge, 1986).

────── 'Concubinage and the Status of Women Slaves in Early Colonial Northern Nigeria', *Journal of African History* 29 (1988).

────── 'Background to Rebellion: The Origins of Muslim Slaves in Bahia', in Paul E. Lovejoy and Nicholas Rogers (eds), *Unfree Labour in the Development of the Atlantic World* (London, 1994).

────── 'The African Diaspora: Revisionist Interpretations of Ethnicity, Culture and Religion under Slavery', *Studies in the World History of Slavery, Abolition, and Emancipation* 2, no. 1 (1997).

────── 'Biography as Source Material: Towards a Biographical Archive of Enslaved Africans', in Robin Law (ed.), *Source Material for Studying the Slave Trade and the African Diaspora*, papers from conference at Centre of Commonwealth Studies, University of Stirling, UK, April 1996, occasional paper 5 (Stirling, UK, 1997).

Lovejoy, Paul E. (ed.), *Ideology of Slavery in Africa* (Beverly Hills, CA, 1981).

Lovejoy, Paul E. and Rogers, Nicholas (eds), *Unfree Labour in the Development of the Atlantic World* (London, 1994).

Mabogunje, Akin and Omer-Cooper, J., *Owu in Yoruba History* (Ibadan, 1971).

Mann, Kristin, 'Women's Rights in Law and Practice: Marriage and Dispute Settlement in Colonial Lagos', in M. J. Hay and M. Wright (eds), *African Women and the Law: Historical Perspectives* (Boston, 1982).

—— 'Owners, Slaves and the Struggle for Labour in the Commercial Transition at Lagos', in Robin Law (ed.), *From Slave Trade to 'Legitimate' Commerce* (Cambridge, 1995).

Manning, Patrick, *Slavery and African Life: Occidental, Oriental, and African Slave Trade* (Cambridge and New York, 1990).

Marcílio, Maria L., 'Sistemas demográficos no Brasil do século XIX', in Maria L. Marcílio (ed.), *População e sociedade* (Petrópolis, Brazil, 1984).

Martin, Susan, 'Gender and Innovation: Farming, Cooking and Palm Processing in the Ngwa Region, South Eastern Nigeria 1900–1930', *Journal of African History* 25, no. 4 (1984).

—— *Palm Oil and Protest: An Economic History of the Ngwa Region of South Eastern Nigeria 1800–1980* (Cambridge, 1988).

—— 'Slaves, Igbo Women and Palm Oil in the Nineteenth Century', in Robin Law (ed.), *From Slave Trade to 'Legitimate' Commerce* (Cambridge, 1995).

McAlister, Lyle N., *Spain and Portugal in the New World, 1492–1700* (Minneapolis, MN, 1984).

McFarlane, Anthony, '*Cimarrones* and *Palenques*: Runaways and Resistance in Colonial Colombia', *Slavery and Abolition* 6 (1985).

Meek, C. K., *Law and Authority in a Nigerian Tribe: A Study in Indirect Rule* (1937; New York, 1970).

Meillassoux, Claude, *Mulheres, celeiros e capitais* (Porto, 1977); also published in English, *Maidens, Meal and Money* (Cambridge, 1981).

—— 'Female Slavery', in Claire Robertson and Martin Klein (eds), *Women and Slavery in Africa* (Madison, WI, 1983).

Mendoza, Irma Marina, 'El cabildo de Pardos en Nirgua: Siglos XVII y XVIII', *Annuario de estudios Bolvarianos* 4 (1995).

Menéndez, Lázara, 'The Freedom of Worship and Respect for All Religious Traditions', *Granma International* (14 June 1992).

—— 'Un cake para Obatalá?' *Temas* (October 1995).

Metraux, Alfred, *Le vaudou Haitien* (1958; Paris, 1968).

Midgley, Clare, *Women against Slavery: The British Campaigns, 1780–1870* (London, 1992).

Miller, Joseph C., *Way of Death: Merchant Capital and the Angolan Slave Trade, 1730–1830* (Madison, WI, 1988).

—— 'A Marginal Institution on the Margin of the Atlantic System: The Portuguese Southern Atlantic Slave Trade in the Eighteenth Century', in Barbara L. Solow (ed.), *Slavery and the Rise of the Atlantic System* (Cambridge, 1991).

Mintz, Sidney W., 'The Socio-Historical Background to Pidginization and Creolization', in Dell Hymes (ed.), *Pidginization and Creolization of Languages* (Cambridge, UK, 1971).

Mintz, Sidney W. and Price, Richard, *The Birth of African-American Culture: An Anthropological Perspective* (1976; Boston, 1992).

Moitt, Bernard, 'Women, Work and Resistance in the French Caribbean during Slavery, 1700–1848', in Verene Shepherd et al. (eds), *Engendering History: Caribbean Women in Historical Perspective* (Kingston, 1995).

Moore, Carlos, *Castro, the Blacks, and Africa* (Los Angeles, 1988).

Moore, Francis, *Travels into the Inland Parts of Africa* (London, 1738).

Morgan, Philip D., 'Black Life in Eighteenth-Century Charleston', *Perspectives in American History*, n. s. 1 (1984).

—— 'The Cultural Implications of the Atlantic Slave Trade: African Regional Origins, American Destinations and New World Developments', *Slavery and Abolition* 18, no. 1 (1997).

Morrissey, Marietta, 'Women's Work, Family Formation and Reproduction among Caribbean Slaves', *Review* 9 (1986).

—— *Slave Women in the New World: Gender Stratification in the Caribbean* (Lawrence, KS, 1989).

Morton-Williams, Peter, 'The Oyo Yoruba and the Atlantic Trade, 1670–1830', in J. E. Inikori (ed.), *Forced Migration: The Impact of the Export Slave Trade on African Societies* (New York, 1982).

Mott, Luiz, *Escravidão, homossexualidade e demonologia* (São Paulo, 1988).

Mouser, Bruce L., 'Women Slavers of Guinea-Conakry', in Claire C. Robertson and Martin A. Klein (eds), *Women and Slavery in Africa* (Madison, WI, 1983).

Mullin, Michael, *Africa in America: Slave Acculturation and Resistance in the American South and the British Caribbean, 1736–1831* (Urbana, IL, 1992).

Newman, Louise M., 'Critical Theory and the History of Women: What's at Stake in Deconstructing Women's History', *Journal of Women's History* 2, no. 3 (1991).

Nicholson, Sharon E., 'Climatic Variations in the Sahel and other African Regions during the past Five Centuries', *Journal of Arid Environments* 1 (1979).

Nwala, T. Uzodinma, *Igbo Philosophy* (Lagos, Nigeria, 1985).

Nwoga, D. Ibe. 'Appraisal of Igbo Proverbs and Idioms', in F. C. Ogbalu and E. N. Emenanjo (eds), *Igbo Language and Culture* (Ibadan, Nigeria, 1975).

Obichere, B. I., 'Women and Slavery in the Kingdom of Dahomey', *Revue française d'histoire d'outre-mer* 65 (1978).

Ogbalu, F. C., *Ilu Igbo: The Book of Igbo Proverbs*, 2nd edn (Ouitsha, Nigeria, 1965).

Ogbomo, Onaiwu, 'Esan Women Traders and Pre-Colonial Economic Power', in B. House-Midamba and F. K. Ekechi, (eds), *African Market Women and Economic Power* (Greenwood, CT, 1995).

Oguagha, Philip A., 'Historical and Traditional Evidence', in Philip A. Oguagha and Alex I. Okpoko (eds), *History and Ethnoarchaeology in Eastern Nigeria* (Oxford, 1984).

Ogunremi, F. A., 'Human Porterage in Nigeria in the Nineteenth Century: A Pillar in the Indigenous Economy', *Journal of the Historical Society of Nigeria* 8, no. 1 (1975).

Ohadike, Don C., *Anioma: A Social History of the Western Igbo People* (Athens, OH, 1994).

O'Hear, Ann, *Power Relations in Nigeria: Ilorin Slaves and Their Successors* (Rochester, NY, 1997).

Okeke, Uche, 'The Art Culture of the Nsukka Igbo', in G. E. K. Ofomata, *The Nsukka Environment* (1978; reprint, Enegu, 1985).

Okeke, Uche and Okechukwu, C. U. V., 'Igbodo Art and Culture', in *The Nsukka Environment* (1978; reprint, Enegu, 1985).

Okpewho, Isidore, *African Oral Literature: Backgrounds, Character, and Continuity* (Bloomington, IN, 1992).

Okpoko, A. Ikechukwu, 'Traditions of Genesis and Historical Reconstruction: The Umueri of Igboland as a Case Study', in B. W. Andah and Ikechukwu Okpoko (eds), *Some Nigerian Peoples* (Ibadan, Nigeria, 1988).

Oldendorp, G. C. A., (ed. Johann Jakob Bossard, trans and eds Arnold R. Highfield and Vladimir Barac) *History of the Mission of the Evangelical Brethren on the Caribbean Islands of St. Thomas, St. Croix and St. John* (Ann Arbor, MI, 1987).

Oldfield, R. A. K., 'Mr. Oldfield's Journal', in M. Laird and R. A. K. Oldfield, *Narrative of an Expedition into the Interior of Africa*, vol. 1 (London, 1837).

Oliveira, Maria Ines Cortes de, 'Viver e morer no meio dos seus: Nacoes e comunidades africana na Bahia do seculo XIX', *Revista USP* (Brazil) 28 (December–February 1995–96).

Olwig, Karen Fog, *Cultural Adaptation and Resistance on St. John: Three Centuries of Afro-Caribbean Life* (Gainesville, FL, 1985).

——— 'African Cultural Principles in Caribbean Slave Societies', in Stephan Palmié (ed.), *Slave Cultures and the Cultures of Slavery* (Knoxville, TN, 1995).

Onwuejeogwu, M. A., 'An Outline Account of the Dawn of Igbo Civilization', *Odinani* 1, no. 1 (1972).

——— 'The Igbo Culture Area', in F. C. Ogbalu and E. N. Emenanjo (eds), *Igbo Language and Culture* (Ibadan, Nigeria, 1975).

——— *An Igbo Civilization: Nri Kingdom and Hegemony* (Lon don, 1981).

Oriji, J. N., 'The Slave Trade, Warfare and Aro Expansion in the Igbo Hinterland', *Transafrican Journal of History* 16 (1987).

———— *Traditions of Igbo Origin: A Study of Pre-Colonial Population Movements in Africa* (New York, 1990).

Oroge, E. A., 'The Fugitive Slave Question in Anglo-Egba Relations 1861–1886', *Journal of the Historical Society of Nigeria* 8, no. 1 (1975).

———— 'Iwofa: An Historical Survey of the Yoruba Institution of Indenture', *African Economic History* 14 (1985).

Orser, Charles E., Jr., *In Search of Zumbi: Preliminary Archaeological Research at the Serra da Barriga, State of Alagoas, Brazil* (Normal, IL, 1992).

———— 'Toward a Global Historical Archaeology: An Example from Brazil', *Historical Archaeology* 28 (1994).

Ortiz, Fernando, *Hampa Afro-Cubana: Los negros brujos* (Madrid, 1906).

———— *Los negros esclavos*, originally entitled *Hampa afro-cubana: Los negros esclavos: Estudio sociológico y de derecho público* (1916; Havana, 1975).

———— 'Los cabildos Afrocubanos', in Julio Le Riverand (ed.), *Orbita de Fernando Ortiz* (Havana, 1973).

———— *Los cabildos y la fiesta Afro-Cubana del Día de Reyes* (Havana, 1992).

———— 'The Afro-Cuban Festival "Day of Kings"', in Judith Bettelheim (ed.), *Cuban Festivals: An Illustrated Anthology*, annotated and trans., Jean Stubbs (New York, 1993).

———— *Cuban Counterpoint: Tobacco and Sugar* (1940; Durham, NC, 1995).

Palmer, Colin A., *Slaves of the White God: Blacks in Mexico, 1570–1650* (Cambridge, MA, 1976).

———— 'From Africa to the Americas: Ethnicity in the Early Black Communities of the Americas', *Journal of World History* 6, no. 2 (1995).

Palmié, Stephan, 'A Taste for Human Commodities: Experiencing the Atlantic System', in Stephan Palmié (ed.), *Slave Cultures and the Cultures of Slavery* (Knoxville, TN, 1995).

———— 'Ekpe/Abakuá in Middle Passage', in Ralph Austen (ed.), *Slavery and Memory* (forthcoming).

Penfield, Joyce, *Communication with Quotes: The Igbo Case* (Westport, CT, 1983).

Perez, Adriana and Cabrera, Norma Garcia (comps and eds), *Abakuá: Una secta secreta: Selección de textos* (Havana, 1993).

Phillips, William D., Jr., *Slavery from Roman Times to the Early Atlantic Trade* (Minneapolis, MN, 1985).

Pike, Ruth, *Aristocrats and Traders: Sevillian Society of the Sixteenth Century* (Ithaca, NY, 1972).

Pla, María del Carmen Borrego, *Palenques de negros en Cartagena de Indias a fines del siglo XVII* (Seville, 1973).

Poovey, Mary, 'Feminism and Deconstruction', *Feminist Studies* 14 (1988).

Posnansky, Merrick, 'West African Reflections on African American Archaeology', in Theresa A. Singleton (ed.), *I, Too, Am America: Studies in African American Archaeology* (Charlottesville, VA, 1999).

Price, Richard (ed.), *Maroon Societies: Rebel Slave Communities in the Americas* (Baltimore, MD, 1979).

'A Ranger's Report of Travels with General Oglethorpe, 1739–1742', in Newton D. Mereness (ed.), *Travels in the American Colonies* (New York, 1916).

Rattray, R. S., 'History of the Ewe People', *Études Togolaises* 11, no. 1 (1967).

Rawley, James A., *Transatlantic Slave Trade: A History* (New York, 1981).

Reddock, Rhoda, 'Women and Slavery in the Caribbean: A Feminist Perspective', *Latin American Perspectives* 12, no. 1 (1985).

Reis, João José, *Slave Rebellion in Brazil: The Muslim Uprising of 1835 in Bahia*, trans. Arthur Brakel (Baltimore, MD, 1993).

Reitz, Elizabeth J., 'Zooarchaeological Analysis of a Free African American Community: Gracia Real de Santa Teresa de Mose', *Historical Archaeology* 28 (1994).

Reitz, Elizabeth J. and Cumbaa, Stephen L., 'Diet and Foodways of Eighteenth-Century Spanish St. Augustine', in Kathleen A. Deagan (ed.), *Spanish St. Augustine: The Archaeology of a Colonial Creole Community* (New York, 1983).

Report on the Debate in Council on a Dispatch from Lord Bathurst to Governor Warde of Barbados (London, 1828).

Richardson, David, Lovejoy, Paul E. and Eltis, David, 'Slave Trading Ports: Towards an Atlantic-Wide Perspective, 1676–1832', in Robin Law (ed.), *The Ports of the Slave Trade (Bights of Benin and Biafra)* (Stirling, UK, 1999).

Robertson, Claire and Klein, Martin A., 'Women's Importance in African Slave Systems', in Claire Robertson and Martin Klein (eds), *Women and Slavery in Africa* (Madison, WI, 1983).

Robertson, Claire and Klein, Martin A. (eds), *Women and Slavery in Africa* (Madison, WI, 1983).

Rodney, Walter, 'African Slavery and Other Forms of Social Oppression on the Upper Guinea Coast in the Context of the Atlantic Slave Trade', *Journal of African History* 7, no. 3 (1966).

—— 'Gold and Slaves on the Gold Coast', *Transactions of the Historical Society of Ghana* 10 (1969).

Rodrigues, Raymundo Nina, *Os Africanos no Brazil* (São Paulo, 1932).

Romero, Sílvio, *Estudos sobre a poesia popular do Brasil* (Rio de Janeiro, 1888).

Saignes, Miguel Acosta, *Vida de los esclavos en Venezuela* (Caracas, 1961).

Sandoval, Alonso de, *De Instauranda Aethiopum Salute: El mundo de la esclavitud en América* (Bogotá, 1956).

—— *Un tratado sobre la esclavitud*, ed. Enriqueta Vila Vilar (1627; Madrid, 1987).

Sanneh, Lamin O., *The Jakhanke: The History of an Islamic Clerical People of the Senegambia* (London, 1979).

Sarracino, Rodolfo, *Los que volvieron a África* (Havana, 1988).

Schwartz, Stuart B., *Segredos internos* (São Paulo, 1988).

Searing, James, *West African Slavery and Atlantic Commerce: The Senegal River Valley, 1700–1860* (Cambridge, 1993).

Sharpe, Barrie, 'Ethnography and a Regional System', *Critique of Anthropology* 6, no. 3 (1986).

Shaw, Thurstan, *Igbo-Ukwu: An Account of Archaeological Discoveries in Eastern Nigeria*, vol. 1 (Evanston, IL, 1970).

—— *Unearthing Igbo-Ukwu: Archaeological Discoveries in Eastern Nigeria* (Ibadan, Nigeria, 1977).

Shelton, Austin J., *The Igbo-Igala Borderland: Religion and Social Control in Indigenous African Colonialism* (Albany, N.Y, 1971).

—— 'Relativism, Pragmatism, and Reciprocity in Igbo Proverbs', *The Conch* 3, no. 2 (1971).

Silva, Eduardo, *Prince of the People: The Life and Times of a Brazilian Free Man of Colour*, trans. Moyra Ashford (London, 1993).

Sinou, Alain and Oloude, Bachir, *Porto Novo: Ville d'Afrique noire* (Marseille, 1988).

Sirman, Eugene, *Colonial South Carolina: A Political History, 1663–1763* (Chapel Hill, NC, 1966).

Slenes, Robert W., 'Escravidão e família: Padrões de casamento e estabilidade familiar numa comunidade escrava (Campinas, século XIX)', *Estudos Econômicos* 17 (1987).

—— 'Malungu, ngoma vem! África coberta e descoberta no Brasil', *Revista USP* 12 (1991–2).

Smith, Abdullahi, 'A Little New Light on the Collapse of the Alafinate of Yoruba', in G. O. Olusanya (ed.), *Studies in Yoruba History and Culture: Essays in Honour of Professor S.O. Biobaku* (Ibadan, 1983).

Smith, M. G., *The Plural Society in the British West Indies* (Berkeley, CA, 1956).

Smith, Robert, 'The Lagos Consulate: An Outline, 1851–1861', *Journal of African History* 15, no. (1974).

—— *Kingdoms of the Yoruba* (London, 1976).

Spiess, Carl, 'Könige der Anloer', in H. J. Helmot (ed.), *Weltgeschichte 3: Westasien und Afrika* (Leipzig and Vienna, 1901).

Spieth, J., *Die Religion der Eweer in Sud Togo* (Leipzig, 1911).

Stone, R. H., *In Afric's Forest and Jungle, or Six Years among the Yorubas* (Edinburgh, 1900).

Sudarkasa, Niara, 'The Division of Labour by Sex in Yoruba Society', in Niara Sudarkasa (ed.), *Where Women Work: A Study of Yoruba Women in the Market Place and in the Home* (Ann Arbor, MI, 1973).

—— 'Status of Women in Indigenous African Societies', in Nancy J. Hafkin and Edna G. Bay (eds), *Women in Africa: Studies in Social and Economic Change* (Stanford, CA, 1976).

Suret-Canale, 'The Western Atlantic Coast, 1600–1800', in J. F. A. Ajayi and Michael Crowder (eds), *History of West Africa* (New York, 1972).

Surgy, Albert de, *La géomancie et le culte d'Afa chez les Evhe du littoral* (Paris, 1981).

Talbot, P. Amaury, *The Peoples of Southern Nigeria*, vol. 1, *Historical Notes* (1926; London, 1969).

—— *Tribes of the Niger Delta: Their Religions and Customs* (London, 1932).

Tardieu, Jean-Pierre, 'Origines des esclaves au Pérou: La région de Lima (XVIᵉ et XVIIᵉ siècle)', in *Colloque international: de la traite négrière au défi du développement: Réflexion sur les conditions de la paix mondiale*, vol. 1 (Ouidah, Bénin, 1994).

Taylor, J. C., 'Journal of the Rev. J. C. Taylor at Onitsha', in S. Crowther and J. C. Taylor, *The Gospel on the Banks of the Niger* (1859; London, 1968).

Taylor, William B., 'The Foundation of Nuestra Señora de Guadalupe de los Morenos de Amapa', *The Americas* 26 (1970).

Terborg-Penn, Rosalyn, 'Through an African Feminist Theoretical Lens: Viewing Caribbean Women's History Cross-culturally', in Verene Shepherd et al. (eds), *Engendering History: Caribbean Women in Historical Perspective* (Kingston, Jamaica, 1995).

Thomas, Northcote W., *Anthropological Report on the Ibo-Speaking Peoples of Nigeria*. 6 vols (1913; New York, 1969).

Thomas, Richard and Bean, Richard, 'The Fishers of Men: The Profits of the Slave Trade', *Journal of Economic History* 34, no. 4 (1974).

Thompson, Robert F., *Flash of the Spirit: African and Afro-American Art and Philosophy* (New York, 1984).

Thornton, John K., 'African Dimensions of the Stono Rebellion', *American Historical Review* 96, no. 4 (1991).

――― 'African Soldiers in the Haitian Revolution', *Journal of Caribbean History* 25 (1991).

――― *Africa and Africans in the Making of the Atlantic World, 1400–1680* (Cambridge, 1992).

――― '"I am the Subject of the King of Congo": African Political Ideology and the Haitian Revolution', *Journal of World History* 4, no. 2 (1993).

Tonkin, Elizabeth, 'West African Ethnographic Traditions', in R. Fardon (ed.), *Localizing Strategies: Regional Traditions of Ethnographic Writing* (Edinburgh, UK, 1990).

Topping, Aileen Moore, intro. and indexes, *An Impartial Account of the Late Expedition against St. Augustine under General Oglethorpe* (1742; Gainesville, FL, 1978).

Trouillot, Michel-Rolph, 'Culture on the Edges: Creolization in the Plantation Context', *Plantation Societies in the Americas* 5, no. 1 (1998).

Turner, Lorenzo D., *Africanisms in the Gullah Dialect* (Chicago, 1949).

Turner, Victor, *Dramas, Fields, and Metaphors: Symbolic Action in Human Society* (Ithaca, NY, 1974).

Valdés, Rafael López, 'Notas para el estudio etnohistórico de los esclavos lucumí en Cuba', in L. Menéndez (ed.), *Estudios afrocubanos* (Havana, 1990).

Van Dantzig, Albert, *The Dutch and the Guinea Coast, 1674–1742* (Accra, Ghana, 1978).

Vansina, Jan, *Paths in the Rainforests: Toward a History of Political Tradition in Equatorial Africa* (London and Madison, WI, 1990).

Venâncio, Renato P., 'Nos limites da sagrada família: Ilegitimidade e casamento no Brasil colonial', in Ronaldo Vainfas (ed.), *História da sexualidade no Brasil* (Rio de Janeiro, 1986).

Venema, L. Bernhard, *The Wolof of Saalum: Social Structure and Rural Development in Senegal* (Wageningen, Netherlands, 1978).

Verger, Pierre, 'Le culte des vodoun d'Abomey aurait-il été apporté à Saint-Louis de Maranhon par la mère du Roi Ghézo?', in *Les afro-américains*, mémoires de l'Institut français d'Afrique noire, no. 27 (Dakar, 1953).

――― *Trade Relations between the Bight of Benin and Bahia, 17th–19th Century* (Ibadan, Nigeria, 1976); first published in Paris as *Flux et reflux de la traite des nègres entre le golfe de Bénin et Bahia de Todos os Santos du dix-septième au dix-neuvième siècle* (1968).

A Vindication of Female Anti-slavery Associations (London, n. d.).

Ward, J. R., *British West Indian Slavery, 1750–1834: The Process of Amelioration* (Oxford, UK, 1988).

Warner-Lewis, Maureen, *Guinea's Other Suns: The African Dynamic in Trinidad Culture* (Dover, MA, 1991).

――― *Yoruba Songs of Trinidad* (London, 1994).

――― *Trinidad Yoruba: From Mother Tongue to Memory* (Tuscaloosa, AL, 1996; Kingston, 1997).

――― 'Posited Kikoongo Origins of some Portuguese and Spanish Words from the Slave Era', *America Negra* 13 (1997).

Webster, J. B., 'Attitudes and Policies of the Yoruba African Churches towards Polygamy', in C. Baeta (ed.), *Christianity in Tropical Africa* (London, 1968).

Wilson, Louis, 'The Bloodless Conquest in South-Eastern Ghana: The Huza and Territorial Expansion of the Krobo in the 19th Century', *International Journal of African Historical Studies* 23, no. 2 (1990).

—— *The Krobo People of Ghana to 1892: A Political and Social History* (Athens, OH, 1991).

Woloch, Nancy, *Women and the American Experience* (New York, 1996).

Woloch, Nancy (ed.), *Early American Women: A Documentary History, 1600–1900* (Belmont, CA, 1992).

Wood, Betty, *Slavery in Colonial Georgia, 1730–1775* (Athens, GA, 1984).

—— 'Some Aspects of Female Resistance to Chattel Slavery in Low Country Georgia, 1763–1815', in Paul Finkelman (ed.), *Women and the Family in a Slave Society* (New York, 1989).

—— *Women's Work, Men's Work: The Informal Slave Economies of Low Country Georgia* (Athens, GA, 1995).

Wood, Peter H., *Black Majority: Negroes in Colonial South Carolina from 1670 through the Stono Rebellion* (New York, 1974).

Wright, Donald R., *The World and a Very Small Place in Africa* (London, 1997).

Wright, Irene, 'Our Lady of Charity', *Hispanic American Historical Review* 5 (1922).

—— 'Dispatches of Spanish Officials Bearing on the Free Negro Settlement of Gracia Real de Santa Teresa de Mose', *Journal of Negro History* 9 (1924).

Wright, Marcia, 'Women in Peril: A Commentary on the Life Stories of Captives in Nineteenth-Century East-Central Africa', *African Social Research* 20 (1975).

Wyse, Akintola, *The Krio of Sierra Leone: An Interpretative History* (Washington, DC, 1991).

Yai, Olabiyi Babalola, 'From Vodun to Mawu: Monotheism and History in the Fon Cultural Area', in Jean-Pierre Chretien et al. (eds), *L'Invention religieuse en Afrique: Histoire et religion en Afrique noire* (Paris, 1993).

—— 'Survivances et dynamismes des cultures africaines dans les Amériques', *Studies in the World History of Slavery, Abolition, and Emancipation* 1, no. 1 (1996).

'Yoruba Culture Is Alive in Cuba', *Granma Weekly Review* (5 June 1987).

Index